In Godzilla's® Footsteps

Japanese Pop Culture Icons on the Global Stage

Edited by

William M. Tsutsui
and
Michiko Ito

First published in 2006 by
PALGRAVE MACMILLAN™
175 Fifth Avenue, New York, N.Y. 10010 and
Houndmills, Basingstoke, Hampshire, England RG21 6XS
Companies and representatives throughout the world.

PALGRAVE MACMILLAN is the global academic imprint of the Palgrave Macmillan division of St. Martin's Press, LLC and of Palgrave Macmillan Ltd. Macmillan® is a registered trademark in the United States, United Kingdom and other countries. Palgrave is a registered trademark in the European Union and other countries.

ISBN-13: 978–1–4039–6461–8 hardback
ISBN-10: 1–4039–6461–0   hardback
ISBN-13: 978–1–4039–6463–2 paperback
ISBN-10: 1–4039–6463–7   paperback

Library of Congress Cataloging-in-Publication Data

In godzilla's footsteps: japanese pop culture icons on the global stage / Tsutsui, William M., and Ito, Michiko.
    p. cm.
Includes bibliographical references and index.
ISBN 1–4039–6461–0—ISBN 1–4039–6463–7 (pb)
    1. Popular culture—Japan. 2. Japan—Civilization—1945– 3. Godzilla films—History and criticism. I. Tsutsui, William M. II. Ito, Michiko.

DS822.5 I485 2006
306.0952'09045—dc22   2005058616

A catalogue record for this book is available from the British Library.

Design by Newgen Imaging Systems (P) Ltd., Chennai, India.

First edition: July 2006

10 9 8 7 6 5 4 3 2 1

Printed in the United States of America.

Transferred to digital printing in 2007.

CREDITS

Contents

LIST OF FIGURES

ACKNOWLEDGMENTS

All but one of the pieces collected in this volume were originally presented at the conference "In Godzilla's Footsteps: Japanese Pop Culture Icons on the Global Stage," held October 28–30, 2004 in Lawrence, Kansas. This international event, marking the fiftieth anniversary of the release of the first Godzilla film in 1954, was sponsored by the University of Kansas (KU) Center for East Asian Studies with generous financial support from the Japan Foundation, the Toshiba International Foundation, the University of Kansas College of Liberal Arts and Sciences, the Hall Center for the Humanities, KU Center for Research, the Kansas Asia Scholars, and the Kansas Consortium for Teaching About Asia. The conference would have been impossible without the tireless work of the staff of the Center for East Asian Studies (and all the members of their families who also helped out): Jun Fu, Randi Hacker, Lea Herron, Nancy Hope, Sheree Willis, and Director Elaine Gerbert. The student workers at the Center also contributed substantially: John Schneiderwind and Ben Duncan above all, but also Tyler Gatewood, Emily Howard, Norma Larzalere, Liz Morel, and Rachel Wilson. Among the dozens of other people who helped make the conference a success and this volume possible, our thanks go out to Chancellor Robert Hemenway, Carl Strikwerda, Victor Bailey, and Jim Roberts at the University of Kansas; Mary Jane Dunlap and the staff at KU University Relations; Mayor Mike Rundle and the City of Lawrence; Consul General Takao Shibata and the (regrettably, now closed) Consulate of Japan at Kansas City; Paul Lim and English Alternative Theatre; student assistants at the KU East Asian Library Pan Bei, Noriko Koga, Haruka Mihara, and Aris Tam; the faculty and staff of the KU Natural History Museum, including Bruce Scherting, John Simmons, and Larry Martin; administrators, curators and students at the Spencer Museum of Art, including Fred Pawlicki, Carolyn Chinn Lewis, Maria Roman Navarro and Kyungwon Choe; and Mike Pennell, Dena Friesen, and Lee Saylor. We are particularly grateful to the other scholars who participated in the conference and who enriched our discussions as well as the quality of the essays published here: Anne Allison, Michael Baskett, Bob Beatty, Chuck Berg, Martin Boyden, Gregory Cushman, Paul Dunscomb, Gerald Figal, Dani Lotton-Barker, and Gregory Pflugfelder.

Anthony (Toby) Wahl of Palgrave was, as always, a model of good judgment, patience, and enthusiasm. Michael Baskett and John Rinnert provided invaluable assistance in preparing the illustrations for this volume. We would especially like to thank all those individuals and organizations who graciously gave us permission to reproduce copyrighted images here.

Notes on Contributors

Mark Anderson holds a Ph.D. from Cornell University and is currently assistant professor of Asian languages and literatures at the University of Minnesota. He is currently completing a book manuscript on international law, media, and Japanese popular culture between 1885 and 1945. His next research project examines the impact of the phonograph and radio broadcasting on popular music in Japan with a particular focus on the shifting relation of the popular music industry to the rise and fall of the Japanese colonial empire.

Joanne Bernardi is director of the Film and Media Studies Program and associate professor of Japanese studies and film in the Modern Languages and Cultures Department of the University of Rochester. She is the author of *Writing in Light: The Silent Scenario and the Japanese Pure Film Movement* (2001).

Theodore C. Bestor is professor of anthropology and Japanese studies at Harvard University. Among his many publications are *Neighborhood Tokyo* (1989), *Doing Fieldwork in Japan* (coeditor, 2003), and *Tsukiji: The Fish Market at the Center of the World* (2004).

Joyce E. Boss is associate professor of English at Wartburg College. Her article "Godzilla in the Details" appeared in *Strategies: Journal of Theory, Culture & Politics* (1999).

Aaron Gerow is an assistant professor in film studies and East Asian languages and literatures at Yale University, specializing in Japanese cinema. He has published numerous articles on early and contemporary Japanese films, and has books forthcoming on *A Page of Madness* and Kitano Takeshi. Other research interests include Japanese manga and popular culture.

Sayuri Guthrie-Shimizu is associate professor of American history at Michigan State University and is the author of *Creating People of Plenty: The United States and Japan's Economic Alternatives, 1950–1960* (2001). Her recent article on the diffusion of baseball in Japan, "For Love of the Game: Baseball in Early U.S.-Japan Encounters and the Rise of a Transnational Sporting Fraternity," appeared in the November 2004 issue of *Diplomatic History* and will be a chapter in her book tentatively titled *Trans-Pacific Field of Dreams: Baseball and Modernity in U.S.-Japanese Relations, 1872–1952*.

Yoshikuni Igarashi is associate professor of history and director of the East Asian Studies Program at Vanderbilt University. He is the author of

Bodies of Memory: Narratives of War in Postwar Japanese Culture 1945–1970 (2000).

MICHIKO ITO is Japanese studies librarian at the University of Kansas.

HIROFUMI KATSUNO is a Ph.D. candidate in anthropology at the University of Hawai'i. He is currently conducting dissertation research on "Robotics and Technofetishism in Contemporary Japan."

BARAK KUSHNER received his Ph.D. in history from Princeton University and taught Chinese and Japanese history at Davidson College. He is the author of *The Thought War—Japanese Imperial Propaganda* (2005), and is now working on a history of ramen. Currently, he is an independent scholar in Washington, DC.

YULIA MIKHAILOVA is professor in the Faculty of International Studies, Hiroshima City University. She is the author of *Motoori Norinaga: His Life and Work* (1988) and *Social and Political Perspectives on Japan, 1860–1880* (both in Russian) and a series of articles on Russo-Japanese mutual images through visual representations, published in *Acta Slavica Iaponica, Asian Cultural Studies*, and other journals.

SUSAN NAPIER is Mitsubishi Professor of Japanese Studies at the University of Texas at Austin. She is the author of *Escape from the Wasteland: Romanticism and Realism in the Fiction of Mishima Yukio and Oe Kenzaburo* (1991), *The Fantastic in Modern Japanese Literature: The Subversion of Modernity* (1996), and *Anime from Akira to Princess Mononoke: Experiencing Contemporary Japanese Animation* (2001).

ERIC C. RATH is an associate professor of premodern Japanese history at the University of Kansas. His research interests include the performing arts and foodways. He is the author of *The Ethos of Noh: Actors and Their Art* (2004). His current research project is on urban farming and cuisine in Kyoto.

WILLIAM M. TSUTSUI is professor of history at the University of Kansas. He is the author of *Manufacturing Ideology: Scientific Management in Twentieth-Century Japan* (1998) and *Godzilla on My Mind: Fifty Years of the King of Monsters* (2004).

KEVIN J. WETMORE, JR. teaches in the Department of Theatre Arts at Loyola Marymount University. In addition to being an actor and director, he is a scholar of Japanese theatre and cinema and African theatre. He is the author of *The Empire Triumphant: Race, Religion, and Rebellion in the Star Wars Movies* (2005), a postcolonial critique of the two trilogies.

CHRISTINE R. YANO is associate professor of anthropology at the University of Hawai'i. She is the author of *Tears of Longing: Nostalgia and the Nation in Japanese Popular Song* (2002) and is currently working on a book on Japanese American beauty pageants in Hawai'i.

INTRODUCTION

William M. Tsutsui

The rise of Japanese popular culture as a global force has been remarkable in its speed and breadth. Japanese anime and manga have become youth favorites internationally; Japanese video games and television series claim devoted followings from Cambodia to Copenhagen; New York City has recently been as charmed by the *otaku* chic of Murakami Takashi's "Little Boy" exhibition as the home run–hitting prowess of Hideki Matsui; sushi is readily available in the supermarket cases of suburban America from coast to coast. As Tim Craig has put it,

> In short, Japanese pop culture is ubiquitous, hot, and increasingly influential. Once routinely derided as a one-dimensional power, a heavyweight in the production and export of the "hard" of automobiles, electronics, and other manufactured goods but a nobody in terms of the "soft" of cultural products and influence, Japan now contributes not just to our material lives, but to our everyday cultural lives as well.[1]

Move over Toyota, Honda, and Hitachi, make way for the "soft" genius of Hello Kitty, Super Mario, and Miyazaki Hayao.

Over most of the past century and a half, the impact of Japanese culture on Western life has generally been figured in terms of elite art forms. In the late nineteenth century, *ukiyo-e* prints famously inspired the French Impressionists; in the early twentieth century, Japanese literary forms influenced American modernist poets and Japanese aesthetics fascinated architects like Frank Lloyd Wright; after World War II, big-city art houses screened the cerebral works of Kurosawa, Mizoguchi, and Ozu. Western scholars, having focused for so long on Japan's sway over European and American high culture, have been caught a little off-guard by the global ascent of "Japanese pop" since World War II. Although academic studies have begun to appear in English on topics from Japanese hip-hop to television dramas to Tora-san films, Western scholars have yet to explore fully what factors explain Japanese popular culture's current worldwide appeal, let alone what forces in postwar Japanese society unleashed the creative energies of manga and anime, *tokusatsu* (special effects) films, and *kawaii* (cute) character goods. Strikingly, the historical roots of Japan's swelling "Gross National Cool," to borrow Douglas McGray's apt turn of phrase, have scarcely been examined at all.[2]

In the postwar advance of Japanese popular culture into international markets and the global consciousness, Godzilla was a pioneer. Although highbrow films (like *Rashōmon*) and exotic stereotypes (the geisha, the samurai) preceded Godzilla abroad, the cinematic monster introduced by Tōhō Studios in 1954 was the first creation of Japan's burgeoning mass entertainment industry to gain large international audiences. *Gojira*, the brooding story of a saurian mutant that ravages Tokyo, was a box office hit in Japan and, as the heavily edited *Godzilla, King of the Monsters*, a version made palatable both linguistically and politically for the American market, filled movie theaters around the world in the mid-1950s. Thus, a franchise was born: over the following five decades, 28 Godzilla movies would be produced by Tōhō (and one, in 1998, by TriStar in Hollywood), making the series the oldest and longest running in world cinema today. Long-time staples of movie palaces, drive-in theaters, and late-night television, the Godzilla films—which evolved over time from sober adult fare to lighthearted children's entertainment to high-tech action thrillers—became cult classics and their giant, radioactive star became a global icon.

Godzilla's initial overseas appeal may well have been rooted in financial expediency and aesthetic familiarity: international film distributors were eager for the inexpensive, readily available, and reasonably high quality sci-fi features offered by Tōhō and Godzilla fit nicely into a genre (the "monster on the loose" creature feature) already well established by Hollywood. Other Japanese pop culture products soon followed in the commercial slipstream created by the king of the monsters: Japanese animation and live-action series proved affordable ways to fill airtime in the early decades of American television, and imports such as Astro Boy (*Tetsuwan Atom*), Ultraman, and Speed Racer (*Mach Go Go Go*) were easily accepted by Western children weaned on Disney, Marvel comics, and superhero movies. By the 1990s, Japanese pop culture products were increasingly embraced for being polished and high quality (rather than cheesy and campy) and for being refreshingly distinct from (rather than derivative of) Hollywood narrative traditions and visual conventions. Yet Godzilla—the man in the rubber suit, the character dismissed by one critic as "a miniature of a dinosaur made of gum-shoes and about $20 worth of toy buildings"[3]—was not only the pioneer that launched the Japanese pop wave, but remained, even 50 years on, a global fan favorite.

For many postwar moviegoers in the United States and Europe, Godzilla was not just their first introduction to Japanese popular culture, but also to Japan itself. A 1985 *New York Times*/CBS News poll famously found that the king of the monsters was one of the three best-known "Japanese people" among Americans.[4] Godzilla was thus something of an ambassador as well as a trailblazer, an unlikely cinematic hero who accustomed generations of global consumers to the excitement, humor, creativity, distinctive sensibility, dark subtexts, and addictive charms of the Japanese pop culture industry. To comprehend the seemingly universal popularity of Pokémon and *Iron Chef*, Mobile Suit Gundam and the Mighty Morphin' Power Rangers, one has to grasp first the world's 50-year-long fascination with Godzilla. And, needless to say, one also needs to appreciate the historical environment—the intertwined political, cultural, economic, and diplomatic contexts—from which the king of the monsters originally emerged.

Considering the longevity, popularity, and significance of the Godzilla series, scholarly writings on the films and their influence have been scarce. Fan publications on Godzilla proliferate in both Japanese and English and, though often useful as research sources (rich as these materials are in images, interviews with production staff, and so forth), they generally tend to be informational, journalistic, intensely personal or creative in nature. Academics, long used to slighting popular culture and dismissing *kaijū eiga* (monster films) as campy kiddie spectacles, devoid of particular artistic, intellectual, or ideological content, have produced only a handful of significant studies of the Godzilla opus. Although Susan Sontag encouraged us to take Japanese creature features seriously as early as 1965, writing memorably of "the aesthetics of destruction . . . the particular beauties to be found in wreaking havoc,"[5] it was more than two decades before any scholars took up her call. Film studies specialist Chon Noriega's 1987 essay, "Godzilla and the Japanese Nightmare: When *Them!* is U.S.," emphasized the series' origins in postwar trauma and cold war anxiety, eclectically blending Freudian analysis with observations on nuclear fear and Japan's uneasy relationship with America.[6] Susan Napier has included the king of the monsters in her influential overviews of postwar Japanese pop culture, most notably in her 1993 article "Panic Sites" that frames the 1954 *Gojira* within the broad science fiction convention of "secure horror" and a specifically Japanese dystopian imagination arising after World War II.[7] More recently, Yoshikuni Igarashi's 2000 examination of *kaijū eiga* in the context of the legacies of war and the consequences of high-speed postwar economic growth is the most important historical analysis of the Godzilla series in English, and William Tsutsui's 2004 study *Godzilla on My Mind* attempts to account for the monster's prominence in U.S. pop culture and longstanding appeal among American fans.[8] Meanwhile, a large and diverse variety of writings on Godzilla have appeared in Japanese, mainly from critics and media commentators, many of them dedicated monster movie *otaku*.[9] Like the English-language literature on Godzilla to date, Japanese sources pose many important questions but only begin to provide much in the way of answers, the kind of scholarly building blocks needed to understand the creation, meanings, and global reach of Godzilla.

The ways in which Godzilla anticipated and influenced later popular culture products from Japan—especially anime and manga, but also films, television, character goods, and even pop art—is a topic largely overlooked by Western scholars and aficionados alike. Although a family tree of Japanese pop culture icons abroad must unavoidably start with Godzilla, the global grand-daddy of Japanese mass entertainment, few commentators (whether discussing Neon Genesis Evangelion, Yu-Gi-Oh!, or Hello Kitty) have addressed the profound thematic legacies of *kaijū eiga*. Godzilla is, after all, most frequently remembered outside of Japan as the bug-eyed slapstick superhero for kids of the 1960s films, not as the somber and politically engaged monster-with-a-message that began the series in the 1950s. But the 1954 *Gojira* clearly established a vocabulary—thematic, visual, and ideological—that would be consistently deployed, explored, and reinforced by the mainstream of Japanese popular culture right up to the present day. Thus, one finds the genetic traces of Godzilla, and particularly that original film, throughout the subculture creations of postwar Japan: the foregrounded nuclear menace, the fascination with mutation, the proximity of apocalypse, a pervasive sense of alienation intertwined with an enduring sentimentality, an honest conviction of pacifism combined with "an obsessive fondness for military weaponry."[10] *Gojira* was an influential, even foundational, text for Japanese popular culture, imaginatively addressing Japan's postwar traumas—atomic bombings, defeat, occupation, dependency, and insecurity in the cold war world—in ways that would become deeply rooted cultural conventions.

As Yoshikuni Igarashi has skillfully delineated, the tone and message of the Godzilla films moved in step with the moods and fortunes of Japanese society in the decades after 1954. The monster itself was "tamed and transformed" in the 1960s,[11] reflecting not just the swelling national self-confidence of the "economic miracle" years but also the changing demographics of the Japanese moviegoing audience and the creeping infantilization—the cute-ification—that is a distinguishing characteristic of postwar Japanese pop culture. At the same time, some might well argue that Godzilla's transformations (from dark and vengeful to goofy and heroic, and then eventually back again) and the monster's increasing identification as "Japanese" may have reflected eco-nomics-induced optimism far less than a kind of cultural resignation, an acceptance of what Murakami Takashi describes as Japan's persistent postwar deformity. The inclusion of Godzilla among *wareware Nihonjin* (we Japanese) may thus symbolize an embrace by the Japanese of what Murakami characterizes as their own monstrosity: "We are deformed monsters," he declares, bemoaning postwar Japan's inability to master the shadows of war, define an independent identity, or overcome subordination to the United States.[12] In a way, then, Godzilla may even have provided a fundamental metaphor for the expression of Japanese identity in the nation's long, unre-solved postwar.

This collection aims to interrogate Godzilla, situating the monster within Japan's historical landscape over the past half century, the postwar rise of Japanese pop, and the unfolding process of cultural globalization. What has Godzilla meant to Japanese audiences? What resonances—political, cultural, social—did the films have with Japanese viewers? Which of these references, influences, and inflections (if indeed any) were accessible to international moviegoers and why did audiences around the world respond to Japanese creature features? How did the 1954 *Gojira* and the film franchise influence the pop culture creations that followed in Godzilla's footsteps, both in the domestic market and on the global stage? What has been the legacy of the king of the monsters on Japanese culture broadly conceived, on international perceptions of Japan, and on the growth of subcultures and fan communities around the world? Why, in short, should that man in a latex lizard suit—not to mention the legions of masked superheroes, giant robots, pocket monsters, and post-apocalyptic mutants who followed in his 50-year-old tracks—matter to us at all?

The first eight essays in this volume deal with Godzilla the movie star, the character, the symbol, the myth, and the pioneer. They demonstrate, as Aaron Gerow observes, that Godzilla was (and is) a mightily "intertextual beast." Explaining Godzilla's intersections with other texts, themes, events, and discourses, these essays establish a variety of contexts in which viewers—both in Japan and abroad, both at the time the films were made and today—have been able to situate and comprehend the king of the monsters. Thus, we discover here the ways in which *Gojira* and the film series that followed were sited in persistent wartime debates over modernity, science, and technology; memories of empire and the shadows of war and defeat; postwar pop culture favorites like Japanese pro-wrestling and manga; cold war politics and nuclear anxiety; the exoticism of the South Pacific and the tensions of rampant consumerism in "high growth" Japan. We also find Godzilla analyzed as a important example of the "monster on the loose" genre, as a commercial boon to American movie exhibitors and television programmers, and as a strong, silent type, an early model of the Japanese pop culture icon who (like the nation from which it came) remained essentially passive and voiceless on the global stage.

Such historical contextualization draws our attention to the multiple and often contradictory fashions in which Godzilla can and has been experienced by audiences in different times, places, and environments (cultural, political, and social). The disjunction is especially stark between Godzilla as frequently seen abroad (cheesy, goofy, and ideologically hollow) and the monster accessible to Japanese viewers, positioned within a matrix of meaning-laden cultural references and political valences. Thus, as Barak Kushner details in his essay here, while Japanese government officials looked to film exports like Godzilla as potent advertisements for a new, thoroughly modern Japan, American audiences largely perceived the king of the monsters (like early postwar Japan itself) as "kitschy, silly, and ultimately unfathomable." Similarly, Aaron Gerow bids us to reconsider the marginalization of the Godzilla films of the 1960s and 1970s as childish and campy, discovering instead a "joyously physical way of watching Godzilla" in the pop culture milieu of the time.

All of the essays on Godzilla in this collection underline the originality of *kaijū eiga* and the remarkable inventiveness of its creators in engaging a range of cultural, political, and social issues while producing highly commercial mass entertainment. Japanese culture in general and contemporary pop culture in particular have often been criticized in the West for being imitative: Joseph Tobin has noted that "unflattering views of the Japanese as passive victims of first Chinese and then Western cultural combinations or, alternatively, as active, underhanded agents of plagiarism" are common in American and European writings.[13] Although Godzilla's detractors have often disparaged

Tōhō "suitmation" as a low-budget knock-off of Hollywood "monster on the loose" classics like *King Kong* and *The Beast from 20,000 Fathoms,* such denigration does not hold up to close scrutiny. Godzilla may initially have been inspired by models from the West but, like the work of Tezuka Osamu or Oshii Mamoru, can hardly be considered derivative. What's more, even though (as Joanne Bernardi observes in her essay) some commentators complain that reading *Gojira* as an antinuclear parable "has become something of a cliché,"[14] the authors in this volume remind us of the depth, subtlety, and complexity of the 1954 film's reflections on the atomic threat, the relationship between science and humanity, and the tolls of war, both past and present.

The last five essays examine Godzilla's legacy in Japanese culture and the ways in which Japanese pop icons following in the king of the monster's global path have reached, inspired, and inflamed international audiences. The pieces by Kevin J. Wetmore, Jr. and Eric Rath explore how the figure and the message of Godzilla have influenced Japanese high culture, specifically the underground theater of the 1980s and the super-kyōgen of the early twenty-first century. Although the appearance of Godzilla in such forms may just affirm Murakami Takashi's notion of a "superflat" erasure of distinctions between high and low in Japan's pop-dominated contemporary culture,[15] these essays suggest not just the pervasiveness of *kaijū eiga,* but also the potential of using a giant cinematic reptile as a means of social critique. Godzilla has, in the hands of playwrights and satirists, become a compelling tool for evoking humor and nostalgia as well as expressing biting political and social satire. Thus, contemporary appropriations of Godzilla have inherited both the solemn moralizing (and implicit anti-Americanism) of the 1954 *Gojira* and the playful absurdity of the monster in the 1960s and 1970s.

Fan communities around the world have also embraced Japanese pop culture creations, using character goods, live-action television series, anime, and manga to craft meanings, identities, and subculture networks. The essays by Christine Yano, Hirofumi Katsuno, and Yulia Mikhailova suggest the wide diversity—and intense local particularity—of responses to icons like Hello Kitty. Case studies of "pink globalization" and its discontents, fandom in the liminal space of Hawai'i, and the uses of Japanese pop to build social status in Russia all demonstrate the importance of gender, ethnicity, social marginalization, and specific political circumstances in shaping the consumption and manipulation of imported popular culture forms. Not only does such research help us to understand better the international reception of the Godzilla series in retrospect, but it also highlights the need for additional scrutiny of the historical evolution of global subcultures since Godzilla's pathbreaking entry into world markets in the 1950s. As Susan Napier encourages us to consider in her chapter, the message and manifestations of "pink globalization" today seem subtly different from those of Godzilla's "green globalization" in the early postwar decades.

In the end, the picture of Godzilla and postwar Japanese pop culture that emerges from this collection is not simple or neat. Most Western observers over the past half century have been quick to pigeonhole Godzilla as an unambiguous metaphor for the United States or The Bomb or nuclear fear, or else as a tasteless (in both its meanings) slice of Japanese cinematic cheese, undeserving of serious consideration. This volume suggests, much to the contrary, that Godzilla is a complex and multifaceted pop idol, embedded in intricate networks of cultural signification and personal meaning, with a profound and lasting global impact unexpected from a low-budget, big-screen creature. That Godzilla's descendants have traced comparable trajectories in the process of globalization—beloved, derided, reimagined, exploited, and eventually integrated into new historical and cultural contexts—should hardly be surprising. The path Godzilla cleared has, in many respects, continued to define the parameters of the global advance of Japanese popular culture right down to the present day.

NOTES

1. Tim Craig, "Introduction," in *Japan Pop! Inside the World of Japanese Popular Culture*, ed. Timothy J. Craig (Armonk, NY: M.E. Sharpe, 2000), p. 5.
2. Douglas McGray, "Japan's Gross National Cool," *Foreign Policy* (May/June 2002), pp. 44–54.
3. Bosley Crowther's review of *Godzilla, King of the Monsters, New York Times*, April 28, 1956.
4. See William M. Tsutsui, *Godzilla on My Mind: Fifty Years of the King of Monsters* (New York: Palgrave Macmillan, 2004), pp. 6–7.
5. Susan Sontag, "The Imagination of Disaster" (1965), in *Hibakusha Cinema: Hiroshima, Nagasaki and the Nuclear Image in Japanese Film*, ed. Mick Broderick (London: Kegan Paul International, 1996), p. 41.
6. Chon Noriega, "Godzilla and the Japanese Nightmare: When *Them!* is U.S." (1987), in *Hibakusha Cinema*, pp. 54–74.
7. Susan Napier, "Panic Sites: The Japanese Imagination of Disaster from *Godzilla* to *Akira*," *Journal of Japanese Studies* 19:2 (Summer 1993), pp. 327–351. See also Susan Napier, *The Fantastic in Modern Japanese Literature: The Subversion of Modernity* (London: Routledge, 1996).
8. Yoshikuni Igarashi, *Bodies of Memory: Narratives of War in Postwar Japanese Culture, 1945–1970* (Princeton, NJ: Princeton University Press, 2000); Tsutsui, *Godzilla on My Mind*.
9. See, for example, Higuchi Naofumi, *Guddo Mōningu, Gojira: Kantoku Honda Ishirō to satsueisho no jidai* (Tokyo: Chikuma Shobō, 1992); Peter Musolf, *Gojira to wa nani ka*, trans. Ono Kōsei (Tokyo: Kodansha International, 1998); Nagayama Yasuo, *Kaijū wa naze Nihon o osou no ka?* (Tokyo: Chikuma Shobō, 2002); Satō Kenji, *Gojira to Yamato to bokura no minshū shugi* (Tokyo: Bungei Shunjū, 1992).
10. Noi Sawaragi, "On the Battlefield of 'Superflat': Subculture and Art in Postwar Japan," in *Little Boy: The Arts of Japan's Exploding Subculture*, trans. Linda Hoaglund, ed. Takashi Murakami (New York: Japan Society, 2005), p. 203. See also Tsutsui, *Godzilla on My Mind*, pp. 94–97.
11. Igarashi, *Bodies of Memory*, p. 121.
12. Takashi Murakami, "Superflat Trilogy: Greetings, You are Alive," in *Little Boy*, trans. Office Miyazaki, Inc., p. 161.

13. Joseph Tobin, "Introduction: Domesticating the West," in *Re-Made in Japan: Everyday Life and Consumer Taste in a Changing Society*, ed. Joseph Tobin (New Haven, CT: Yale University Press, 1992), p. 3.

14. Cynthia Erb, *Tracking King Kong: A Hollywood Icon in World Culture* (Detroit: Wayne State University Press, 1998), p. 28.

15. Alexandra Munroe, "Introducing Little Boy," in *Little Boy*, pp. 244–245.

1

When Godzilla Speaks

Susan Napier

In 1956, Clifford Simak, an American science fiction writer, published *Strangers in the Universe*, a collection of short stories that included the piece "Shadow Show." The story describes a group of scientists who have been sent to a lonely asteroid and commissioned with the task of creating life, specifically sentient human life that could take alien form, thus allowing humans to populate inhospitable planets throughout the universe. To keep the scientists amused and also psychologically sound, an entertainment known as the Play has been created for them in which they can mentally project images of made-up characters onto a screen and have them interact with the mental projections of the other scientists. The characters projected by the scientists are a varied group, ranging from the grotesque—such as the "Alien Monster"—to the comic, the so-called Out at Elbows Philosopher. In the story's surprise denouement the scientists realize that they have indeed succeeded in creating life, not through their experiments but through the machine that enables the Play. In a shocking reversal, the characters declare independence from their creators and begin to speak and act for themselves, coming down from the screen and appearing on the stage. At the end of "Shadow Show," Bayard Lodge, the story's protagonist, walks down the auditorium to meet his projected persona, the "Rustic Slicker."

Simak ends "Shadow Show" with Lodge's stunned thoughts:

> In just a little while the characters would step down off the stage and would mingle with them. And their creators? What would their creators do? . . .
> What would he say to the Rustic Slicker?
> What *could* he say to the Rustic Slicker?
> And more to the point, what would the Rustic Slicker have to say to him?[1]

At the turn of the twentieth century Oscar Wilde wrote, "[t]he whole of Japan is pure invention,"[2] implying that the Japanese and their culture were simply Western projections, shadows on the screen of the Western mind, incapable of life of their own. This perception of Japan as a voiceless Other has continued through much of the last century. In 1970, for example, the

French semiotician Roland Barthes described Japan as an "Empire of Signs," essentially silent, needing the Western interpreter to understand its signifiers. As Barthes says in a typically enthusiastic passage, "[t]he murmuring mass of an unknown language constitutes a delicious protection, envelops the foreigner in an auditory film—the unknown language . . . forms around me as I move, a faint vertigo, sweeping me into its artificial emptiness, which is consummated only for me."[3]

Wilde and Barthes are not the only ones to whom Japan speaks in special ways just for them. The nineteenth-century American writer Lafcadio Hearn loved Japan so much that he became a Japanese citizen, taking on a Japanese name. But Hearn too seems to have created his own Japan, in this case a fairy land with, as he says, "its people a fairy folk" and he discusses with pleasure the joy of "[f]ind[ing] oneself suddenly in a world where everything is upon a smaller and daintier scale than with us, a world where all movement is slow and voices are hushed . . . a realization of the old dream of a World of Elves."[4]

To Hearn the Japanese in general have "hushed voices." For many other Western men it was the "hushed voice" of the Japanese woman that was particularly entrancing. In his 1956 novel *Sayonara*, James Michener has his hero, the American flying ace Lloyd Gruber, muse about the differences between Japanese and American women. To Gruber the postwar American girl is loud and hectoring, destroying her husband's manhood by her nagging bitchiness. In contrast, the Japanese woman's actions speak louder than words. Gruber envisions how his friend Airman Kelly's Japanese wife takes care of him through the simple act of bathing him quietly, giving him back the confidence he needs through this silent expression of affection.

Turning to popular culture, we see that the rule of silence seems to hold here as well. Certainly the star of this volume, Godzilla himself, comes across as the strong and silent type (aside from his trademark roar). Our first view of him in the 1954 film that began it all is of an enormous dark scaly head rising above the hills of a Japanese coastal town, and this scene is made all the more menacing by Godzilla's total silence. Like the ideal Japanese woman, Godzilla's actions speak louder than words. His massive footprint, his steady advance, and above all the destruction that he leaves behind are both terrifying and impressive. Many scholars, myself included, believe that the initial Godzilla—with his links to nuclear testing and radiation—may in many ways be seen as a displaced version of the atomic bomb.[5] His story and its ultimately happy outcome—Godzilla is vanquished through Japanese science—may, therefore, be read as a form of cultural therapy, allowing the defeated Japanese to work through the trauma of the wartime bombings in the scenes of panic or destruction and, with the film's happy end, giving them a chance to reimagine and rewrite their devastating defeat. The total voicelessness of Godzilla in this film may remind us of John Treat's quotation from a survivor of Hiroshima who describes the day of the bombing when she looked up in the sky and thought, "[o]h look there's an enemy plane coming" and then says, "[t]hereafter there were no more words."[6]

To Americans and to other non-Japanese, Godzilla may be equally complicated, even if we are not consciously aware of all that he suggested or continues to suggest. To give a perhaps typical example of Americans' reaction to Godzilla, let me turn to the American humorist Dave Barry who wrote about his youthful impressions of the Japanese in his book *Dave Barry Does Japan.*

> The point is that my initial impression [which he had received from watching old World War II movies on television] of the Japanese was not favorable. Fortunately, as I grew older, my intellectual horizons broadened, and I no longer received information about the outside world exclusively from television; I also started going to horror movies. From these I learned that Japan was not just a weird foreign country that had tried to kill us, it was also a weird foreign country that was for some reason under almost constant attack by giant mutated creatures. Godzilla was the most famous one, of course, but there were also hyperthyroid pterodactyls, spiders, etc, all of which regularly barged into Tokyo and committed acts of mass destruction. I imagine this eventually became so commonplace that Japanese TV weathermen included it in their forecasts ("Partly cloudy this afternoon, with a 60% chance that Tokyo will be leveled by immense radioactive worms.").[7]

To Mr Barry's young eyes, Japan was indeed a land of monsters, threatening America, a vision that changes somewhat in the course of his book, as he concludes with a paean to the civility and safety of modern Japanese society. But even here he feels compelled to add, "[w]hich is not to say that Japan isn't still a little scary."[8] It is possible that Barry's early vision of Godzilla still lingers on the edges of his consciousness.

If the idealized female was the "good" side of Japan in American eyes in the 1950s—vulnerable, grateful, and self-sacrificing—Godzilla is what the Japanese scholar Takayuki Tatsumi describes as the "ultimately disastrous other" linked both to the atomic bomb and, as Tatsumi goes on to describe, to "help[ing] the postwar Japanese . . . reconstruct a national identity by making themselves into victims and resistors against an outside threat."[9] But this national identity has been problematic even in Japan (as we can see from the way Godzilla's symbolic position changes in the postwar period) and became the basis for numerous distortions among non-Japanese as the postwar era continued. Nevertheless, the monstrous figure of Godzilla, as William Tsutsui chronicles in *Godzilla on My Mind,* has remained an icon for both the Japanese and the West, especially the United States, right up to the present time.

To the Japanese, as Tatsumi relates, "the image of Godzilla, the oversized public enemy in the 1950s, was displaced with that of Godzilla the national superhero in the economic high growth period."[10] For Americans, however, while Godzilla's representation may include both the camp and the cute, for many it is still at heart an image of terrifying otherness, invoked to describe everything from the "Godzilla" earthquake that flattens a future Japan in William Gibson's novel *Virtual Light* to the notorious "Bridezilla" so ubiquitous in magazine columns of wedding do's and don'ts (Bridezilla is a "don't," by the way). But, perhaps, most stable has been the image of Japan as a monstrous Godzilla-esque Other. This image is not always seen in specifically Godzilla-related terms but certainly in ones close to it. Thus, when Japan was still seen as an economic superpower, *Newsweek* once ran an article on Japan that included a quotation describing the Japanese as the "economic terminators" of the future, the terminator, of course, being yet another image of the unstoppable power.[11] The Japanese critic Ueno Toshiya has suggested that a recent stereotype of the Japanese might be what he calls the "Japanoid," a robotic entity largely based on the rise of technology and information capitalism.[12]

Whether Japanoid, terminator, or simply Godzilla, these monstrous beings are still essentially silent, gigantic, but passive, shadows onto which the West and possibly Asia project their own dreams and nightmares of Japan. It is my contention, however, that in the last decade or so, this silence has begun to be broken. In fact, and I fear I may sound blasphemous, given the topic of this volume, I would suggest that the silent menacing Godzilla of old may be a little out of date as an icon for contemporary Japan. Or perhaps a more felicitous suggestion would be that Godzilla's descendants are beginning to talk back.

Indeed, I would assert that, from at least the beginning of the 1990s, Japan in the form of its immensely rich contemporary culture has begun to speak with a new authority. Over the last decade, fashion designers, toy makers, artists, video game designers, manga artists, and animators have begun to export what Douglas McGray in his famous article in *Foreign Policy* calls Japan's Gross National Cool. Developing his ideas from the political scientist Joseph Nye's vision of "soft power," that is, economic and cultural, in opposition to "hard power," that is, military, McGray suggests that "Japan is reinventing superpower."[13] On the one hand, he points out that Japanese culture has "transcended U.S. demand," becoming an artistic and commercial force in both Europe and Asia. On the other hand, he asserts that Japan has also "made deep inroads into American culture, [a culture] which is usually written off by the rest of the world as aggravatingly insular."[14] Incredibly, McGray manages not to include even a single mention of Godzilla in reference to Japanese superpower, but the implication is clear—derided through the 1990s for its weak economy, Japan is now back and is exercising increasing cultural and even, to some extent, economic influence throughout the world.

The statistics and anecdotes speak for themselves: Japan's global entertainment industry, according to Ken Belson and Brian Bremner, is worth between $400 billion and $500 billion a year, or up to 10 percent of the country's gross domestic product in 2002. The Hello Kitty empire alone generates about half of her parent company Sanrio's $1 billion in sales.[15] Young people all over the world are not only buying Japanese products but also making pilgrimages to Japan to get the real experience of Japan and, incidentally, buy hard-to-obtain products. The magazine *Shūkan Tōyō Keizai* profiled a young Parisian woman who travels to Japan, not to visit Kyoto or to eat Japanese cuisine, but to visit the consumer electronics mecca of Akihabara and the specialized manga emporia of Shibuya. In my own research I have heard of young Americans going on "anime tours" of Japan, visiting such sacred sites as Studio Ghibli or buying the Meiji candy drops highlighted in the anime *Grave of the Fireflies.*

Back in the West, the prestigious French luggage manufacturer Louis Vuitton commissioned the popular Tokyo artist Murakami Takashi to create an animated film for its stores featuring a girl who falls into a tunnel decorated with (surprise!) Louis Vuitton logos. At the same time, a spokesman for Christie's auction house in Japan suggested that Murakami had become a name brand—"like Picasso." In 2003, the popular manga magazine *Shōnen Jump* began to be published in English and has spawned a vast manga boom among American girls and boys. Earlier that year, the Japanese animated film *Spirited Away* won the Academy Award for best animated film, beating out four American entries including two from Disney. In the summer of 2003, the anime fan convention Otakon ("Convention for the Otaku Generation") drew almost 20,000 colorfully dressed American fans to Baltimore. I know because I was there and it was one of the more memorable experiences of my life, fighting my way through a convention center filled with Hamtaros, No-Faces, Goddesses, and so forth.

How is it that Japanese popular culture has begun to take on an autonomous life of its own? And what does it mean that Japan, rather than say France or England or China, has begun to "speak"? And who or what are the real heirs to Godzilla? Before investigating these questions it might be useful to remind ourselves that Japan has long had a powerful imagistic force in Western culture from artists and architects, such as the French Impressionists—who found in Japanese woodblock prints a world of inspiration and enrichment—to the great literary modernists, such as Ezra Pound or Wallace Stevens, who used Japanese haiku to begin a revolution in American poetry. In the postwar period, visions of Japanese geisha girls from the 1950s were transformed into Japanese pop idols in the works of cyberpunk writers, such as William Gibson, whose fictional versions of a technologized, media-driven Japan have helped us to imagine our own future as modern Americans. But most of these visions, even Gibson's, have still kept Japan as passive, a place of rich fascination that still must be mediated through Western eyes. (The hologram heroine of Gibson's novel *Idoru,* for example, while mysterious and mischievous is still largely silent.)

Nevertheless, it is around the same time as the development of cyberpunk in the 1980s, I would argue, that Japan does begin to take on a more autonomous role in Western culture. Perhaps surprisingly, my first example of this would be Ridley Scott's 1982 film *Blade Runner.* As many critics have noted, Scott's vision of Los Angeles in 2019 is a distinctly Asian one,[16] beginning with the first scene in which the detective Deckard is introduced arguing with the Japanese-speaking chef of a sushi bar. (In the non-director's cut of the film, in fact, the first word that Deckard speaks in voiceover is

Japanese—"Sushi, cold fish, that's what my ex-wife called me.") But it is not the Asian mise-en-scene nor even the giant simulacrum of a Japanese woman that floats in the sky above Deckard, but rather Deckard's prey that is the most intriguing for the purposes of this essay. Deckard is hunting "replicants," androids who are stronger, smarter, more loyal, and fundamentally more *competitive* than we "humans" are. Perhaps it is not too much of a stretch to think that the replicants are really the Japanese as "we" envisioned them in the 1980s? In this regard it is interesting that the replicants are particularly linked with the notion of sight, as when the chief replicant, Batty, tells Deckard as he (Batty) starts to die, "I've seen things with these eyes that you wouldn't believe: starships on fire off the shoulders of Orion. C-beams at the Tannhauser Gate," and then finishes on a remarkably lyrical note: "all these memories, lost in time, like tears in the rain." In America's rather paranoid vision of Japan during the 1980s, the Japanese seemed to "see" our weaknesses more clearly than we ourselves could.

The replicants may be seen as honorable heirs to Godzilla, magnificent, terrifying, and utterly Other, but, unlike Godzilla, immensely articulate. In the period following *Blade Runner* we may discern two strands in what might be called Godzilla's descendants—the cuddly cute who tend to be on the silent side and consist of cartoon and other so-called characters, and the interestingly articulate, the protagonists of Japanese animation and its related artistic form, manga.

Turning to cuteness first, how can we not begin with Hello Kitty? In their book *Hello Kitty: The Remarkable Story of Sanrio and the Billion Dollar Feline Phenomenon*, Belsen and Bremner, perhaps inevitably, compare Kitty with Godzilla, noting that during the 1980s when it seemed that Japan was taking "leadership positions in one core manufacturing industry after another . . . it wasn't Hello Kitty that symbolized Japan, it was Godzilla."[17] In certain ways, Hello Kitty makes sense as the next Japanese symbol. Like Godzilla, she is ubiquitous—appearing, as Christine Yano helpfully informs us in her essay (chapter 11) in this volume, on everything from stationary to vibrators. She is also, as the first Godzilla movie became when it had American footage with Raymond Burr added to it, something of a hybrid. Although designed and manufactured in Japan, Kitty is actually from London and her surname is "White." Indeed as with Godzilla, Kitty has been tweaked somewhat for the American market, changing her fashion tastes to pink and lavender, for example, rather than the Japanese favorite red and blue. Also like Godzilla, Kitty is silent, in fact, she has no mouth. But perhaps Kitty is too sweet to be associated with Godzilla?

Perhaps not. In the twenty-first century, Kitty's silence is considered problematic. Particularly among certain young women, her lack of mouth is considered an affront, yet another version of the passive Japanese female. Thus, in 2002, Jaime Scholnick created a piece of performance art in which Kitty talks back. Entitled "Hello Kitty Gets A Mouth," the story begins with Kitty using her Hello Kitty vibrator. Unfortunately, not having a mouth, Kitty is unable to vocalize her pleasure so she begins a journey to find one, ultimately ending up at a plastic surgeon's office in Beverly Hills. Other art pieces and web sites suggest that Kitty may not be always so cute and cuddly. Perhaps she is a legitimate descendant of Godzilla after all.

Another obvious candidate for Godzilla's heir would have to be Pikachu of Pokémon. Pokémon itself stands for "Pocket Monsters," so could we see Pikachu as a kind of junior Godzilla? Once again we have the problem that Pikachu is awfully cute and child oriented to be a reasonable Godzilla symbol. Also, unlike Godzilla, Pikachu, far from being a silent loner, is very much part of a team. Yet, according to Christine Yano, Pokémon can strike fear in the hearts of Americans in almost Godzilla-esque fashion. As she explains it, many parents see the Pokémon phenomenon as a "monster out of control."[18] Pokémon even polarizes politically. The left finds the game embodying the evils of consumer capitalism, whereas the right, especially fundamentalist Christians, see it as nothing less than Satanic, promoting "non-Christian" concepts, such as ghosts, psychics, and hypnosis, and diagnosing a child's Pokémon addiction and demonic influence by watching for symptoms that include "hostility, anger or rage when asked to leave the game."[19] With this kind of negative publicity, Pokémon is beginning to seem more monstrous than Godzilla ever was!

To my mind however (and obviously this is related to my own biases as a researcher on anime and anime fandom), the most interesting descendants of Godzilla are the characters who populate anime and manga. Not only can we say that the enormous pop culture that constitutes anime and manga—reaching as it does around the world—represents an almost Godzilla-esque phenomenon in its own right, but the actual characters in anime and manga—who range from the alien to the girl next door—are examples of how Japan has started to speak for itself.

As film scholar Susan Pointon had commented, Japanese animation (and I would argue manga as well) is a non-Western cultural product that has remained uncompromisingly true to its native origins.[20] This is worth pondering for a moment. The last time I saw young Americans excited about another country's culture was in the 1960s when my older brother was growing out his hair in Beatles style and playing the Kinks (badly) on the bass guitar. But England is still a lot closer to America than Japan is.

What we are looking at when we see the blooming Japanese animation and manga subculture in the United States (and actually all over the world) is nothing less, I would submit, than a genuine social phenomenon. At a time when many thinking Americans are lamenting what they perceive as American parochialism, this deep fascination with a non-Western cultural product, a fascination that often, as I have discovered in my research, turns into a fascination with the country itself, is truly stunning and genuinely heartening. In my interviews with anime and manga fans throughout the country I have encountered an enormous number of them who have started studying Japanese, have become interested in other Japanese practices, from martial arts to the tea ceremony, and have been to or want to go to Japan.

What accounts for this fascination? A very short answer would be the explanation that Japanese animation and manga are both different and universal at the same time. The fans comment on the beauty of the artwork or the sophistication of the music. But most of all, the stories and the characters speak to them. For those of you who have not encountered anime or manga this may come as a surprise but, in fact, many Americans can find in the enormous range and variety of manga and anime something (perhaps a lot) with which they identify.

And very specifically, I might add, as became clear when I examined the answers to my question, "Do you identify with any anime characters?" The answers varied greatly, from a young man who identified with the neurotic Shinji, the anti-hero of the immensely popular series *Neon Genesis Evangelion* (Shinseiki Ebuangerion), because he empathized with Shinji's problems dealing with his father and with women, to a teenage girl who wrote that she identified with the fighting heroine of *Revolutionary Girl Utena* (Shōjo kakumei Utena) because she was "strong and brave, and wanted to use her powers to help other people." As is obvious, the types of characters in anime vary hugely, but this array allows for an infinite variety of material from which young fans can begin to construct their own identities.

Another reason for the popularity of anime is the universality of its themes. Although I cannot explore this at great length here, I have found in my research that anime can very broadly be categorized into three modes: the apocalyptic, the carnivalesque, and the elegiac, and I would like to discuss a brief example of each type.

We will begin with Ōtomo Katsuhiro's 1988 film *Akira*, not only because it is the first anime that garnered critical and popular attention in the West and ultimately ushered in the anime boom, but also because it is intimately related to Godzilla. In fact, Alan Cholodenko in his article "Apocalyptic Animation: In the Wake of Hiroshima, Nagasaki, *Godzilla* and Baudrillard" calls *Godzilla* the major precursor for *Akira*, not only because *Akira* also inscribes the war, Hiroshima, The Bomb, and the U.S. Occupation, but also because *Akira* was only the second Japanese film to break into the Western mass entertainment market, the first being *Godzilla*. Although the plot of *Akira* is immensely more complicated than *Godzilla*, it too offers the viewer a sense of overwhelming power and otherness, especially in the person of Tetsuo, the young delinquent biker, who takes on telekinetic powers of such an awesome scale that he lays waste to Tokyo even more destructively than did Godzilla. As Cholodenko says, "Avatar of Godzilla—character and film—Akira—character and film—is The Bomb, at once more and less the Bomb than The Bomb, that explodes/implodes both America and Japan, even as it revivifies/reanimates them, even as Tetsuo, the monster-on-the-loose avatar of Godzilla and Akira takes up his nuclear-powered, chain-reactive absorbing place within that lineage, donning a red cape to complete the highly loaded tricolour—red, white, and blue—in that process metamorphosing . . . himself . . . into something 'eternally incomprehensible,' enigmatic, Radically Other."[21]

Although we may find Cholodenko's formulation a little strong, there is no question that the end of the world is a major theme in postwar Japanese culture and is particularly well suited for the medium of animation. To turn to an example of the carnivalesque, we find, wrapped in anarchic comedy, another quasi-apocalyptic vision. This example is from the immensely popular series *Urusei Yatsura* about a beautiful space alien named Lum, who, like Godzilla, has roots in Japanese folklore—she is in fact a kind of Japanese demon called an *oni*, who threatens to take over the world unless a hapless human named Ataru can beat her in a game of tag. Ultimately, through subterfuge, he does beat her and the world is saved—until the next episode.

Urusei Yatsura plays on our fears of apocalypse in a lighthearted way that is ultimately comforting, whereas *Akira*'s scenes of destruction may be considered cathartic, but in both cases they resonate with both Japanese and American audiences. (Intriguingly, in my course on the "Cinema of Apocalypse" I have found the largest number of apocalyptic films to be produced either in Japan or America—perhaps not surprising given our shared heritage of the atom bomb.)

My last example, from the elegiac mode, is of the world ending on a personal level—the deaths of a family at the end of World War II in *Grave of the Fireflies*. In this film, two children struggle to survive during the war only to die at the very end. Although in some ways a very "Japanese" film, with its strong regional details, this is one of the favorite films among American anime watchers, speaking to them in a quieter and more evocative tone than the more bombastic apocalyptic or comic works.

So, with anime and manga, Japan/Godzilla is not only talking back but also speaking to the rest of the world in an unprecedented fashion. Not only young Americans, but Malaysians, Mexicans, French, and Chinese are finding something that they do not find in their own cultures. It helps, of course, that we are now part of an enormous global system where entertainment flows seamlessly and almost instantaneously toward a large and hungry public. Anime and manga, like Godzilla, are nothing if not commercial.

But there may be yet another reason for the popularity of Japanese culture today and this may be found in what I believe is a new approach to what we used to call the "real world," an approach that increasingly accepts, perhaps even celebrates, the fluidity between the material and the virtual. In her article "Cuteness as Japan's Millennial Product," Anne Allison makes a fascinating point concerning the differences between the construction of fantasy in children's entertainment in Japan and America. As she writes, "[i]n the States, the trend is for greater realism and clear-cut borders (for example in plots that emphasize battles between good and evil). In Japan, by contrast, the preference is for greater phantasm and ambiguity, characters and stories that would be unimaginable in real life."[22] But, as the popularity of Pokémon, Kitty, anime, and manga make clear, this phantasmatic ambiguity is embraced by American children as well, perhaps increasingly so. An anime fan, whom I interviewed a few years ago, put it strikingly; "Anime," she said, "is more realistic than live action film." In the contemporary world where the boundary between the real and the virtual is increasingly porous, where life is fluctuating, transformative, and above all uncertain, she may well be right. The fantastic may have as much relevance to us as the material. In his book on Godzilla, William Tsutsui stresses the ambiguity of Godzilla. This is not a monster that can be easily characterized or categorized, much like humanity itself.

Perhaps the younger generation in America is beginning to understand this and, perhaps for this reason, they are willing to let Japan speak and speak in many voices. We are after all, not so very different. Joseph Tobin writes that "[t]he Japanese have been adapting Western cultural products long enough and well enough that by the beginning of the new millennium there is no longer a clear fixed boundary between Western and Japanese things or ideas. Japanese culture . . . is a hybrid construction that, like all cultures, is continuously reinventing itself."[23]

Nevertheless, it is also true that American culture is a hybrid construction that reinvents itself, as our recent embrace of Japanese culture makes clear. As this volume symbolizes, Godzilla is as American as he is Japanese.

In conclusion, I would like to return for a moment to Simak's story "Shadow Show." As Baudrillard in *The Evil Demon of Images* says, "[t]o begin to resemble the other is to take on their appearance, is to seduce them, since it is to make them enter the realm of metamorphosis despite themselves."[24] At one point in Simak's story, Lodge, the angst-ridden scientist who fears creating human life, has an evil dream: he is talking to a monster, a creature utterly unlike him but one that insists on claiming human affinity. He wakes up screaming, and mixes himself a drink.

> "Come on," he said to the monster of the dream. "Come on friend, I'll have that drink with you." He gulped it down and did not notice the harshness of the uncut liquor. "Come on," he shouted at the monster. "Come on and have that drink with me." He stared around the room waiting for the monster. "What the hell," he said, "We're all human, aren't we?"
> "Us humans," he said, still talking to the monster, "have got to stick together."[25]

In Simak's vision, the moment when the Other begins to speak is fraught with terror because it suggests a continuum of identity in an infinite "realm of metamorphosis." In the postwar period such a notion casts doubt on some of our most fundamental conceptions of ourselves. In our postmodern world, however, the notion of a fixed, separate identity is no longer taken for granted. Even though all of us may not yet be able to embrace Godzilla (the Other), we are at least able to listen to him when he begins to speak.

NOTES

1. Clifford Simak, *Strangers in the Universe* (New York: Simon & Schuster, 1956), p. 45.
2. Oscar Wilde, quoted in Frank Nute, *Frank Lloyd Wright and Japan* (London: Routledge, 2000), p. 100.

3. Roland Barthes, *Empire of Signs* (New York: Hill & Wang, 1982), p. 9.

4. Lafcadio Hearn, *Glimpses of Unfamiliar Japan* (Rutland, VT: Charles E. Tuttle, 1976), p. 7.

5. See Susan Napier, "Panic Sites: The Japanese Imagination of Disaster from *Godzilla* to *Akira*," in *Contemporary Japan and Popular Culture*, ed. John Treat (Honolulu: University of Hawai'i Press, 1996), pp. 235–262.

6. John Treat, *Writing Ground Zero: Japanese Literature and the Atomic Bomb* (Chicago: University of Chicago Press, 1995).

7. Dave Barry, *Dave Barry Does Japan* (New York: Random House, 1992), p. 7.

8. Ibid., p. 205.

9. Takayuki Tatsumi, "Waiting for Godzilla: Chaotic Negotiations between Post-Orientalism and Hyper-Occidentalism," in *Transactions, Transgressions, Transformations: American Culture in Western Europe and Japan*, ed. Heide Fehrenbach and Uta G. Poiger (New York: Berghahn Books, 2000), p. 228.

10. Ibid, pp. 230–231.

11. Bill Powell, "Don't Write Off Japan," *Newsweek* 919 (1992), p. 48.

12. Ueno Toshiya, "Japanimation and Techno-Orientalism," http://www.t0.or.at/ueno/japan.htm.

13. Douglas McGray, "Japan's Gross National Cool," *Foreign Policy* (May/June 2002), p. 46.

14. Ibid.

15. Ken Belson and Brian Bremner, *Hello Kitty: The Remarkable Story of Sanrio and the Billion Dollar Phenomenon* (Singapore: John Wiley & Sons, Asia, 2004), p. 5.

16. See, for example, Giuliana Bruno, "Ramble City: Postmodernism and *Blade Runner*" in *Alien Zone*, ed. Annette Kuhn (London: Verso, 1990), pp. 183–195.

17. Belson and Bremner, *Hello Kitty*, p. 25.

18. Christine Yano, "Panic Attacks: Anti-Pokémon Voices in Global Markets," in *Pikachu's Global Adventure: The Rise and Fall of Pokémon*, ed. Joseph Tobin (Durham, NC: Duke University Press, 2004), p. 113.

19. Ibid, p. 127.

20. Susan Pointon, "Transcultural Orgasm as Apocalypse: *Urotsukidoji*: The Legend of the Overfiend," *Wide Angle* 19:3 (1997), p. 45.

21. Alan Cholodenko, "Apocalyptic Animation: In the Wake of Hiroshima, Nagasaki, *Godzilla* and Baudrillard," in *Baudrillard West of the Dateline*, ed. Victoria Grace, Heather Worth, and Laurence Simmons (Palmerston North, New Zealand: Overmore Press, 2003), p. 239.

22. Anne Allison, "Cuteness as Japan's Millennial Product," in *Pikachu's Global Adventure*, p. 44.

23. Joseph Tobin, "Conclusion: The Rise and Fall of the Pokémon Empire," in *Pikachu's Global Adventure*, p. 259.

24. Jean Baudrillard, *The Evil Demon of Images*, trans. Paul Patton and Paul Foss (Sydney, Australia: The Power Institute of Fine Arts, 1987), p. 15.

25. Simak, *Strangers in the Universe*, pp. 29–30.

2

Mobilizing *Gojira*: Mourning Modernity as Monstrosity

Mark Anderson

This essay discusses the first film in Tōhō's Godzilla series, *Gojira* (1954). Some important recent readings of Godzilla, such as those of Takahashi Toshio and Yoshikuni Igarashi, have turned toward historicizing the film in relation to memories of the Asia Pacific War and the cold war.[1] While trying to sustain their attention to struggles over constructions of the Japanese and American past in the present, particularly as regards the issue of mourning and melancholy, I will focus on a tension foregrounded in the film between science, technology, and Japaneseness. I will compare and contrast *Gojira*'s treatment of these issues with their status in a wartime debate on these same topics from just twelve years before—the overcoming modernity debate.[2]

The phrase "mourning modernity as monstrosity" in the title refers to a Japanese romantic position in the debate associated with Kamei Katsuichirō and Hayashi Fusao that modernity was a foreign pathology that brought with it a loss of traditional values. Modernity was to be mourned as a loss of spiritual presence and resisted by a missionary, evangelistic variety of Shintō. The phrase "mobilizing Godzilla" refers to a position in the debate associated with Shimomura Toratarō that overcoming modernity in a Japan that has made science its own would have to be a self-overcoming. Shimomura argues that Japan should be even further rationalized and technologized in the course of total wartime mobilization, but that such a strategy of ultramodernity also offers the possibility of overcoming any spiritual loss produced by earlier forms of modernity in Japan. For Shimomura, technology and spirit are aligned in a proto-cybernetic alternative modernity that will also help with the war.

Juxtaposing the film and the overcoming modernity debate reveals an important, non-Western genealogy for contemporary discourses of neo-liberalism and neo-conservatism in support of globalization—that they, like the positions in the debate—were developed for the purposes of interpreting the stakes of World War II. The shadow of competing interpretations of World War II falls every bit as heavily upon the contemporary U.S. political formation as it does on Japanese affairs. *Gojira* gives these issues a postwar, radioactive twist, but takes the wartime debate as a point of departure in important ways.

A reader might reasonably ask, "Why discuss *Gojira* in the context of the overcoming modernity debate? Isn't this imposing an extraneous issue from another period onto a 1954 film?" I see at least five reasons to consider the wartime debate and the film in relation to one another:

1 In the context of Japan's defeat in World War II and many of its leaders having been convicted of and executed for war crimes, the film poses the question of how Japan may defend itself in an ethical way and the consequences of this issue for Japan's proper relation to both science and tradition. In my reading, the overcoming modernity debate centrally turns on a discussion of the proper status of science in relation to Japanese culture for the purpose of defending Japan in 1942. The film foregrounds these very issues raised in the debate, in the shadow of ethical questions arising from the very same war.

2 The atomic era depicted in *Gojira* (1954) shared significant continuities with the wartime period of the debate (1942). The United States, Germany, and Japan all had nuclear research programs in progress at the time the overcoming modernity symposium was held. The war they were attempting to interpret in the debate was concluded with the use of atomic weapons by the United States on the Japanese.[3] *Gojira* implicitly raises questions about the ethics of the United States and U.S. scientists in pursuing the Manhattan Project and enabling the subsequent arms race that awakens Gojira.

3 *Gojira*'s year of release, 1954, was just two years after the end of the U.S. occupation. The *Lucky Dragon* incident (in which a Japanese fisherman died from the fallout of U.S. H-bomb testing in the Pacific in March 1954) and the release of the film *Gojira* (in November of the same year) were two of the first public occasions on which the Japanese people began to discover the facts of Hiroshima and Nagasaki after the suspension of U.S. occupation censorship in 1952.[4] Later scenes of the film depict a publicly broadcast funeral service for civilian Japanese victims of Gojira that may easily be interpreted as stand-ins for civilian Japanese war dead that could not be publicly mourned under foreign occupation, or even as a publicly broadcast funeral service for Japanese victims of war crimes committed by the United States at Hiroshima and Nagasaki. In other words, the frame of the debate serves to underline that the film's deep engagement in the work of mourning the dead produced in World War II, in a certain sense, doubles the mourning of modernity as spiritual loss that already constituted the significance of modernity for Kamei and Hayashi and against which they defined the significance of the war.

4 The action in the second half of *Gojira* revolves around Japanese civilian, scientific, and military mobilization in response to an external threat.

The overcoming modernity debate was precisely a discussion of the proper approach to civilian, scientific, and military mobilization during World War II. The film industry was itself central to the mobilization effort and many of the supporting and featured cast and crew of *Gojira* were active in making films for the purpose of wartime mobilization under the direction of the Japanese state.[5] To the degree that *Gojira* unified Japanese viewers in relation to the cold war or interpretations of World War II, the 1954 film itself may be interpreted as a work of Japanese national mobilization as well as national mourning. It both depicts the media system of wartime mobilization and itself performs a related function on its audience in 1954.

5 The overcoming modernity debate as I interpret it was an articulate and important non-European response to the issue of globalization and its impact on cultural identity. Framing discussion of *Gojira* in terms of the overcoming modernity debate thus allows us not only to situate *Gojira* more precisely in relation to the history of globalization's effects on Japanese national culture, but also to draw larger connections between the debate and the film's roots in the very same issues of culture, globalization, and national defense in the context of World War II that gave rise to the proglobalization neoliberalism of F.A. Hayek and the neoconservatism of Leo Strauss that have been so important to rationalizing the U.S. invasion of Iraq. I suggest that the Japanese debate from 1942, the Japanese film from 1954, and the seemingly very contemporary political philosophies of Hayek and Strauss were all articulated as competing interpretations of and responses to World War II. Reading *Gojira* in the context of the overcoming modernity debate can thus help give us perspective on the powerful neoliberal and neoconservative ideologies so militantly clamoring for hegemony in our own time. Their claims to legitimacy and to ideological power consistently turn on their claim to best account for World War II. In other words, I argue that contemporary U.S. citizens live in the shadow of World War II every bit as much as the Japanese civilians depicted in *Gojira* and the Japanese viewers of the film in 1954. Hopefully, this essay will allow us to draw some conclusions about how that shadow falls across Americans today as well as Japanese in 1942, 1954, and 2005.

The conference, entitled "Overcoming Modernity" (Kindai no chōkoku), was hosted by the journal *Bungakkai* (Literary World) in 1942. For participants in the debate, such as Kamei Katsuichirō and Hayashi Fusao, modernity itself was seen as pathological. Japan's only hope was to overthrow the foreign corruption of the Japanese body politic by returning to Japan's tradition and roots as best it could. They articulated an antimodern political theology designed to restore faith to a modern Japan suffering from secular humanism.[6] Others, such as the philosopher of science, Shimomura Toratarō, argued that the Japanese body and the Japanese social formation had already significantly incorporated modernity and technology. The modern Japanese body had even been extended and combined with the machine such that traditional concepts of spirit were no longer adequate to theorize it. He presented a pro-modern political theology of alternative modernity that held out the possibility of technology enabling the restoration of spirit to a modern Japan suffering from secular, liberal humanism.[7]

For Kamei and Hayashi, the presence of modernity in Japan was a monstrosity that brought with it the subversion of Japanese tradition and mores. They argued that wartime mobilization must be an explicit and self-conscious repudiation of modernity itself to the degree that remained possible. For Shimomura, Japanese victory required even further rationalization of Japanese society and promotion of science. Any Japanese overcoming of modernity would have to be an overcoming of an already highly modernized Japanese social formation—it would have to be a criticism and an overcoming of present-day Japan itself. Overcoming in any meaningful sense could not be confined to a projection of Japanese social contradictions onto a foreign body. For Shimomura, I will suggest, it was the sort of hybridity represented by Gojira's relation to technology that needed to be even further radicalized for successful Japanese mobilization that might hold out the prospect of overcoming contemporary Japanese modernity. Both sides of the debate were centrally concerned with reconnecting contemporary Japanese culture to a supramundane spirit that transcended secular humanism and the enlightenment in ways that I find quite resonant with the political theology of American fundamentalists and neoconservatives.[8]

One of the central points of the wartime debate is that science and technology (including communications media) have transformed the Japanese social formation. *I suggest that* Gojira *is notably a film that stages the media system within which it was produced*—in this sense, its content is in large part other media systems. The form in which *Gojira* is shot consistently cannibalizes other media. In other words, I argue that, in *Gojira*, the media is the message—or at least one of the important messages. I further insist, however, that the media in the film are consistently bounded by a notion of Japanese national space and community even as they aspire to a universal humanist concern for all mankind. Thus, media in the film serve as a platform on which events staged within the film and for us as viewers become national Japanese events: events such as national emergencies and rituals of mourning on a national scale.

U.S. response to the attack on the World Trade Center on September 11 must surely reinforce our concern for just how central the media are in the incredibly powerful production and framing of national emergency and spectacle. The constant invocation of Pearl Harbor, the phrase Ground Zero, the arguably kamikaze style of the attacks on the towers, the reenactment of the flag-raising at Iwojima as a symbol of reconstruction of the Twin Towers, and the presentation of occupied Japan as a model for occupied Iraq also insist that remembrance of the Asia Pacific War as traumatic loss and Allied victory remains at least as central to foundational narratives of postwar U.S. self-understanding as it does to competing narratives of postwar Japan.

Gojira, the film, almost serves as a documentary on the Japanese media system of 1954. Central aspects of this media system, such as emergency radio broadcasting and an expansion of popular radio ownership, were initially developed for the explicit purpose of psychological mobilization and civil defense during the Asia Pacific War.[9] Parts of it, such as the television broadcasts that *Gojira*'s film camera intermittently dissolves itself into, were new to Japan in the mid-1950s but were integrated as part of the preceding system.

Gojira's presence in the film is first presented as a flash of light when a fishing boat is overcome. Notice of this incident is relayed to Japanese maritime authorities by radio-transmitted Morse code. Maritime authorities employ the radio to track a series of missing ships and the location of the mysterious agent later known as Gojira. Gojira's footprint is exposed to a Geiger counter and determined to be radioactive. Various characters hear radio reports of Gojira's location, apparent heading, and emergency warnings to evacuate Tokyo. Evacuation is organized and nationalized through the media. Interestingly, when the film was remade for the U.S. market, an additional layer of media coverage was added with Raymond Burr as a foreign correspondent who makes live tape recordings for later publication in print.

The plot of the film ultimately turns around the scientist Serizawa and attempts by his ex-lover (Emiko) and her fiancé (Ogata) to persuade him to use his oxygen-splitting invention to destroy Gojira. He does not want to deploy it. He is afraid that once it has been used others will reproduce it and yet another lethal technology will be unleashed upon the world in the manner of the H-bomb that clearly produced the monster Gojira itself. The cycle would simply be repeated. Emiko persuades Serizawa to deploy his personal invention (as opposed to its being the more historically plausible product of a state-funded research program, for example). Serizawa solves the dilemma by destroying his research notes and committing suicide in the course of killing Gojira. At least one Japanese scientist thus proves himself to be more ethically engaged and concerned for others than the implicitly negligent U.S. scientists who unleashed the A-bomb and the H-bomb upon humanity in general and Japan in particular.

Two of the dramatic highlights of Gojira's rampage through Tokyo are his toying with a train, and his destruction of a radio and television broadcast tower as a Japanese announcer plunges to his death in mid-broadcast. When the scarred scientist veteran Serizawa sacrifices his life for the sake of defending Japan with science, yet without endangering the rest of humanity, we hear a funeral dirge as we are shown pictures of Japanese victims receiving medical treatment. Soon we see a choir singing funeral music in a ceremony of national mourning. Soundtrack music becomes diegetic as we hear and see the ceremony as a television broadcast. In *Gojira*, the nation is brought together as one through a cinematic depiction of the new medium of television (in 1954) and the repeated presentation of emergency radio broadcasts established during the Asia Pacific War.

The longest continuous programming broadcast within the diegetic world of the film is a funeral ceremony. Gojira, Serizawa, and countless civilian victims have died. The entire population and infrastructure of Tokyo have been devastated. The film lets the object of its mourning go without saying, allowing the viewer to make his or her own connections to a degree. Samuel Weber finds that television overcomes distances in a matter that transcends the spatial limitations usually associated with the body. It serves as a surrogate for the body, such that perception takes place in more than one place at a time. It is a simultaneity of transmission, but a simultaneity that splits the unity of place, bodies, and subjects.[10] The film registers a certain disorientation as it jumps from the filming of action to the filming of radio listening, to the filming of television viewing, to the filming of action we shortly discover to have been from the perspective of a television camera in the course of a broadcast, and back to the direct filming of action we simultaneously understand to have been orchestrated for televisual consumption. This unsettling migration of the camera registers the effects of the multiplication of sites of the viewers' perception even as the perceptual unity of the individual's body is itself split by way of various media prosthetics that the film camera jumps back and forth between.

In *Mourning and Melancholy*, Freud argues that "mourning is regularly the reaction to the loss of a loved person, or to the loss of some abstraction which has taken the place of one, such as fatherland, liberty, an ideal, and so on."[11] Melancholy is a symptom of hostility originally felt for an other, but internalized and directed at oneself. It differs from normal grieving in that the sufferer relentlessly attacks him or herself.[12] For Rickels, when introjection fails to assimilate the corpse of the dead, the subject begins a process of incorporation. Without acknowledging pain or loss, the subject is inhabited by the incorporated deceased whose virtual presence on the inside is shared outside with an alien other. This occult connection is then established by communications media that externalize and reverse death wishes, often in the form of the undead.[13]

Gojira: Kenkyū tokuhon (The Godzilla Research Reader) asks the following important question: Even if we accept that there may be some tenuous scientific causality that connects the revival of Gojira to the H-bomb, given that the film tells us Gojira lived closely enough to Ōdo Island that legends concerning him survive, why would he then head toward the main island of Japan and the capital, Tokyo, rather than just head back to Ōdo Island?[14] It seems we are forced to look for a psychic rather than physics-based chain of causality.

It is difficult not to read the appearance of the monster Gojira and the longevity of the film series itself as, at least partly, symptoms of a national Japanese melancholia. A melancholic has ambivalent feelings of love and hate for the other. After destruction and defeat at the hands of the United States, after a would-be war of liberation was redefined as a crime against humanity, after the Japanese troops that had been held up as paragons of virtue were accused of war crimes, is there any doubt that Japanese feelings toward the

United States and their own war dead must have involved ambivalent feelings of both love and hate? This process of melancholia could involve a refusal to name a perceived loss of traditional Japan and nature to the predations of modernity and the treaty powers since the 1850s even as the occupation government embarked on modernization as liberation, a refusal to name the loss of the ideal of Japanese world leadership as a force for justice now reframed by the outside world as a historical injustice, or the inability to directly express hostility toward its enemy, the United States, once this relationship was redefined as one of military occupation and cold war alliance. Once Japanese actions in the war were framed as injustice, it also became extremely difficult to publicly express or mourn the loss of Japanese colonial empire and international hegemony.

It is instructive to read the scenario for *Gojira* in relation to the wartime overcoming modernity debate. Kamei Katsuichirō and Tsumura Hideo, for example, had argued that Japan's problems stemmed from the flood of corrupting foreign influences that had adulterated Japanese culture and mores by way of mass media, such as Hollywood films and American jazz music.[15] Kamei and Hayashi prescribed a displacement or nativization of foreign elements and increased research and thought seeking an authentic Japanese response to the contradictions of modernity—class antagonism, the breakdown of community, and the perceived loss of a clearly demarcated national cultural identity. War in China was popularly conceived as a struggle between the forces of Western, colonial modernity and the moral force of a resurgent Asia, in the guise of Japan. The Japanese romantics looked to Japanese spirit as the secret weapon that would enable military and ideological victory.

The sections of the film set on Ōdo Island featuring native ritual and the commentary of the local elder resonate with the Japanese romantic position in the debate. The elder suggests that Gojira is a god known to folk tradition and that proper ritual observation in accordance with tradition is a necessary prerequisite for any hope of peace. A young island woman scoffs at his belief that folk monsters might be real and implicitly at his belief in tradition itself. This section of the film also resonates with the Yanagita Kunio school of folklore studies. During the war, Yanagita had argued that Okinawa and the Pacific islands were likely origins of Japanese culture and should be studied as such.[16] In this light, the lecture of the island elder could also stand in for a Japanese folklorist lecturing on the consequences of the loss that comes with neglecting traditional ways, and failing to respect and sustain indigenous, non-European-American identity.

Further, with the loss of the empire, entire limbs of the Japanese media system were chopped off. To the degree that *Gojira* is a film centrally concerned with psychic structure as a function of Japanese media systems, perhaps we can also say that it is a film that stages the psycho-mediated trauma of amputating the Japanese colonial media system down to domestic, national media system proportions. Nine years before the film was made, the territory in which U.S. H-bomb testing was conducted fell within the bounds of the

Japanese empire and its media system. In this regard, the appearance of Gojira somewhat resembles the experience of a phantom limb of the Japanese media. The newly domesticated and shrunken Japanese media system is getting signals from the imperial media system that it has recently amputated. In other words, *Gojira* stages ghosted messages from an outside that was formerly inside.

The segments depicting Gojira's victims clearly evoke Hiroshima, Nagasaki, and the firebombing of Tokyo for the viewer, but also foreshadow the potential consequences of nuclear attack on Japan as a result of cold war conflict. We are directly presented with the loss of Serizawa and Gojira. It is worth noting that Serizawa's self-sacrifice is evocative of the scenario of spiritist films of the war time that insistently evoked personal sacrifice for the sake of the empire.[17] The primary difference would be that where the later spiritist films insisted on depicting loss of life for the sake of the emperor as a cause to be celebrated, in *Gojira* the loss of life is very clearly experienced as wrenching trauma, as grief to be ritually recognized and mourned by the nation. This scenario is interestingly continuous with wartime understandings, however, insofar as participants in the overcoming modernity debate such as Nishitani Keiji, Suzuki Shigetaka, and Shimomura Toratarō saw wartime sacrifice for the empire as itself already sacrifice for the sake of a truly universal humanism.

It is important to consider the scientist characters in *Gojira* in relation to Shimomura Toratarō's discussion of science in the overcoming modernity debate. He clearly dissented from the Japanese romantic position. Shimomura was a philosopher of science whose first book was a monograph on Leibniz. Shimomura took the stance that the complex division of labor and integration of technology into the Japanese social formation in the course of military mobilization required seeing contemporary Japan as itself of a piece with modernity. For Shimomura, a Japanese overcoming of modernity would necessarily have to be a self-overcoming. The contradictions of modernity had already been incorporated into the Japanese social formation. He argued that antimodernist positions were a voluntaristic evasion of the issues that imagined all contradiction in Japanese modernity could be projected onto a foreign space. He insisted that further rationalization and promotion of science were going to be necessary for Japanese success in the war effort. He felt that spiritism was distorting and, by calling for such intellectual monstrosities as uniquely Japanese science, served to undermine the development of the very science and technology that Japan needed to perfect in order to win the war.[18]

As a philosopher of science, Shimomura held that technological extensions of man, while creating problems, also offered a potential solution. For Shimomura, a radical rationalization of Japanese society and an even more extensive incorporation of ultramodern technology might perhaps allow for a reintegration of the national body in a manner compatible with the emperor (e.g., using science and media to ideologically reintegrate the Japanese social body, thus undoing the damage to emperor-oriented tradition caused by

previous incarnations of science and media in modern Japan). He explicitly
conceived this process as transcending the individual, as an issue to be
resolved in sociological or even theological terms. The important point is
that Shimomura argued that modernity could only be overcome by further
modernization: technological, prosthetic extensions of man were to be even
further augmented. It was through the pursuit of a political theology of
Japanese ultramodernity that Shimomura considered the modern dystopia of a
Westernized secular, liberal humanist Japan might potentially be overcome.[19]

It is intriguing to compare Shimomura and Marshall McLuhan on this
point. Both Shimomura and McLuhan argue that technology, in general, and
communications technologies, in particular, function as extensions of the
human body. Both figures had intellectual ties to English New Criticism[20]
and opposed technology to culture, but both men developed intellectual
positions for which this Manichaean dichotomy could be to some extent
resolved through the further application of technology. For McLuhan this
took the form of retribalizing society by way of electronic media. For
Shimomura, the Japanese social formation was to be re-gathered into a theological, imperial state through the further deployment of technology.
McLuhan's transition took place in the 1950s as he became increasingly
familiar with cybernetics and information technology. With cybernetics, the
opposition between the ghost and the machine is resolved into a distinction
between programming and hardware. Both are integral parts of a single
information system. Shimomura was writing ten years earlier and still uses the
language of spirit, but his position resonates with that of McLuhan insofar as
he directly relates the question of spirit to the status of the technologized
body in the manner of Henri Bergson. Further, by connecting social engineering to theology and the emperor, Shimomura in effect foreshadows
McLuhanite political theology of cybernetic ultramodernity *avant la lettre*.

Yamanouchi Yasushi has argued for far-reaching parallels between the
social control projects of Ōkōchi Kazuo in wartime Japan and Talcott
Parsons in the United States.[21] He finds that situated in the context of the
overcoming modernity debate, Ōkōchi takes up essentially the same position
as Shimomura. For both thinkers, further modernization is the antidote or
path to overcome modernity. From the perspective of the Japanese debate,
I argue that McLuhan is postmodern in the specific and novel sense that *he
claims modern communications technologies lead to a retribalization of social
formations*. Societies alienated by modernity and print media will become
increasingly oral and village-like. *From the perspective of the Japanese overcoming modernity debate, McLuhan literally claims that cybernetics and communications technology overcome modernity* conceived as urban alienation and
anomie. This seems important given the way in which McLuhan's phrase
"global village" has become an uncontroversial frame of reference for many
cheerleaders of globalization.[22] Shimomura calls for a similar project, but one
that would make a modern, technologized Japan compatible with a spirit
appropriate to the emperor. Both Shimomura and McLuhan thus see
technology as potentially enabling the production of a premodern spiritual

immediacy that overcomes the opposition between Japan and the West (Shimomura) or Africa and the West (McLuhan). Shimomura's position requires Western recognition of Japanese agency and modernity, however, whereas McLuhan does not particularly address the issue of non-Western agency.[23]

Let us return to the two scientists depicted in the film. On the one hand, we have the fatherly archaeologist, Yamane Kyōhei, who is sympathetic to Gojira and concerned to save his life for the sake of scientific knowledge, but also through identification with him as a fellow victim of nuclear war who is thus at least metaphorically Japanese. On the other hand, we have the scarred, one-eyed war-veteran, Serizawa, who devises the weapon that destroys Gojira, but sacrifices his own life in the process so that the price of saving Japan won't be the infliction of yet another arms race upon the rest of mankind.

The archaeologist Yamane is determined to find out what Gojira can tell us about the natural world, what the past can tell us about the present.[24] He argues that all three are intertwined. His concern to save the monster's life appears to arise out of an identification with a fellow war victim who is metaphorically Japanese, and also as a source of as yet untapped scientific knowledge that unthinking destruction will eliminate before it can be decoded. (Implicitly, the Japanese people themselves thus have a scientific value as a people who have survived nuclear attack.)

At different points, Yamane says, "Do you want to kill an H-bomb survivor?" and "He is not an aggressor, he is a victim!" These statements suggest that the Yamane character situates both Gojira and Japan as victims rather than as aggressors, certainly in the cold war context, but potentially and psychically, perhaps in World War II context as well. Insofar as we pursue Yamane's interpretation of Gojira as metaphorically a Japanese victim of U.S. attack, in the World War II context, Yamane is implicitly suggesting that the current Japanese government should challenge the reigning melancholy that forecloses the implication of the United States in the suffering of Japanese war dead as a consequence of the ongoing security alliance with the United States and effective military occupation. In the cold war context, it suggests that continued Japanese alliance with the United States may be enforcing a melancholia that forecloses asking why Japanese alliance with the United States is a good idea in the 1950s. It suggests that the Japanese government is in a sense repeating the spiritist bureaucracy's wartime refusal to listen to the voice of science yet again in the postwar period.

Serizawa is marked as a veteran of World War II by his eye-patch, but in terms of film-genre convention, this also marks him as an abnormal, mad scientist type. His basement laboratory strongly evokes the underground lab of countless Hollywood incarnations of Dr. Frankenstein. The mad scientist role also seems important for situating Serizawa vis-à-vis the melodramatic subplot involving the lapsed understanding that he would marry Yamane's daughter, Emiko.

Emiko's engagement to the new fiancé, Ogata, represents a triumph of love marriage over arranged marriage, the choice of an emotionally attentive partner as opposed to the seemingly asexual Serizawa, who carries on a nearly monk-like devotion to science even when he has concluded that its fruits cannot be shared with anyone else for ethical reasons. At the same time, Emiko's new fiancé is the male character whose concern for the security of the Japanese nation forces the breakthrough with both Emiko and Serizawa that determines Serizawa's secret technology will be deployed to prevent the further suffering of the Japanese people at the hands of Gojira.

As an individual, Serizawa is certainly Japanese, but as an ethical scientist he is depicted as irrevocably tied to modernity and universal humanism. He is determined to prevent the suffering of all mankind from a future arms race. Serizawa is a scientific genius, but his genius has produced a technology of potential mass destruction. Where does Serizawa fit in the context of the overcoming modernity debate?

Serizawa's initial position is that both the conceptual dissemination of his monstrous science and its technological deployment would be unethical. Serizawa initially thought that if he just kept his research to himself, he could prevent at least one monstrous product of modernity from even further threatening life on earth. Because of the specter of yet another arms race, Serizawa appears not to allow for the possibility that the science might be innocent, but its use might be criminal. It is the dissemination of the scientific knowledge itself that he fears, apparently because he sees its technological production and deployment as nearly inevitable.

It is Yamane's daughter, Emiko, who betrays Serizawa's secret. She and her fiancé persuade him to recognize a sense of responsibility for saving Japanese lives now. *He has his change of heart about deployment of his weapon as a direct result of watching the national television broadcast of a funeral ceremony for victims of Gojira's rampage.* This change of heart about one-time deployment to save Japan does not alter his view that the science itself is intrinsically dangerous, however.

In the end, Serizawa's position is quite distant from that of Shimomura, McLuhan, Ōkōchi, and Parsons. For all of them, modernity can only be overcome with further modernization and rationalization. Whereas these thinkers see science and technology as potentially resolving the contradictions of modernity, Serizawa is not willing to go that far. He settles on a compromise formation. Where Shimomura understands the ethics of science to be a question of the morality of the ways in which it is applied, Serizawa implicitly holds that science with weapons applications is intrinsically unethical and that to enable or contribute toward its dissemination would be wrong in itself.[25]

In the short run, Serizawa *will* act as Shimomura would call for and deploy his new technology, thus realizing its immediate benefit to the social formation, but at the same time he will destroy his work, kill himself, and take the dark fruit of modernity, he is personally responsible for, to his grave. Where Shimomura recognizes a dark, deterritorializing aspect to technology, he also holds out hope that science may resolve the contradictions that it creates through its responsible application and further development. Serizawa appears to insist that the dark side of science and technology with weapons applications cannot be redeemed, at least not directly. The aspect of modernity that this form of science represents is thus itself intrinsically malignant. Shimomura's take on science—that ethics is a question of the uses to which it is put (which roughly parallels the official U.S. position of the 1950s)—is thus rejected by the character Serizawa.

Through his sacrifice, the film presents Serizawa as a national hero who has saved Japan and martyred himself as a consequence of his concern for humanity at large. He is a martyr to modernity and to a Japan that identifies with universal humanism, but who also recognizes the pathological limitations of modernity. He recognizes that he is of modernity, but that modernity is pathological. There is no cure, at least as long as H-bomb testing continues. He deploys and then retracts the little piece of modern science over which he has personal control. History in *Gojira* is thus ultimately cast as tragedy or melodrama rather than as progress.

Serizawa's character stages the drama of an individual scientist who would more likely have been part of a larger national military research project. It is interesting that the film presents him as independent of the Japanese state. Shimomura was concerned with the development of classic modern science and technology that would then be put in the hands of the state for more effective and far-reaching military mobilization, but also with a larger, more idealistic and spiritual scientific project that necessarily must transcend national needs to be true science.[26] Indeed, Japan had its own atom bomb project during World War II and Japanese scientists did take part in it, albeit with a sense of resignation regarding the likelihood that it would produce a weapon soon enough to help the Japanese war effort.[27] Framing Serizawa's project as private erases the deep connection between scientific development and state military mobilization that Shimomura emphasized.[28]

Now let us revisit the question of media and monstrosity. In *Gojira*, it is the media infrastructure that allows Gojira's emergence to generate a sense of national threat, national hysteria, national mobilization, and national mourning. If a tree falls in the forest and no national Japanese media are there to report it, it will not be a news story of concern to the entire nation at one and the same time. Similarly with *Gojira*, the film stages the manner in which national mobilization is inseparable from the question of national media.

It is only on the stage of a modern media system that the question of modernity can be raised as a national question. Absent the media, we are absent the nation. But *Gojira* doesn't just stage the print media nation, although newspaper headlines do flash across the screen periodically. Within the diegetic world of the film, much of the action is broadcast live through the airwaves on both radio and television. The time delay of the "we" of national community in a print-based system is a matter of days. Print-based media allow the reader a certain autonomy of reception; broadcasting intrinsically forms a community of simultaneity. If you hear a broadcast, you hear it at exactly the same time the rest of the nation (or market) hears it.[29] This allows national trauma and ritual to feed back on themselves as they unfold in ways that the print media do not allow.

For us as viewers, the film itself adds yet another layer in its directly filmed representation of those events that it does not depict as radio or TV broadcasts. Within *Gojira*, the entire nation is consistently depicted as "tuned in" to the developing situation. Given that the film was released in 1954, it is conceivable that some Japanese saw their first television "broadcast" within this very film. If Gojira is monstrous because he or she responds to or designates a threat to the Japanese nation, we may conclude that it is ultimately an effect of the media system whose broadcasts interpellate and reiterate the nation that is endangered. If Gojira pulled the plug and radio, television, and print media ground to a halt (Gojira does tear down power lines upon entering Tokyo), would the status of the Japanese nation be transformed?

But we know that this is not how the film ends. The broadcasts continue and the filming rolls on. The nation gains a Japanese martyr to modernity in Serizawa, and an agent of nature martyred by the United States and modernity in Gojira. Gojira is an honorary Japanese citizen by virtue of suffering nuclear attack by the United States as did the Japanese, but is also a part of nature. We can read Gojira as a proxy for the natural purity and moral beauty that the Japanese romantics were attempting to recover through the study of Japanese antiquity, contemporary spiritual practice, and the conduct of war. In the world of *Gojira* and H-bomb testing, modernity has contaminated this same nature and it is no longer possible that it may be retrieved in its premodern purity. Nature itself, the definition and source of Japanese purity, has been rendered monstrous and impure. In other words, a site marked as premodern and as an alternative to modernity by the Japanese romantics—nature—has itself been made monstrous by the nuclear science and cold war politics of American modernity that has corrupted the Japanese social body beyond repair. Thus *Gojira* the film irradiates multiple positions laid out in the overcoming modernity debate, while refusing to resolve any of them.[30]

The film *Gojira* tells us Japan is under attack; we know because the media tell us so. It tells us Japan suffers from modernity. Yet for Shimomura, science and technology may conceivably overcome modernity if used correctly. *Gojira* takes issue with Shimomura and McLuhan in the following respect: for both Shimomura and McLuhan, technological extensions of man may literally resolve the contradictions of modernity. The imperial state may potentially be techno-theologically recuperated; the globe of the alienated modern urban center may potentially become a village in spirit. In *Gojira*, we know the most recent threat has been successfully fended off, but at a very steep price. Modernity, technology, and consequently nature have become pathological and contaminated. The film rejects Shimomura's claim that modernity and science are recuperable when used responsibly in favor of the position that modernity is intrinsically pathological and must be stopped in its tracks. In the world of *Gojira*, Japan is placed in a double-bind. Neither modernity nor nature remains unproblematic or hopeful alternatives. In addition to the work of mourning the Japanese dead, this perhaps accounts for the deeply melancholy tone of the film.

Yet the problem is posed such that Japan is the passive object of an external onslaught. In this sense the film is conceived within the worldview of Japanese romanticism and rejects the agency that Shimomura insists on attributing to Japanese appropriations of modernity, science, and technology. Within the world of *Gojira*, the contamination of modernity ultimately comes from outside, and from the United States, situating Japan as a passive, perhaps even heroic, victim of the cold war and perhaps World War II as well.

This seems to suggest that perhaps melodrama is not only the master narrative of *Gojira*, but of Kamei and Hayashi's variety of Japanese romanticism as well. The family-state suffers a trauma at the hands of an alien interloper, or alternatively, a family member is rendered mutant by an alien interloper. Perhaps the *Gojira* series is centrally a melodrama of Japanese family-state suffering, in this installment at the hands of the United States in both World War II and the cold war. And as in more conventional melodrama, power, politics, and economics are translated into the language of morality, of good and evil, of martyrdom, sacrifice, and of the boundary between speakable and unspeakable personal loss, between mourning and melancholy.

The composer of the soundtrack, Ifukube Akira, explicitly connected the *Gojira* figure to the souls of Japanese servicemen lost in the Pacific during the war.[31] The soundtrack for *Harp of Burma*, a narrative released two years later that specifically mourns the Japanese war dead, has a very similar tone and atmosphere and was written by the same composer. This adds an element of the Gothic to *Gojira*'s melodrama of familial suffering. The Gojira monster and its soundtrack thus figure the living dead of World War II trapped by the state of national melancholia created by U.S. occupation censorship over the previous nine years.

For many older, conservative Japanese, in losing the war, not only did fathers, husbands, and brothers die, but also Japan and the world lost a world historical alternative attempting to throw off the yoke of white supremacy in East Asia. For Marxists, Koreans, and Chinese, the world lost an alternative colonial master with an Asian identity crisis. But the *Gojira* story arguably does not end with the fall of the Japanese empire or Gojira's vaporization in Tokyo Bay.

Contemporary master narratives of globalization and Middle East "conquest as liberation" take their point of departure in the writing of neoliberals such as F.A. Hayek and neoconservatives such as Leo Strauss. Both thinkers developed their positions in response to the challenge of interpreting the world historical significance of World War II. Hayek's most widely read work, *The Road to Serfdom*, was published during the war and excerpts from it were reprinted in *Reader's Digest* in 1946. Strauss's work explicitly draws parallels between relativism in postwar U.S. thought and the onset of the Nazi regime in Weimar Germany. In this sense, the proponents of globalization and neo-Straussian cheerleaders of Iraqi conquest have always already been in dialogue with the Japanese debate on overcoming modernity.

The hegemonic narrative claims that where fascism and Keynesianism sought to supplement capital with the welfare state, neoliberalism and neoconservatism call for supplementing capital with technology and doing away with state interference in the market place to the greatest extent possible. Indeed, it claims that only capital can successfully innovate in the manner technological development demands. Technological innovation is supposed to be the evolutionary imperative that only the private sector can purportedly meet. Keynesianism is metaphorically tied to fascism and communism as similarly weighed down by a premodern feudal imaginary of centralized planning and social control.[32]

My exploration of the overcoming modernity debate suggests that the wartime positions of Ōkōchi and Shimomura placed as much faith in technology and social rationalization as do contemporary neoliberal proponents of globalization and the communications revolution, or neoconservative proponents of an expanded U.S. military grounded in distributed intelligence that is so efficient and superior to any conceivable opponent that military solutions to problems of U.S. foreign policy are simply more practical than diplomatic ones. Insofar as the television broadcast of the funeral scene in *Gojira* and the screening of the film itself played a part in mourning the losses and the suffering of the Japanese family state, in rearticulating Japan's relation to technology, modernity, and national spirit, perhaps the film *Gojira* also presumes a certain faith in the ability of media technology to overcome modernity.

As regards communications revolutions, I'm tempted to amend Thomas Friedman's account of globalization to include not only the Lexus and the olive tree, but also *Gojira*. I would like to close with advice from an essay by Arif Dirlik. He writes that "[n]either memory nor forgetting is entirely innocent—nor is the historical consciousness that they inform. A central question for the present, I think, is how to distinguish critical memories of the past that also allow for a critique of the present from those memories that conform to the predispositions of the present and serve to legitimize contemporary configurations of power."[33] I think today we have a particular obligation to recognize the diversity of memory of those who fight wars on the ground even as we endeavor to challenge nation-state policies grounded in theological terms—whether they be grounded in a theology of antimodernity or ultramodernity. Either one effectively obscures the responsibility of particular leaders making decisions and the citizens who let them get away with it.

NOTES

1. Takahashi Toshio, *Gojira no nazo* (Tokyo: Kodansha, 1998); Yoshikuni Igarashi, *Bodies of Memory* (Princeton, NJ: Princeton University Press, 2000), pp. 114–122. Other works on this topic in English include Susan Napier, "Panic Sites: The Japanese Imagination of Disaster from *Godzilla* to *Akira*," in *Contemporary Japan and Popular Culture*, ed. John Treat (Honolulu: University of Hawai'i Press, 1996); Chon Noriega, "Godzilla and the Japanese Nightmare: When *Them!* is U.S.," in *Hibakusha Cinema*, ed. Mick Broderick (London: Kegan Paul International, 1996); Jerome Shapiro, *Atomic Bomb Cinema* (London: Routledge, 2002), pp. 272–280.

In Japanese, see Fujikawa Yūya, *Gojira-jiheitai-kessenshi* (Tokyo: Kōjinsha, 2004); Higuchi Naofumi, *Guddo mōningu, Gojira* (Tokyo: Chikuma Shobō, 1992); Inoue Hideyuki, *Gojira tanjō* (Tokyo: Asahi Sonorama, 1994); Noma Norikazu et al., eds., *Gojira: Kenkyū tokuhon* (Tokyo: Paradigm, 2000); Takarada Akira, *Nippon Gojira ōgon densetsu* (Tokyo: Fusōsha, 1998).

2. The July 1942 conference "Overcoming Modernity" was sponsored by the journal *Bungakkai* (Literary World) and was attended by Nishitani Keiji, Kikuchi Masashi, Kobayashi Hideo, Miyoshi Tatsuji, Moroi Saburō, Shimomura Toratarō, Kamei Katsuichirō, Tsumura Hideo, Kawakami Tetsutarō, Suzuki Shigetaka, Yoshimitsu Yoshihiko, Hayashi Fusao, and Nakamura Mitsuo. It was published in the September and October issues of the journal, *Bungakkai* 9:9 (September 1942) and *Bungakkai* 9:10 (October 1942). A reedited version was published in book form the following year: Kawakami Tetsutarō, ed., *Kindai no chōkoku* (Tokyo: Sōgensha, 1943).

Secondary works on the debate in English include: Kevin Doak, *Dreams of Difference: The Japan Romantic School and the Crisis of Modernity* (Berkeley: University of California Press, 1994); Andrew Feenberg, *Alternative Modernity* (Berkeley: University of California Press, 1995); Harry Harootunian, *Overcome By Modernity: History, Culture, and Community in Interwar Japan* (Princeton, NJ: Princeton University Press, 2001); James Heisig, *Philosophers of Nothingness* (Honolulu: University of Hawai'i Press, 2001); Minamoto Ryōen, "The Symposium on 'Overcoming Modernity,' " in *Rude Awakenings: Zen, the Kyoto School, and the Question of Nationalism*, ed. James Heisig (Honolulu: University of Hawai'i Press, 1995).

In Japanese, see Hashikawa Bunzō, *Nihon romanha hihan jōsetsu* (Tokyo: Miraisha, 1965); Hiromatsu Wataru, *Kindai no chōkokuron* (Tokyo: Kōdansha Gakujutsu Bunko, 1989), pp. 24–29, 34, 41–47, 198–201, 236, 239; Kosaka Kunitsugu, *Nishida tetsugaku to gendai* (Tokyo: Mineruba Shobō, 2001), pp. 1–29; Takeuchi Yoshimi, "Kindai no chōkoku," in *Kindai no chōkoku* (Tokyo: Chikuma Gyōsho, 1983); Nakamura Yūjirō, *Nishida tetsugaku no datsukōchiku* (Tokyo: Iwanami Shoten, 1987), pp. 189–215.

3. Gar Alperovitz, *The Decision to Use the Atomic Bomb* (New York: Random House Value Publishing, 1997).

4. "Throughout the occupation the U.S. military enforced a representational silence over the subject of the atomic bombings." Abe Mark Nornes, "The Body at the Center—*The Effects of the Atomic Bomb on Hiroshima and Nagasaki*," in *Hibakusha Cinema*, p. 152; pp. 152–155 cover the suppression of this particular footage in more detail.

The *Lucky Dragon* was a tuna boat caught in the fallout from a U.S. H-bomb test on Bikini Atoll that took place on March 1, 1954. It returned to port on March 14. The crew members suffered from radiation sickness and one died. Tuna stocks in Japanese fish markets was disposed of as contaminated "H-bomb tuna." U.S. H-bomb testing in the Marshall Islands began in November 1952 and two more tests were conducted after the *Lucky Dragon* returned to port. Tests were finally suspended in April 1954. This account is based on Inoue, *Gojira tanjō*, p. 31.

5. Tsurubaya Eiji was in charge of *Gojira*'s special effects. He had worked under the director Yamamoto Kajirō on the pivotal wartime film, *The Sea War from Hawai'i to Malaya* (Hawai-Marei oki kaisen, 1942). Tsuburaya first worked on a set with *Gojira*'s director, Honda Ishirō, during the next Yamamoto directed film, *Kato's Falcon Fighters* (Katō hayabusa sentōtai, 1944). Many of the films they later

worked on together incorporated elements from these films, including a wartime setting, a semi-documentary feel, and the centrality of special effects. Both films featured and were promoted on the basis of their cutting edge special effects, and these had been supervised by Tsuburaya. Higuchi, *Guddo mōningu, Gojira*, pp. 149–156. These films also come up for discussion in Peter High, *The Imperial Screen* (Madison: University of Wisconsin Press, 2003), pp. 382–408.

6. I use "political theology" here to indicate an appeal to a supernatural, suprascientific spirit for the purpose of framing modernity as a process of secularization that must be reversed. I in no way mean to suggest that Shintō and Christianity are interchangeable, rather that in Hayashi and Kamei's positions, the Shintō of the emperor cult performs a function closely analogous to that of the Catholicism of Yoshimitsu Yoshihiko and Carl Schmitt in their respective political theologies—it is explicitly appealed to as a salutory source of spirit in opposition to the modernity that their positions frame as secular. Rather than reject a too secular aesthetics for a more spiritual aesthetics in the manner of the German Romantics, the early 1940s work of Kamei and Hayashi nearly dispenses with aesthetics altogether in favor of their personal varieties of Shintō/emperorist theology. Kamei Katsuichirō, "Gendai seishin no oboegaki" and Hayashi Fusao, "Kinnō no kokoro" in *Kindai no chōkoku*, ed. Kawakami, pp. 3–18 and pp. 90–120.

Kamei refers to modernity and mechanization as a poison and an enemy on pp. 6 and 9. Hayashi states that the individualism and liberalism of the Civilization and Enlightenment movement of the Meiji period (1868–1912) was a forgetting of the tradition and blood lineage of a Japanese person on pp. 99–100. On p. 118, denial of the gods, humanism, rationalism, subjectivism, and individualism are all listed as ways of thinking that reject the divinity of the Japanese national essence (*kokutai*). Naturalist writers and leftists who act in this manner have committed unforgivable sins (*zaiaku*). On p. 120, Hayashi declares that the literature of modernity poisons youth, leading the Japanese people to lose their self-confidence. The essay is presented as a prayer calling for youth to achieve historical and racial self-consciousness, and above all, to worship the Japanese gods through loyalty to the emperor.

7. Shimomura Toratarō, "Kindai no chōkoku no hōkō," in *Kindai no chōkoku*, ed. Kawakami, pp. 121–127.

8. The antiliberal, antisecular, antimodernism of American fundamentalists is closer to the position of Kamei and Hayashi, the antidemocratic, alternative modern "true Oriental liberalism" of Nishida and Nishitani closer to the "true democracy" of Straussian neoconservatism that excludes enlightenment conceptions of equality on principle. All four groups are thus engaged in competing projects of "overcoming modernity."

9. Tsuganesawa Toshihiro finds that radio served as an organ of emperor-state fascism in Japan during the 15-year state of wartime emergency after the Manchurian Incident (1931) and proved to be the most powerful weapon of wartime "national spiritual mobilization." It was reorganized around a German national socialist model in 1934. Tsuganesawa Toshihiro, *Gendai Nihon mediashi no kenkyū* (Tokyo: Mineruba Shobō, 1998), pp. 78–79.

10. Samuel Weber, *Mass Mediauras* (Stanford, CA: Stanford University Press, 1996), pp. 114–117.

11. Sigmund Freud, "Mourning and Melancholia," in *A General Selection from the Works of Sigmund Freud* (New York: Doubleday Anchor, 1957), p. 125.

12. Tammy Clewell, "Mourning Beyond Melancholia," *Journal of the American Psychoanalytic Association* 52:1 (Spring 2004), p. 60. Friederich Kittler and

Laurence Rickels have pointed to the way in which media technology both reproduce and model Freud's psychic systems. Haunting, mourning, and the development of media technology go hand in hand with articulation of the unconscious.
Laurence Rickels, *The Case of California* (Baltimore: Johns Hopkins University
Press, 1991), pp. 13–14.

13. Ibid., p. 4.
14. Noma et al., eds., *Gojira: Kenkyū tokuhon*, pp. 18–20.
15. Kamei, "Gendai seishin no oboegaki," p. 5; Tsumura Hideo, "Nani wo yaburu
    bekika," in *Kindai no chōkoku*, ed. Kawakami, pp. 133–138.
16. Murai Osamu, *Nantō ideorogī no hassei* (Tokyo: Ōta Shuppan, 1995).
17. High, *The Imperial Screen*, pp. 385–396.
18. Shimomura Toratarō, "Kindai no chōkoku no hōkō," pp. 121–127. Shimomura
    addresses these points in a more extended fashion in "Kokusaku toshite no
    kagakuron ni tsuite," in *Shimomura Toratarō chosakushū*, vol. 1 (Tokyo: Misuzu
    Shobō, 1992), pp. 123–140. The latter piece was first published in the journal
    Chūō Kōron in January 1943.

    The secondary literature on Shimomura is limited but the more important
    writing includes Ōhashi Ryōsuke, *Nishida tetsugaku no sekai—arui wa tetsugaku
    no tenkai* (Tokyo: Chikuma Shobō, 1995) and Kobayashi Toshiaki, *Nishida
    Kitarō no yūutsu* (Tokyo: Iwanami Shoten, 2003), pp. 173–190.
19. Shimomura, "Kindai no chōkoku no hōkō," pp. 124–127.
20. Shimomura refers to Eliot's *The Metaphysical Poets* in "Kindai kagakushi ron,"
    in *Shimomura Toratarō chosakushū*, vol. 2, p. 259.

    Marshall McLuhan received his graduate education at Cambridge University
    working with the pioneering new critics F.R. Leavis and I.A. Richards. In the
    1940s, McLuhan took the Leavis line on almost everything. Phillip Marchand,
    Marshall McLuhan: The Medium and the Messenger (New York: Tickner & Fields,
    1989), p. 94.

    Leavis's broader cultural preoccupation was consistently with the perceived
    dangers of "technologico-Benthamite" civilization. His early booklet *Mass
    Civilization and Minority Culture* (1930) stressed the unprecedented character
    of the machine age and challenged its leveling effects in the press, film, and liter-
    ature. The susceptibility of the majority to such standardizing trends meant that
    a small, independent-minded minority was forced to maintain access to cultural
    tradition on behalf of society as a whole. Leavis's work employed a conception of
    "organic community" in which work and life were a harmonious totality that he
    felt had been supplanted by industrial forms of mechanized and alienated labor.
    This stance later proved important for McLuhan's writing on the side of the
    Southern Agrarian movement in the United States in such outlets as *Sewanee
    Review*. McLuhan clearly took up Leavis's opposition to the "blind drive onward
    of material and mechanical development" as his own cause (see Robin Jarvis,
    "F.R. Leavis," http://www.press.jhu.edu/books/hopkins_guide_to_literary_
    theory/f._r._leavis.html). McLuhan's New Critical background familiarized him
    with Eliot and his conception of language's resonance with the past. Marchand,
    Marshall McLuhan, p. 95.

    Like Shimomura and Nishida, McLuhan thinks about language and communica-
    tions media in terms of technology and the body. Like Shimomura, he points to
    World War II as an occasion for the acceleration of technology's application to
    people and things, both psychologically and mechanically. Communications and
    transportation technology enable the stock market, international armies, worldwide

news-gathering organizations, and the emotional mobilization of the public by the press necessary to contemporary world war. For McLuhan, sports and marketing are peacetime analogues of the technologies of military mobilization. Marshall McLuhan, *The Mechanical Bride* (New York: Vanguard Press, 1951), p. 7.

McLuhan explicitly notes that Wiener has declared the rivalry between mechanism and vitalism to be dead. Like Shimomura, McLuhan claims that quantum and relativity physics depart from Newtonian physics in depicting a world "that is not unilateral, monistic, or tyrannical. It is neither progressive nor reactionary, but embraces all previous actualizations of human excellence in a simultaneous present." McLuhan too, is concerned with an integrating world order and its impact on culture: "No longer is it possible for modern man, individually or collectively, to live in any exclusive segment of human experience or achieved social pattern." "From one point of view, the fashion parade can be seen as a preview of a world society being born from the destruction of all existing cultures." McLuhan, *The Mechanical Bride*, pp. 34, 87, 75.

McLuhan married technology to theology in a manner reminiscent of Shimomura. McLuhan maintained to the end that his media schemes were Thomistic (Marchand, *Marshall McLuhan*, p. 82). His approach was partially inspired by a reading of Teilhard de Chardin, who was formatively influenced by Bergson. "As de Chardin explains in his *Phenomenon of Man*, new invention is the interiorization in man of the structures of earlier technology; and therefore it stockpiles, as it were. What we are studying here is the interiorization of print technology and its effect in shaping a new kind of man. De Chardin speaks of our own day when there are so many new technologies to be interiorized." Marshall McLuhan, *The Gutenberg Galaxy* (Toronto: University of Toronto Press, 1997), p. 174.

21. Yamanouchi Yasushi, "Total War and Social Integration," in *Total War and "Modernization,"* ed. Yamanouchi Yasushi, J. Victor Koschmann, and Narita Ryūichi (Ithaca, NY: Cornell University East Asia Program, 1999), pp. 23–26.

22. The term "global village" appears in McLuhan's *Understanding Media* on pp. 272, 326, and 366. "Radio provides a speed-up of information that also causes acceleration in other media. It certainly contracts the world to village size, and creates insatiable village tastes for gossip, rumor, and personal malice. But while radio contracts the world to village dimensions, it hasn't the effect of homogenizing the village quarters. Quite the contrary.... The effect of the radio as a reviver of archaism and ancient memories is not limited to Hitler's Germany.... Radio is not only a mighty awakener of archaic memories, forces, and animosities, but a decentralizing, pluralistic force, as is really the case with all electric power and media." McLuhan, *Understanding Media* (New York: McGraw-Hill, 1964), p. 326.

23. Shimomura, "Kokusaku toshite no kagakuron ni tsuite," pp. 123–140.

24. I would like to thank Michael Molasky for encouraging me to pursue the issues that the Yamane character raises for my problematic.

25. Shimomura, "Kindai no chōkoku no hōkō," pp. 123–124.

26. Shimomura Toratarō, "Kagakushi no tetsugaku," in *Shimomura Toratarō chosakushū*, vol. 1, p. 294.

27. Robert Wilcox, *Japan's Secret War* (New York: Marlowe and Company, 1995).

28. Interestingly, the oxygen-based technology that slays Godzilla in the film does have a vague semantic resonance with actual wartime events. The Japanese naval torpedo design recognized as superior to anything that the Allies or the Germans possessed was powered by compressed oxygen gas.

29. Takeyama Akiko presents some thoughts on the distinct temporality of print and broadcast media in Takeyama Akiko, *Rajio no jidai* (Tokyo: Sekai Shisōsha, 2002), pp. 44–45. Broadcast media require a publicization of the broadcast schedule and an adjustment of the consumer's personal activity to the time of the broadcast in a way without precedent in print media. In *The Imperial Screen*, Peter High puts together an important discussion of the electric media event in the 1930s Japan as producing new forms of social behavior connected to the development of synchronized broadcast networks. High, *The Imperial Screen*, pp. 26–39. Satō Takumi discusses the idea of *gleichsaltung* or coordination and growing interdependence within Japanese, German, and U.S. media in "Kingu no jidai," in *Taishū bunka to masu media*, ed. Aoki Tamotsu et al. (Tokyo: Iwanami Shoten, 1999), pp. 218–219.

30. It is worth pointing out that Gojira not only comes from a natural setting, but destroys urban areas. Takahashi, *Gojira no nazo*, pp. 160–162. The Japanese romantics explicitly found fault with urban ways of life as sites of a contaminating modernity. Yasuda Yojūrō goes so far as to argue that war literature recording the experience of soldiers on the battlefield allows us access to a premodern Japanese emotional authenticity otherwise unavailable. The soldier is thus also aligned with nature and the premodern. Yasuda Yojūrō, *Kindai no shūen* (Tokyo: Shogakkan, 1941), pp. 76–77. If we follow Ifukube's reading of Gojira as embodying the spirit of dead Japanese soldiers, they are precisely the figures that the H-bomb testing disturbs, angers, and contaminates. It is important to remember that Yasuda's discussions of nature and Japan take the concept of irony as their point of departure so his early writings cannot be equated with the fairly direct and theologically based attempt to return to the past that characterizes the later work of Kamei and Hayashi.

   It would be possible and quite interesting to develop a very different reading of Gojira as a figure of Yasuda's "Japan as irony"—as figuring authentic Japanese modernity through the necessary but impossible gesture of reviving the past in the present, as a gesture toward the authenticity of the past that will necessarily be always already contaminated, whose very failure gives rise to the necessity of the gesture. Yasuda is very close to Miguel de Unamuno in this regard.

31. Igarashi, *Bodies of Memory*, p. 116.

32. "The balance of power in the eternal conflict between industry and meddling feds had been irreversibly altered, Wriston argued: Technology itself had wandered in and 'changed everything,' had launched an 'information revolution' as all-transforming as the Industrial Revolution had been, and had in the process made all efforts to regulate industry as outmoded as the sundial. Markets would be the real ruler in the nineties, forcing upon every government everywhere the same laissez-faire policies for which the Republican Party, USA, had fought for so many years." Thomas Frank, *One Market Under God* (New York: Anchor Books, 2000), p. 54.

33. Arif Dirlik, *Postmodernity's Histories* (Lanham, MD: Rowman & Littlefield, 2000), p. 20.

3

GOJIRA AS JAPAN'S FIRST POSTWAR
MEDIA EVENT

Barak Kushner

Why should we care about *Gojira*, arguably just a monster movie with a guy lumbering around in a rubber suit? Why should we stop and take note of a movie that has an obvious multicultural appeal and spawned a series of similar movies for more than five decades? My own understanding of *Gojira* (1954) is from the perspective of a bridge between Japan's imperial war from 1931 to 1945 and the postwar. In my work on the cultural and political continuities between the war and the postwar, *Gojira* becomes an interesting case study as a media event. In fact, it was Japan's first international postwar media event. *Gojira* is a way for me to extend my research from the war into the postwar, but to explain the popularity and the film's longevity we have to grapple with Japan's postwar media, its international image, and the understanding that foreign communities had of Japan in the early postwar period. I examine the film historically, not as a film scholar or film critic. Yoshimi Shunya and others explain that a media event is an event in which the original event is outpaced by the attention that the media pay to the event as it continues to linger in the public mind, the news, and the social psyche. In Yoshimi's estimation, media create the reality of an event through the dissemination, distribution, and diffusion of the event itself. It is important to note that the media need not be privately owned, nor can it only be the news agencies that create a media event. Governments as well as international organizations can accomplish this task equally as well. *Gojira* was a popular hit in Japan; it traveled abroad, returned to Japan, and became a franchise unto itself. *Gojira* marks Japan's return to the international stage—before the 1964 Olympics, before the success of the *shinkansen* (bullet trains), and before the postwar economic miracle that launched headlines about Japan's dominant workforce.

Along the lines of this type of reasoning, what is interesting is that early reception in Japan, box office receipts, demonstrated that audiences enjoyed *Gojira*, but critics panned it. Why were they critical of it? The milieu at the time was critics who wanted films that would promote a modern Japan. But why, therefore, does Godzilla live on? *Gojira* was like a Zen hit, a hit that was not a hit. So why should we care about it?

In 1954 *Gojira* became a popular hit in Japan, setting a record by selling 9,610,000 tickets, but the critics and the media mostly disparaged it. According to the November 3, 1954 *Asahi* newspaper, "Only the concept is interesting."[1] The article negatively compared Japan with America, in that Japan produced few science fiction films, but the *Asahi* reporter could not be entirely dismissive because the film evinced a few imaginative qualities that made for interesting viewing. Not that the poor film script allowed the monster to develop any "personality," and as far as monster films went, it paled in comparison to *King Kong*, but the writer suggested that it was not a total flop. As much as it was disliked by early critics, popular acclaim for the film grew and as a result, *Gojira* is the only monster film consistently ranked as one of Japan's greatest films.[2] In addition, the monster film has retained a strong following over the decades and remains a favorite internationally as well. During the 1950s, an age when cinema did not compete with television for audiences, Godzilla's dominance in the market was a significant cultural marker because in 1952 Japan produced 303 motion pictures showing in 4,438 cinemas. This era was, after all, the beginning of the golden age of Japanese films. In 1954, production expanded to 348 films.[3] The fact that Godzilla rose to the top amidst this avalanche of films should force us to take notice.

When *Gojira* first illuminated screens in the late fall of 1954, it faced serious artistic competition; so the fact that it garnered any audience, let alone serious box-office statistics, requires analysis. When we think of Japan in the 1950s, our minds naturally turn to top-ranked films like the other early 1950s prizewinners: *Seven Samurai, Ikiru,* and *Rashōmon*. In 1954 the darling of the movie review industry and art world was director Kinugasa Teinosuke's *Gate of Hell*, which was based on a novel by renowned writer Kikuchi Kan. *Gate of Hell* even went on to win the Grand Prix at Cannes. *Rashōmon* had previously garnered praise in Europe, taking the grand prize at the 1950 Venice Film Festival. But who sees students walking around with *Rashōmon* T-shirts, or children playing with little action figures from the *Seven Samurai*. Although *Rashōmon* was a great film, it did not launch a franchise and it could not market character goods. However, *Gojira* did. *Gojira* was the first postwar Japanese film to go international, to be free of occupation censorship restrictions, and to make it successfully to the foreign screen to spawn an industry in its name.

The Japanese film industry, and, more importantly, the recognition it received abroad, even made it into National Diet debates. At the end of 1952, when Japan was preparing to reenter international society after a six-and-a-half year hiatus following the Allied occupation and loss of sovereignty, *Gojira* and the international fame that the monster brought Japan succeeded despite lackluster political support. The Japanese government, at least as expressed in Diet debates, salivated over the potential impact Japanese films held in influencing foreign attitudes toward Japan, not to mention generating the sorely needed hard currency films received abroad. The image most elite Japanese, elected officials, and bureaucrats hoped to peddle abroad was that of a progressive Japan, a Japan with artistic verve and style. According to members of Japan's parliament, films that emphasized traditional Japan primarily embodied these notions of Japanese culture that the authorities felt made Japan look good. The Japanese public and Japanese elites reacted to postwar Japanese cinema differently. Japanese politicians loved *Rashōmon* and they believed that it "helped foreigners understand the psychology of Japan," even though the plot centered on an eleventh-century incident.[4] (These comments came out in two December 1952 parliamentary debates concerning foreign affairs and the image of Japan abroad.) In several early postwar parliamentary debates, when discussion of postwar Japanese culture abroad surfaced, the talk quickly turned to *Rashōmon* or similar motion pictures. A third debate at the end of 1952 pushed this even further when Diet member Matsuda Takechiyo explained that "[i]t is imperative that we promote toward foreign countries ideas concerning the 'goodness' of Japan."[5] Primarily, Matsuda and others wanted to impress upon the international body of nations that Japan had regained its sovereignty and was therefore a "good nation."

One caveat with the international release of modern Japanese films centered on the issue of language. Film critics and theorists writing in *Kinema Junpō* felt that Japanese films abroad held limited interest for the mass audience, or that viewers were essentially limited to the intellectual classes, because of subtitles. While Japanese audiences read films, Japanese reviewers assumed that foreigners preferred to avoid this chore. We need to dub our films to make them internationally palatable, Japanese film reviewers emphasized.[6] Groups discussed how Japanese films provided for an excellent source of hard currency income and economic fortune, if only these obstacles could be surmounted. Certainly, in the early 1950s, Japanese films were being prized around the world. The Ministry of Foreign Affairs attended such festivities, but the prime minister did not once send anything except a formal plaque of congratulations. "If Japan desires to export more film, the government needs to be more protective of its film production companies or the situation will worsen," filmmakers cried.[7] *Gojira* signified the end of appealing Japanese films that stayed away from modern topics and the film announced Japan's return to the international cultural and political scene. In terms of dubbing, by avoiding the artsy while embracing the popular, and by not appearing to be a "traditional" Japanese movie, *Gojira* fit the bill in all regards. It served as a bridge film to mainstream audiences in a way that exotic period-piece Japanese films never could. *Rashōmon* would not have been popular with dubbing, nor would it have been accepted, but since Godzilla did not speak and because the film was modern, dubbing did not essentially ruin the artistic product.

Not everyone agreed that traditional Japanese films bolstered the correct understanding of Japan abroad. The Japanese intelligentsia swarmed over this debate and it manifested itself in unusual ways. Oya Sōichi, a renowned

Japanese wartime and postwar journalist, visited the Middle East in the mid-1950s and on one sojourn stopped by a small kibbutz in Israel. In the middle of the sands of the Gaza, within a small country fighting for its survival, the Israelis had the time to learn about Japan. But, they were being educated not about modern Japan, but about medieval Japan. Oya then realized that a large gap existed abroad between the image of Japan in foreign lands as a historical existence and the reality of Japan as a modern nation. The kibbutz inhabitants had greeted Oya with shouts of "Rashōmon, Rashōmon," which they had seen three days earlier. The incident struck Oya as telling and he wrote that because of this experience he learned that the best way to augment this already pro-Japanese cultural sentiment sweeping the world was to produce more quality Japanese movies and ship them abroad.[8] Oya wanted to see *modern* Japanese film abroad since he felt that traditional Japanese films showed Japan as being backward. He was part of a larger Japanese academic argument that wanted to reinsert Japan into the pantheon of nations, but in a different way from the Japanese government. These postwar intellectuals wanted to divorce foreigners from their view of a backward prewar Japan and demonstrate how the new Japan had shed its traditional heritage. At a time when factions in the Japanese parliament greatly debated the international image of the nation, the notion of Japan as an image of postwar modernity was paramount. The gap between what the elites wanted and what the government proposed reflected a fairly divided social mandate about how to go about correcting Japan's wartime mistakes. In 1954 Japan was technically sovereign once again after the signing of the San Francisco Peace Treaty, but the 600,000 internees detained in Siberia had not yet returned. The Liberal Democratic Party had not yet completed its domination of the political landscape with the 1955 system. In short, Japan had not yet overcome its wartime intellectual, physical, and political baggage. The Korean War had ended, the Communists in China were successful in vanquishing the nationalists, and the Soviets looked poised to strengthen further their grip on Eastern Europe.

For the producers and staff that worked on *Gojira*, the film was not only a major media event but it was also a serious film about the threat of war and social insecurity. In many ways, I believe that *Gojira* was a Japanese precursor to what the Chinese in the 1970s labeled as "scar literature," or *shanghen wenxue*, the prose written just after the conclusion of the Cultural Revolution. This form of literature acted like a social catharsis, aiding individuals in venting their long-repressed fears and anger, producing artistic works for public consumption. Like *Nikudan* (Human Bullet), *Nobi* (Fires on the Plain), and other postwar Japanese films of the antiwar genre, *Gojira* was not about war; it was about fear—fear that war could happen again, fear that mankind was not in control. Fear was a universal construct, but in a way different from your average horror movie. Takarada Akira (who played Ogata, Emiko's love interest in the film *Gojira*), Tōhō star of over 100 films and who took the lead role in the first four Godzilla movies, admitted in an interview that he shed tears during his first viewing of *Gojira*. "Godzilla himself wasn't evil and he didn't have to be destroyed. . . . Godzilla was a warning to mankind."[9] To Takarada and Japanese moviegoers of the 1950s, *Gojira* appeared as a mainstream film with social commentary. Honda Ishirō was also not some half-baked director, but the assistant director to Kurosawa Akira. (In fact, years later after a dozen Godzilla movies had been made, Kurosawa and Honda again paired together to film the acclaimed *Kagemusha* and *Ran*.) Even the actors in *Gojira* dripped with prestige and talent, separating the film from its B-class American monster film counterparts. Shimura Takashi, Dr Yamane in the original Japanese version, achieved international acclaim as the government bureaucrat who discovers the meaning of life just as he is told he has terminal cancer in Kurosawa's *Ikiru*. Shimura should also be well known to Japanese movie fans as the leader of the samurai in the equally famous *Seven Samurai*. Clearly, *Gojira* was not your average monster movie with such an illustrious cast and crew. Even Godzilla the monster was serious. In a 2001 interview with a popular Japanese magazine, Nakajima Haruo, who played Godzilla in the early years, said that once he learned of his appointment to play Godzilla, he spent an entire day at the zoo watching animal movement to learn how to move inside a constricting monster suit. Nakajima also wanted to gauge popular reception of the film and went to a theater in Shibuya for the opening. The ticket line stretched long; the theater was filled to standing room only and people spilled into the hallway. The audience remained silent as the monster approached and eyes widened as Godzilla filled the screen.[10] Hiring serious actors does not necessarily indicate that the studio aimed for a high cultural output and did not intend for the film to be campy, but most postwar Japanese accounts stress the thought put into the movie, whereas American and foreign audiences focus on the monster and its product placements. Director Honda did not even think of making a sequel, since his original intent was not focused on profit, but "a sincere protest against nuclear destruction."[11]

The *Gojira* that Honda and Tsuburaya Eiji produced also reified many wartime assumptions. As Michael Baskett and other scholars in Japan have detailed in their research on wartime Japanese popular culture, imagination about the South Pacific played a large role in media such as manga, film, radio broadcasts, and even toys during the war from 1931 to 1945. This tendency continued into the postwar period. Out of 26 postwar films that Tsuburaya made after *Gojira*, fully half of them, in some way, dealt with the South Pacific, jungles, and similar images to what made it into the pages of *Bōken Dankichi, Norakuro,* and other popular wartime adventure comics. (It seems that Tsuburaya settled on making *Gojira* as a quid pro quo to later make his long-awaited film concerning a giant octopus in the Indian Ocean.) Tsuburaya's film career had actually begun with wartime propaganda. In 1935 he traveled as an embedded director/journalist with the Japanese Navy on naval exercises for six months around the world. As a sailor he visited Java, Fiji, and Hawai'i, and his film was released as a documentary of sorts with the title *Sekidō o koete* (Crossing the Equator).[12] Footage in the film included

Japan's own colony Taiwan and the islands it received the mandate to control after World War I, the Marianas Islands. Tsuburaya also recorded images of the lifestyles of various natives whom, according to the narration of the film, were better off after the introduction of Japanese guidance and leadership. Scholars debate whether *Gojira* is a war film or not, and this is a worthwhile discussion determining where the factors for audience appreciation hide. At the same time an alternative mode of analysis might be postwar Godzilla's relation with Japanese wartime propaganda. *Gojira* is a slippery and complex film with multiple easily identifiable themes. It is a multifaceted film, broad enough to span competing interpretations and I assert that Tsuburaya and Honda are examples of that slipperiness.

Gojira was such a domestic Japanese hit that Columbia pictures felt it could gain more viewers across the Pacific. Although not much is know about the specific strategies to sell Godzilla across the ocean, we can still divide the audiences into two distinct categories: in Japan *Gojira* was popular at the box office whereas in the States, Godzilla's popularity grew from the creation of fandom and the ensuing merchandising, not from the film precisely.[13] It took a while, but eventually the movie spawned a tertiary industry across the ocean. The Japanese media reported in 1978, once again, that a Godzilla craze was sweeping across America with T-shirts for sale and other character goods.[14] (Hello Kitty started in 1974 so it was not a far reach for Godzilla goods to also become pop icons, divorced from the original content of the film.) Americans even liked the monster enough to recreate their own version of it.

Not until a year and a half after its domestic release, in 1956, did Godzilla really became known internationally with the release of the dubbed and narrated American version *Godzilla, King of the Monsters* with its addition of Raymond Burr in edited scenes. Since the American public never had access to the original Japanese version, at least until very recently, the United States made this film a popular franchise without a majority of the audience seeing the real film. Due to the fact that the film's international success was based on two entirely different sets of criteria, what was it about Godzilla that struck foreign viewers as a good film? This idea leads me to my next discussion regarding understanding the popularity of the film outside of Japan.

International audiences appreciated and waxed poetic for the cinematic masterpieces that *Rashōmon* and *Gate of Hell* represented, but *Gojira* was the first Japanese film to gain an international appeal that lasted. *Gojira* developed a devoted audience, a cult following, and its popularity and trademark have never weakened. However, in contrast to Pokémon and Ultraman, *Gojira* "smells" of Japanese culture.[15] This "smell" of culture is what Iwabuchi Kōichi writes about when he identifies the features of Japanese culture that either repel or attract international consumers. In his work on nationalism and culture, Iwabuchi does not specifically discuss *Gojira*; he focuses more on contemporary electronic and popular culture gaining a large market share in the Far East and Southeast Asia. But I feel his theory about the spread of culture is useful here. In his lucid commentary on the international influence of popular Japanese culture, Iwabuchi asserts that Japanese popular culture and consumer electronics have spread, in major part, because they are "culturally neutral," meaning that they do not emit a specific odor of Japaneseness.

However, I aver that Japanese monster films of the 1950s specifically attracted audiences, at the outset, because of their exoticism. America's recent relationship with Japan grew out of World War II, when most still believed that all Japanese were samurai with *chonmage* (topknots) and walked around in the company of white-painted geisha. Conversely, *Gojira*, though not exotic in the traditional sense, maintained its following precisely because it was so Japanese. No film could be more Japanese since only Japan had the atomic bomb dropped on it, and only the Japanese understood the deep-seated fear of sliding back into war again. In fact, as Terrence Rafferty noted in the *New York Times*, the original Japanese version of Godzilla, not the poorly dubbed American one, is the quintessential Japanese film. It is insular to the extreme. In the film, there is "no occupying army, no United Nations representatives, no heavy-set Caucasian reporters," only Japanese.[16] In other words, the film is rank with Japaneseness. Tomiyama Shōgo, producer of the last Godzilla movie, *Godzilla Final Wars*, hammered this point home in the publicity for the culmination of the five-decade-long Godzilla series when he remarked that Godzilla "was received enthusiastically throughout the world as a 'Made in Japan' property that represents postwar Japan."[17]

The smell of *Gojira* as exotic, I think, accounts for the initial success of the film. However, that is not the same set of values that governs its continued success. The longevity of *Gojira* and one of the goals behind its promotion abroad was to advertise a modern Japan, but this has proven impossible since once icons are removed from their cultural context and displaced abroad, their significance changes. Godzilla suffers the same fate as American icons outside of our national borders—their inherent cultural markers are not exported with the show and much of it becomes kitschy. This "smell" of Japanese culture and its connections to Godzilla, icon worship, and the proliferation of character goods like Hello Kitty and others, has also led to a national fatigue concerning Godzilla that might explain the end of the series in 2004. Much to Japanese higher society's chagrin, the image of Japan, in places, has become a situation where "those wacky Japanese" predominates. This idea that Japanese culture is strange and filled with funnily dressed men and women engaging in bizarre behavior, running away from monsters, or playing on silly game shows has been strengthened in recent years with Spike TV's rerelease of nighttime Japanese television programming, usually involving a Beat Takeshi variety show where contestants competing in games make fools of themselves. Ironically, in a situation similar to *Gojira*, Americans are not watching the original Japanese television show but a redubbed version catering to American concepts of Japanese comedy. This effort is similar to what Woody Allen did in *What's Up Tiger Lily?* when he took a Japanese detective/suspense movie and dubbed it into a murder mystery surrounding the search for the ultimate egg salad recipe. Allen was culturally building on the American notion that Japanese films were kitschy, silly, and ultimately unfathomable to American audiences.

What Americans bought in Godzilla was not representative of the Japan that parliamentarians wanted to export because the monster morphed in transition across the ocean, turning funny and wacky. Eventually, Godzilla became a friendly monster since there was no fear in the American sense and the films turned entertaining in the derisive sense, reaffirming American notions about Japan that the country is a joke. Godzilla was not serious, it was cheesy. But, before you laugh, let us consider this notion of cheese. We should take cheesiness seriously.

One reason for Godzilla's longevity on the international scene might also be due to its perceived cheesiness. As Annalee Newitz, a public intellectual, defines cultural cheese, it is "the production of, and appreciation for, what is artificial, exaggerated, or wildly, explosively obscene." Cheese "describes a way of remembering history, a kind of snide nostalgia for serious cultures of the past."[18] To Americans, Godzilla became cheesy, but the Japanese, including the man inside the plastic costume, took the film seriously enough. In Japan *Gojira* was not cheese. Was *Gojira* popular abroad because it was cheesy? There is certainly an element of veracity to the assertion. Indeed, we must assume that the Japanese audience in 1954 was much more attuned to the historical antecedents that made *Gojira* appealing upon its domestic Japanese release, than was the foreign audience when the film arrived on American shores, edited within an inch of its life, dubbed, narrated with a central American character, and stripped of its original meaning and intention. Certainly the cheese factor distinguishes the Japanese film released abroad, with its poor dubbing and tiresome editing, but fads like that tend to die out after a few seasons and Godzilla has not only survived the century, but age as well. Cheese did not motivate North Korean dictator Kim Jong Il to kidnap well-known South Korean director Shin San-Ok and force him to direct a remake of the Japanese film along Marxist lines. In fact, the North Korean version, *Pulgasari*, may be the only time that North Korea has willingly copied any facet of Japanese popular culture, a fact that should not go ignored. So appealing and strong is the Godzilla trope that the North Koreans swallowed their historical animosity toward Japan and produced their own domestic version of Godzilla.[19] Godzilla may be cheesy for Americans, but it is also serious to the Koreans.

Godzilla was also popular in different ways in Japan than America due to the nature of the two national histories. To the Japanese, Godzilla appeared indomitable but they eventually subdued it. Former prime minister Suzuki Kantarō announced when he left office, just after Japan's surrender in August 1945, that the reason behind Japan's defeat was not a defective military or an absence of martial spirit, but because the country lacked a sufficient scientific spirit. Though many see *Gojira* as an antiwar film, it is also indicative of the way in which wartime Japanese social attitudes influenced the postwar social ethos.

Those who have viewed the original *Gojira* should note that Japan's new Defense Forces (not self-defense forces) do not provide assistance in the monster's final destruction. Only a scientific discovery by a Japanese scientist, Dr Serizawa and his "oxygen destroyer," saves the day. Take careful notice of the fact that the doctor with the oxygen destroyer is a Japanese scientist who wins the day; foreign science does not make an appearance. Dr Serizawa's sacrifice of self to save the nation seems cruelly similar perhaps to how Ivan Morris once described a Japanese cultural trait to persevere in the face of certain doom as "the nobility of failure." He realizes that he will die, but, unlike the wartime Japanese pilots, Serizawa wants to save the nation, not the emperor. Thus his sacrifice is not in vain as death is depicted in *Human Bullet* and *Fires on the Plain*.[20] At the same time we need to remember Godzilla's path of destruction from Shinagawa through the center of Tokyo where the monster lays waste to the national Diet building. After stomping on the parliament, the beast makes its way over to Asakusa, following an interesting detour around the imperial palace, and eventually slipping back into the Sumida River. Had the moviemakers really desired to make an antiwar film, they could have chosen to destroy the emperor's residence. Perhaps recent occupation censorship policies were still fresh in the minds of Honda and Tsuburaya or perhaps their own experiences as wartime cinematic propagandists impeded them from having the plot follow this lead.[21]

Ironically, even though the international version of *Gojira* lost its "Japanese smell" upon reaching American movie theaters, during the time that Godzilla developed into the archetype for monster movies, or rather became the mother of all monsters, the movie icon slowly seemed to regain its cultural identity. We cannot ignore the fact that it has already become a common cultural joke in America to mock bad dubbing in Japanese films. (Everything wacky is inherently labeled Japanese—bad TV, strange foods, funny games. It is still seen as a land of monsters, though now they are machine made or stand as vending machines.) In many ways the fear that Japanese elites demonstrated just after the war—that Japan would not be taken seriously by the world—has come true. Godzilla helped usher Japan in to new world markets, but by the time Woody Allen's 1960s kitsch remake of the Japanese detective film made audiences giggle, Godzilla and an awareness of Japan were not unusual. Allen's redubbing of a Japanese detective thriller banked on American attitudes that Japanese movies were inherently cheesy and, in many ways, the release of *Gojira* on American shores set that tone. However, back on Japanese shores, the film represented a different perspective on postwar life and it is important to remember that, at one time, Godzilla was *the* monster, the king of monsters, in fact.

NOTES

1. *Asahi Shinbun* (Tokyo, evening edition), November 3, 1954.
2. *Kinema Junpō*, the industry standard film magazine, listed it as one of the top 20 greatest postwar Japanese films, and forty-third in the class of all-time best Japanese films. Kinema Junpō, ed. *Sengo kinema junpō besuto ten zenshi, 1946–2002* (Tokyo: Kinema Junpōsha, 2003).

3. Bureau of Statistics, Office of the Prime Minister, ed., *Japan Statistical Handbook* (1954), pp. 479–481.

4. [001/024]15—Shū–gaimuiinkai—4gō, Showa 27nen 12gatsu 10nichi (Uehara's statements), National Diet Debate Records.

5. [003/024]15—Shū–gaimuiinkai—11gō, Showa 27nen 12gatsu 19nichi (Matsuda's statements), National Diet Debate Records.

6. "Kaigai ni okeru nihon eiga (zadankai)," *Kinema Junpō* (January 1, 1955), p. 43.

7. Ibid., p. 47.

8. Oya Sōichi, "Sekai wa shojochi ni michite iru," *Kinema Junpō* (February 15, 1955), p. 37.

9. Stuart Galbraith IV, *Monsters Are Attacking Tokyo* (Venice, CA: Feral House, 1998), p. 30.

10. Nakajima Haruo, "Shodai Gojira wa watashi data," *Bungei Shunjū* (January 2001), pp. 186–188.

11. Mark Schilling, *The Encyclopedia of Japanese Pop Culture* (Tokyo: Weatherhill, 1997), p. 58.

12. "Bunka Bazar," *SPA* (March 12, 1997), p. 143.

13. Sayuri Shimizu's article in this volume speaks more to the issue of how America marketed Godzilla.

14. "Ano [Gojira] ga nichibei de ijō ninki! raishun ni wa shinsaku tōjō," *Shūkan Josei* (July 25, 1978), p. 146; "Hito to jiken," *Shūkan Gendai* (December 8, 1977), p. 52.

15. Koichi Iwabuchi, *Recentering Globalization, Popular Culture and Japanese Transnationalism* (Durham, NC: Duke University Press, 2002), p. 24.

16. Terrence Rafferty, "The Monster that Morphed into a Metaphor," *New York Times*, May 2, 2004.

17. http://www.godzilla.co.jp/english/index.html, accessed September 8, 2004.

18. Annalee Newitz, "What Makes Things Cheesy? Satire, Multinationalism and B–movies," *Social Text* 18:2 (2000), p. 59.

19. For more on this film, see Satsuma Kenpachirō, *Gojira ga mita Kita Chōsen kinseinichi ni shuen shita kaijū yakusha no yo ni mo fushigi na taikenki* (Tokyo: Nesuko, 1988).

20. Ivan Morris, *Nobility of Failure: Tragic Heroes in the History of Japan* (New York: Holt, Rinehart & Winston, 1975); Emiko Ohnuki-Tierney, *Kamikaze, Cherry Blossoms, and Nationalisms: The Militarization of Aesthetics in Japanese History* (Chicago: University of Chicago Press, 2002).

21. Nagayama Yasuo, *Kaijū wa naze Nihon o osou no ka?* (Tokyo: Chikuma Shobō, 2002), p. 28.

4

Lost in Translation and Morphed in Transit: Godzilla in Cold War America

Sayuri Guthrie-Shimizu

Godzilla—an old geezer who turned 50 in 2004 with no prospects of ever collecting his social security—is arguably among the pop culture icons most enduringly inscribed into the experiential memories of a generation of Americans. How many baby-boomers could join Peter Musolf—the author of *Gojira to wa nani ka* (The Godzilla Question) published in Japan on the eve of release of the ballyhooed 1998 Hollywood blockbuster *Godzilla*—in remembering bleary-eyed, late-night television sightings of the cheesy-looking saurian monster venting its fiery wrath on shoddy-looking buildings and screaming crowds notable for their stylized scrambling? How many Americans schooled in the evolving TV culture of the 1960s and 1970s can recall, as do many a nameless blogger reminiscing in cyberspace, their local TV stations airing Godzilla movies in the local versions of "Creature Feature" or "Chiller Theater" every weekend?[1]

The ubiquity and enviable staying power of this cultural and cult icon is readily demonstrated with various indices of commercial success in our time. The series that bears Godzilla's name, launched in Japan in 1954 and culminating in the ballyhooed 2004 fiftieth-anniversary release, is the longest running in world movie history. Since 1963, its franchise has spawned a multitude of media products and kids' (and sometimes adults') toys and collectibles, reportedly grossing hundreds of millions of dollars each year. Godzilla's menacing images and beastly metaphors have infiltrated some of the most familiar sites of popular culture production in contemporary America, such as parade floats, soft drink ads, rock and roll lyrics (remember Blue Öyster Cult's *Godzilla?*), Valentine's Day novelty gifts, tattoo motifs, and political cartoons like Mike Luckovich's famous 1990 satire of the Japanese ownership of MCA and Columbia Pictures.[2]

Americans of Generation X and younger, who know Godzilla in its 1998 TriStar incarnation, may not realize that this Hollywood-rendered creature with a character tie-up with Taco Bell originated in Japan in the immediate wake of a prolonged international "police action" commonly known as the Korean War. Indeed, the degree to which Godzilla has become embedded in Americans' collective consciousness and everyday practices suggests that it has, as the dean of Godzilla-ology, William Tsutsui, has persuasively argued in his recent homage, become an "inalienable part of American popular culture" over the past 50 years, a period known to historians as the latter half of the American century.[3] One might add that Godzilla commands its present status as a global multimedia icon precisely because it has come to occupy such a prominent cultural niche in the United States, the center of worldwide media information flows.[4]

Exactly when did America's romancing of Godzilla begin? Godzilla first "raided" American cities in 1956, hitting theaters in New York City in April, the greater Boston area and Washington, DC a month later, and other key metropolitan areas from coast to coast by mid-summer. Godzilla's U.S. debut came a year and a half after Tōhō's original version was released in Japan to unexpectedly robust commercial success, reportedly commanding a paying viewership of 6 million. It ranked third among Tōhō movies in annual gross (152 million yen) that year, after Kurosawa Akira's critically acclaimed *The Seven Samurai* and Inagaki Hiroshi's *Miyamoto Musashi*. The American version, dubbed and heavily edited, also grossed a respectable $2.5 million, far more than the run-of-the-mill monster B-movies playing everywhere in the United States at the time. The movie stands among the earliest, little known cases of dollar-earning postwar exports from Japan, then on the cusp of postwar economic take-off as a newly anointed member of the General Agreement on Tariffs and Trade (GATT).

Godzilla's not-so-shabby trans-Pacific cinematic debut in the mid-1950s compels a question: why did this culture product, imported for $25,000 (a pittance by the American industry's standards of the time, yet a major financial coup for the exporting party at the prevailing exchange rate of 360 yen to the dollar, when the differential in average hourly wages between the national workforces stood at 10 to 1)[5] from a country with which America's "Greatest Generation" had only a decade earlier fought a bloody and hate-inspiring war, find a receptive audience to inaugurate a long and illustrious, if ridiculed, movie (and later television) career?

To untangle this historical puzzle one must plunge into the crosscurrents of social, cultural, and economic forces in the United States at mid-decade, when society was infused with a curious blend of peacetime euphoria and primal fear of the perceived threat to homeland security that was the cold war. With this objective in the background, this essay first queries how this decidedly populist Japanese movie classic, invested by its makers with loaded memories of, and political commentaries on, the war with the United States and the dark shadows of the unfolding thermonuclear age, found unexpected resonance in the country it implicitly (indeed rather explicitly in the Japanese original) criticized. This opening inquiry will be followed by an overview of disparate forces churning in U.S. society between the mid-1950s and mid-1970s (when the deaccelerating and degenerating Godzilla series was forced into a decade-long hiatus) to probe how they constituted a historical matrix amenable to Godzilla's much derided popularization among a youthful demographic cluster. The 50-year-old Japanese monster (who retired in 1995, but resumed an active work life only three years later) thus gives us a lens through which a profile of cold war America can be projected and the braided, consumption-mediated postwar histories of the United States and Japan be brought into magnified view.

* * *

When the American version of the 1954 original, retitled *Godzilla, King of the Monsters!* (note the exclamation mark), hit theaters in the United States in the spring and summer of 1956, it was unabashedly pitched as another mindless monster movie, a cinematic genre rapidly proliferating in the United States as a sure-fire money maker. In New York and Washington, DC, for instance, it first appeared in local movie listings as a Japanese monster movie or a "sci-fi melodrama from the Orient." In the key metropolitan areas in the Midwest, it was billed as part of *Bestial Monster Madness,* coupled with *Man Beast: Sub-Human Monster,* and it played at open-all-night theaters. The caption next to the fire-breathing Godzilla read: "It's Alive! Raging through the World on a Rampage of Destruction!" On the West Coast, where it opened in the early summer for matinees and showings at drive-in theaters, the hyperbole was ratcheted up a few notches: "See it crush . . . See it kill . . . A mighty city of 8 million wiped out by its death ray blasts! Enjoy the thrill of your life!!"[6]

The marketing of *Godzilla, King of the Monsters!* (*Gojira* in the Japanese original) as a gore-ridden creature film was, however, far from what its Japanese progenitors had intended for their handiwork. According to producer Tanaka Tomoyuki (who would produce many of the Tōhō monster movies in the following decades), Godzilla's Japanese creators—himself, director Honda Ishirō, and the author of the original novel Kagawa Shigeru (a former finance ministry career bureaucrat)—had been inspired by the sorrows of the recent war and the horrors of the hydrogen bomb, terrifyingly dramatized by the radiation poisoning, in March 1954, of the crew of the Japanese fishing vessel *Lucky Dragon No. 5* when it came too close to U.S. testing on Bikini Atoll. The incident triggered a firestorm of anti-American hostility across Japan and aroused fears of dire diplomatic repercussions at the highest echelon of President Dwight Eisenhower's Republican administration.[7]

Director Honda had been deeply affected by the unspeakable destruction wrought on Hiroshima, which he passed through on his return to Tokyo in early 1946 after eight years of military service. By his own account, Honda invested his sense of horror about war's senselessness and the monstrous potential of nuclear weaponry into *Gojira* and never, even remotely, envisioned children and youth as the film's intended audience. Similarly, Kagawa's original novel left little ambiguity about the link between Godzilla's emergence from the depths of the Pacific Ocean and American hydrogen bomb testing. The cinematic team thus wove profound themes—nuclear annihilation, environmental degradation, and the apocalyptic potential of modern science run amuck—into the film at a cost of 1.3 trillion yen (no low-budget B-movie by contemporary Japanese standards). As critic Kawamoto Saburō later noted, *Gojira* was a quintessentially "early postwar Japanese film" in that Tokyo's Godzilla-flattened landscape was eerily reminiscent of the fire-bombed Tokyo of barely a decade before, and victims of Godzilla's rampages in the movie resembled survivors of the atomic-bombings corralled in shattered field hospitals in Hiroshima and Nagasaki's aftermath.[8]

The presence of another key player on the Japanese production team, pioneer special-effects expert Tsuburaya Eiji, further epitomized the weighty baggage brought to the cinematic world of the 1954 *Gojira*. Having honed his craft in the filming of wartime feature films glamorizing Japan's naval advances in the Pacific, Tsuburaya was ready to take up a role as a technical genius of peacetime popular entertainment.

The diplomatic circumstances under which Tōhō Studio made *Gojira* also evinced the unresolved nature of Japan's reconciliation with the recent war. Godzilla was put on Tōhō's drawing board only after the Indonesian government, still seeking a settlement on World War II reparations, forced the abandonment of a feature film about a former Japanese soldier participating in the Indonesian war for independence.[9] Given the World War II vestiges in which the movie was incubated and crafted, the initial Japanese reviews of *Gojira* as "dark and eely" and "leaving a bad taste in [my] mouth" come as no surprise, for its wartime genealogy was palpable in its every constitutive element.[10]

Gojira's entry into the American movie market as *Godzilla, King of the Monsters!* 17 months later shares a trajectory with other "cheap" foreign movies, from such places as Mexico and Italy, that made their way into double-bill showings in the United States in the mid-1950s. When executives of a relatively upstart East Coast movie distributor, Embassy Pictures, learned of the huge commercial success of *Gojira* in Japan through foreign news clips, it approached an all-too-eager Tōhō and bought the distribution rights for North America for $25,000. Thus began the historic transmogrification of *Gojira* into *Godzilla, the King of Monsters!*, a creature film with only a few scenes that were, as opined in an early U.S. review, "banzai-worthy."[11] In the hands of Embassy Pictures' executive producer Joseph Levine (along with producers Harold Ross, Richard Kay, and writer/director Terry Morse), the movie—the deliberate message of which was bound to offend the mainstream American audience—received a relatively quick and inexpensive makeover into an inoffensive object of mass entertainment and was marketed as such through radio saturation campaigns.[12]

Concerned that Godzilla, as depicted in the Japanese original, was not "powerful enough" to satisfy the prevailing popular craving for monster fare with a flare, Levine enlarged Godzilla in the Embassy Pictures' marketing pitch from a monster standing 50 meters (150 feet) tall to a towering behemoth of 400 feet in height, which would "make King Kong look like a midget." Fortunately for Levine and his production staff, the terms and conditions of the Tōhō-Embassy Picture contract gave the American side infinitely wide latitude in what they could crop, add, and superimpose, reflecting metaphorically the reality of contemporary power relations between the two countries. As denizens of a vanquished nation desperate to replenish its war-depleted reserves of the now almighty U.S. dollar, Tōhō's executives were willing to sell almost anything to tap into an American movie market that would remain alluring through the 1960s and early 1970s. One of the commodities sold was artistic integrity and pride, resignedly foresworn by *Gojira*'s cinematic progenitors.[13]

The result of this not-so-unwitting trans-Pacific collusion was the now-famous insertion of pre-Perry Mason, pre-Ironside Raymond Burr into the original Japanese cast. The relatively unknown American actor's big screen presence was fortified (or eviscerated, depending on one's point of view) by the poorly executed English dubbing, which from the very first run of *Godzilla, King of the Monsters!* every key metropolitan movie reviewer made a point of ridiculing.[14] Not surprisingly, the roughly 30 minutes excised from *Gojira* contained several explicit references to Hiroshima and Nagasaki. The implied linkage between the amphibious prehistoric monster from the Mesozoic era thawing in the depths of the Pacific Ocean and the recent American H-bomb testing also disappeared. Instead, 20 minutes worth of screen time showing Burr on a junket as a reporter in exotic Asia witnessing the unfolding disaster was added, probably enough to satisfy what Christina Klein calls the cold war Orientalism infiltrating America's middle-brow culture in the early postwar decades.[15]

Godzilla, King of the Monsters! suffered mostly belittling reviews ("a dinosaur made of gum-shoes and about $20 worth of toy buildings and electric trains," "cheap cinematic horror stuff . . . it is too bad that a respectable theatre has to lure children and gullible grown-ups with such fare," "If you're a horror devotee, 'Godzilla' should go on your shopping list," etc.).[16] The U.S. alterations perhaps made it deserving of these comments. Still, the degree to which the Japanese production team's cinematic intent was obscured as a result of Embassy Picture's creative redaction and addition was astounding. A *New York Times* reviewer's pontification provides a particularly telling example:

Perhaps if we wished to seek a reason, we might note that the film was produced in Japan and Godzilla is explained as a freak offspring of nature, dislodged and reactivated by H-Bombs. One might remotely regard him as a symbol of Japanese hate for the destruction that came out of nowhere and descended upon Hiroshima one pleasant August morn. But we assure you that the quality of the picture and childishness of the whole idea do not indicate such calculation. Godzilla was simply meant to scare people.[17]

Embassy Picture's recasting of *Gojira* into a standard monster-on-the-loose flick devoid of any social relevance revealed several currents powerfully channeling the U.S. movie industry at the time. The monster entered the U.S. market exactly at the moment when a cinematic genre specifically targeting young audiences was expanding aggressively. This juvenilizing trend was reflective of the segmentation of American consumer markets amid the unprecedented postwar economic boom and the rise of the teenager as a discrete category of consumers with free time and increasing discretionary money (and thus worthy of specialized catering).[18]

The harbinger of this new cinematic/marketing attention to the market segment driven by juvenile tastes and interests was Hal Chester's *The Beast from 20,000 Fathoms*. Released in June 1953, this archetypal Warner Brothers low-budget creature film, deploying Ray Harryhausen's special effects, grossed a then spectacular 5 million dollars. This movie adaptation of a 1951 short story by Ray Bradbury featured a prehistoric dinosaur, awakened from its eternal sleep deep in the Arctic ice by a nuclear test, migrating toward its old breeding ground, the present-day New York City, which it would destroy. The hugely successful movie established a winning formula for capturing—and merchandising—the amorphous anxiety about nuclear testing and homeland assault pervasive among Americans in the heyday of the cold war. In June 1954 *Them!*, another Warner Brothers movie, picked up on the nuclear-mutation theme. This one featured giant ants originating in New Mexico and attacking Los Angeles. The motif of radiation-morphed mega creatures was also employed in such youth-oriented exploitation films as *It Came from Beneath the Sea* (1954), *Tarantula* (1955), *X the Unknown* (1956), *Mole People* (1956), *The Deadly Mantis* (1957), *Beginning of the End* (1957), *Attack of the Crab Monsters* (1957), and *The Cyclops* (1957). Clearly, *Gojira* had to be retooled into this mold if it was to successfully enter the orbit of the monster/sci-fi horror movie mania in 1950s America.[19]

Besides the engineered fit into a proven formula, *Gojira*'s nuclear-age theme had a reason to resonate in cold war America at a deeper emotional level. Tanaka's 1954 original (with appropriate alteration, of course) could tap into the preexisting American paranoia about the nuclear arsenal and its threats, real or imagined, to "homeland security." Although America's atomic-age anxiety was fed not by haunting memories of actual A-bomb destruction, as was the case with Japan, but by the prospect of potential attacks by a hostile outsider, it was nuclear paranoia nonetheless. As historian Laura McEnaney has masterfully demonstrated in her study of civil defense in the United States in the 1950s, fears of a nuclear attack penetrated deeply into middle-class American households. Because of the Republican administration's ideological proclivity against federal funding for civil defense and civic education programs about the danger of nuclear weaponry, the bulk of these efforts were left to civic organizations and public schools.

The American home became a paramilitary unit, a site for cold war military readiness where Dad talked of building a nuclear bomb shelter in the backyard, Mom and Mrs Jones next door stocked the survival kit in the basement, and the kids routinely practiced "duck and cover" at school. The menacing and deadly potential of nuclear power thus seeped into the mainstream American home and school through everyday practices of civil defense and awareness campaigns. In this milieu, the idea of a giant lizard-like, H-bomb morphed reptile threatening one's home and mankind was not something that lay entirely outside the realm of the imaginable possibilities or lacked in verisimilitude for American school-age children.[20]

The prominence of science-run-amuck motifs in American popular culture also fostered an ambient market receptiveness to Godzilla. With the advent of V-II rockets and atomic weapons at the end of World War II, a significant change took place in America's mass thinking about science and nature. Science and its systematic application to instruments of destruction and carnage entered the speculative horizons of ordinary Americans. Instruments of carnage were no longer the special province of mad scientists or science fiction writers. Mainstream Americans' simultaneous fascination with science and anxiety about its ominous potential were manifested in many forms, including sightings of flying saucers, encounters with space aliens (as reported in mass-circulating magazines), and the growing popularity of sci-fi and space war movies. At about the same time, the American mass media began to be saturated with images of mass-scale violence in easily consumable visual packages. When Godzilla made its debut in the United States, various breeds of giant reptiles, amphibians, insects, and other "scientifically-enhanced" biological entities were traversing the silver screen in droves and destroying American cities such as New York and Los Angeles, all with the stalwart assistance of special-effects technologies.[21]

The plethora of monster/sci-fi movies geared toward juvenile viewers in the 1950s also reflected a structural change then taking place in the American movie business. As the phenomenal growth of movie attendance, fueled by the early postwar economic boom, showed signs of losing steam in the face of television in the early 1950s, the American movie-going population began to diversify into more stratified groups. Many factors contributed to this segmentation, key among them a realignment of the movie distribution system compelled by federal regulatory oversight. Since the late 1930s, the Justice Department had sought to loosen the grip that the major Hollywood studios held on film distribution through antitrust prosecution. When the U.S. Supreme Court upheld a lower court antitrust ruling in *United States vs. Paramount* (1948), the Big Five studios had no choice but to divest themselves of their theaters over the next six years. The majors also began to move away from B-movie production because this category of cinematic merchandise was deemed only marginally profitable.[22]

Public policy imperatives and private market considerations combined to open up the field for smaller movie exhibitors and distributors, such as Embassy Pictures, Godzilla's initial shepherd into the U.S. market, and American International Pictures (AIP). AIP, which would handle several of the Godzilla movies in the 1960s and 1970s, specialized in double-bills, in 1956 pairing *The Day the World Ended* and *The Phantom from 10,000*

Leagues, and unleashed a cycle of horror films based on the Edgar Allan Poe stories and a string of teen films, beginning with *Beach Party*, in the early 1960s.[23] These industry upstarts navigated the shifting business terrain mostly by catering to specialized target audiences, such as the youthful demographic bloc. The substantial growth in teenagers' discretionary spending in the 1950s and 1960s assured the viability of this business strategy. The stock in trade of such entrepreneurial distributors consisted of art-house opuses and B-movies, many of which came from overseas.[24]

The stratification of the movie-delivery infrastructure was accompanied by other centrifugal forces. Historians of twentieth-century consumerism have noted that the multiplying sites and modes of consumption accelerated the segmentation of American mass markets in the postwar period.[25] This seemingly inexorable force affected media products as well, including Godzilla and its spin-offs. Drive-in theaters, an entertainment offshoot of suburbanization, road improvements, and expanding family car ownership in mid-century America, became a key outlet for low-budget B-movies. This new venue of film viewing was particularly friendly to working and middle-class American families with multiple children, a core element of what historian Lizabeth Cohen has conceptualized as the citizen-consumer in the United States. In the comfort of their own cars, Americans were able to practice vaunted "family togetherness" while consuming, among other things, spectacles of UFOs, radiation-engorged creatures, and monsters projected onto huge outdoor theater screens. Saturday matinee double-bills at indoor theaters proved a lifesaver for young parents in need of an affordable way to keep their carousing offspring entertained on the cheap. Godzilla movies were but handy fodder at these sites of parentally sanctioned American juvenile consumerism.[26]

Around the time the first Godzilla sequel *Gojira no gyakushū* (1955) was released in the United States as *Gigantis the Fire Monster* (1959),[27] *Godzilla, King of the Monsters!* began to appear in Wednesday late night and weekend television listings in major metropolitan newspapers.[28] The dramatically quick ascent of television in American society was a boon to Tōhō's string of Godzilla-featured movies, which would coalesce into the company's flagship monster movie series in the early 1960s. Americans in stunning numbers bought television sets in the 1950s. The percentage of American homes with TV sets jumped from only 0.4 percent in 1948 to 9.0 percent in 1950 and 34 percent a mere two years later. By the end of the decade, nine out of every ten American households owned a "home screen." By 1965, about a quarter of American homes were equipped with more than one set, which enabled family members with divergent TV viewing preferences and styles to fulfill their specialized needs at times of their own choosing. In the words of media historian James Baughman, television produced an "unprecedented acceptance of a new household technology," even compared to other staples of the twentieth-century American household, such as the radio, the telephone, and the automobile. What was more, income levels hardly served as a predictor of TV ownership by the mid-1950s.[29]

Godzilla movies and other visual products that commanded relatively cheap fees for air rights came in handy for the operators of the newest information/entertainment medium on the block. In the early 1950s, most major movie studios were determined to battle this upstart medium and refused to sell their films to TV stations eager to run them on weekend afternoons and in the late evenings. Smaller studios, however, generally broke with Hollywood's TV boycott. As a consequence, local TV stations tended to schedule cheap B-movies or old Hollywood feature films to fill their late afternoon and late-evening non-network time slots. Their need for cheap and available fillers with a proven formulaic appeal explains, at least in part, the frequent late-night TV appearances of Godzilla and its ilk, especially after the number of small and marginally viable local stations increased dramatically in the mid-1960s.[30]

In infiltrating these diverse venues, the Japanese monster found children and young teenagers to be its most reliable clientele. Many Godzilla purists are known to lament that as series sequels won over Japanese children in the 1960s, the saurian protagonist's character profile took a benign and even gratuitously playful turn. The fourth movie of the series, *Godzilla vs. the Thing* (1964), marked something of a watershed as the monster's fearsome image temporarily receded to make way for a Superman-esque heroic/good-guy persona. The malign effects of the juvenilizing Japanese fan base were detectable as early as 1955, when an SP song record coupling *Gojira-san* (Dear Godzilla) and *Uchi no Angirasu* (You are just like family, Angilas) was released in Japan to coincide with the latest sequel's release. The record's lyrics all but conjured up the image of Godzilla and its battle foe as something akin to household pets, contained and domesticated, rather than deadly monsters threatening to crush homes.[31]

This early sign of domestication became a lasting mark when, in the early 1960s, Tōhō's business executives made a calculated decision to tone down Godzilla's villainous image and credentials and cultivate a following among children. This cinematic reorientation of the Godzilla series may have been shameless pandering, but it was also a telling index of Japan's dizzyingly precipitous ascent into the period of high-speed economic growth that accompanied the advent of mass-consumer society. In this phase of postwar Japanese history, children, students, and young working adults became, as was the case in the United States, distinct market categories with their own subcultural needs for merchandise and services.[32] But even before Tōhō's decision to go juvenile, Godzilla's critics in the United States were already deriding *King Kong vs. Godzilla* (1963) for the subtly childish and comic profile they perceived in the Japanese monster battling America's bestial icon of the 1930s.[33]

By the time *Godzilla vs. the Thing* was brought to U.S. audiences, media commentaries on the repeated arrival of outlandish and endearingly poorly dubbed creature films from Japan regularly associated the nationally recognizable brand with a "comic book treatment" for children. The emasculation of Godzilla's menacing and war-inspired origin was so complete and the beast's recasting as family-friendly kiddy fare so widespread by the mid-1960s that the appropriateness of giving Godzilla an A-1 (family) rating was not contested even by the rating system's harshest critics. After this "comic turn," Godzilla came to be coupled in the United States with now-familiar epithets like "happy horrors for children," "combination of horror and hokum," and "strictly for the comic set," spawning an array of merchandise on toy counters and sugar-coated chocolate monsters in the supermarket candy aisle. A public Halloween children's party in Chicago even played *Godzilla vs. the Thing* as its main attraction in 1969. In both its native land and its transplanted country, Godzilla became an enduring, constitutive part of a vastly commercialized childhood and home life.[34]

The interlocking web of social, cultural, political, and economic forces that shaped cold war America and directed its evolutionary change prepared the way for the radiation-morphed and later comical and familiar monster brand to lodge itself in the American mass cultural landscape and occupy a corner of a collective generational memory. In other words, America in the 1950s was "ready" and "wired" for Godzilla and all its physical and metaphorical evolutions. As historian Warren Susman put it, a house in the sprawling suburbs, complete with a multitude of electrical appliances and a car or two in the garage symbolized "the world of new possibilities" in mid-twentieth-century America. Our favorite fire-spewing Japanese monster stomped into this world of new possibilities with an earth-shattering roar.

NOTES

1. Peter Musolf, *Gojira to wa nani ka*, trans. Ono Kōsei (Tokyo: Kodansha International, 1998), pp. 13–17; entries at a nostalgia site called Resurrected Memories, http://www.geocities.com/dzilla1964/ResurrectedMemories. html; http://gammillustrations.bialand.com/mk_reg/colton_mk.html; http://thegalleryofmonstertoys.com/70swing/70smainpage.html.

2. *Tatootime* 4 (1987), p. 14; Laurence Biegelsen and John Neuffer, *Komikku Nichibei masatsu*, trans. Ono Kōsei (Tokyo: Kodansha, 1992); Howard Chau-Eoan, "Lending a Hand to Godzilla: The Fed Pitches in as the Daiwa Scandal and Other Ills Shake up Japan's Banks," *Time* 146 (October 30, 1995), pp. 69–70; Tim Carvell, "How Sony Created a Monster," *Fortune* 137:11 (June 8, 1998), pp. 162–168.

3. William M. Tsutsui, *Godzilla On My Mind* (New York: Palgrave Macmillan, 2004), p. 114.

4. Higuchi Naofumi, *Guddo mōningu, Gojira: Kantoku Honda Ishirō to satsueisho no jidai* (Tokyo: Chikuma Shobō, 1992), p. 204.

5. Tanaka Tomoyuki, "Tanaka Tomoyuki oini kataru," *Kinema Junpō* 857 (April 1983), pp. 95–97.

6. *New York Times*, April 23 and 27, 1956; *The Washington Post and Times Herald*, April 30, 1956; *Christian Science Monitor*, May 4 and 3, 1956; *Los Angeles Times*, July 4, 9, and 11, 1956; *Chicago Daily Tribune*, August 4–6, 1956; *Detroit Free Press*, October 5, 1956.

7. Tanaka, "Tanaka Tomoyuki oini kataru," pp. 95–96.

8. "Honda Ishirō kantoku o kakonde," *Kurosawa Akira Kenkyūkaishi* 10 (1992); Kawamoto Saburō, "Gojira ha naze 'kurai' noka," *Sinefuronto*, 23:7 (July 1998), pp. 16–18; "Kaijū eiga ni idonda otokotachi," *Sukurin tokuhenban Tōhō kaijū gurafiti* (Tokyo: Kindai Eigasha, 1991), p. 36.

9. Tanaka, "Tanaka Tomoyuki oini kataru," p. 96; Higuchi, *Guddo mōningu, Gojira*, p. 176.

10. Miyamoto Haruo, *Sengo hīrō-hiroin densetsu* (Tokyo: Asahi Shinbunsha, 1995), pp. 64–66; *Asahi Shinbun*, November 1, 1954; Tanaka, "Tanaka Tomoyuki oini kataru," p. 96; *Kinema Junpō* (December 1954).

11. Anthony Slide, *The American Film Industry* (Westport, CT: Greenwood Press, 1986), p. 110; *The Washington Post*, April 30, 1956.

12. Tsutsui, *Godzilla on My Mind*, p. 39; Obituary of Terry Turner, *New York Times*, December 1, 1971.

13. "Kaijū eiga ni idonda otokotachi"; "Japan Film Chief Cites Homeland Cinema Gains," *Los Angeles Times*, July 4, 1956; "Japanese Movies Focus on Past and Present," *New York Times*, April 19, 1959; "Designed in Japan for the U.S.A.," *New York Times*, March 6, 1960.

14. *New York Times*, April 28, 1956; *Christian Science Monitor*, May 3, 1956; *Los Angeles Times*, July 12, 1956.

15. Kusanagi Satoshi, "Ganso Gojira no Beikoku jōriku," *Asahi Sōken Ripōto* 169 (June 2004), pp. 74–75; Christina Klein, *Cold War Orientalism: Asia in the Middlebrow Imagination, 1945–1961* (Berkeley: University of California Press, 2003).

16. *New York Times*, April 28, 1956; *Christian Science Monitor*, May 3, 1956; *Los Angeles Times*, July 12, 1956.

17. *New York Times*, May 6, 1956.

18. For the making of the discrete social category "teenagers," see Thomas Hine, *The Rise and Fall of the American Teenager* (New York: William Morrow, 1999).

19. John Brosnan, *The Primal Screen: A History of Science Fiction Film* (London: Orbit Books, 1991), pp. 85–108; Studio 28, ed., *Monsuta mekazu: Hariuddo kaijū kokusatsushi* (Tokyo: Yōsensha, 2000), pp. 47–88; Robert Marrero, *Godzilla: King of the Movie Monsters* (Key West: Fantasma Books, 1996), pp. 12–16.

20. Laura McEnaney, *Civil Defense Begins At Home: Militarization Meets Everyday Life in the Fifties* (Princeton, NJ: Princeton University Press, 2000).

21. Brosnan, *The Primal Screen*, pp. 44–84.

22. James L. Baughman, *The Republic of Mass Culture* (Baltimore: Johns Hopkins University Press, 1997), pp. 40–41.

23. Slide, *The American Film Industry*, p. 16.

24. Thomas Doherty, *Teenagers and Teenpics: The Juvenilization of American Movies in the 1950s* (Boston: Unwin Hyman, 1988), pp. 16–19.

25. For overviews of this point, see Gary Cross, *An All-Consuming Century* (New York: Columbia University Press, 2000) and Lizabeth Cohen, *A Consumer's Republic* (New York: Knopf, 2003), especially chapter 7.

26. Stephanie Koontz, *The Way We Never Were* (New York: Basic Books, 1992); *The Washington Post*, September 20, 1959, November 20, 1960; *Los Angeles Times*, September 17 and 19, 1964; *New York Times*, November 26, 1964.

27. The second Godzilla movie released in the United States went by Gigantis because Warner Brothers opted to cut costs by not paying for the rights to use the name Godzilla. Kusanagi Satoshi, "Amerika no Gojira: Kaijū eiga to iu bunka

yushutsu," *Asahi Sōken Ripōto* 132 (June 1998), p. 129; "Supplemental Notes by Shane Ballmann," in Morrero, *Godzilla*, p. 23.

28. *Los Angeles Times*, May 7, 1959; *Chicago Daily Tribune*, September 19, 1961.
29. Baughman, *The Republic of Mass Culture*, pp. 30–31, 41–42, 91.
30. *New York Times*, October 12, 1958, October 12, 1965, September 11, 1966; March 27, 1967; Baughman, *The Republic of Mass Culture*, pp. 79, 103.
31. Takahashi Toshio, "Gojira, watashitachi o tōitsuzukeru daikaijū," *Shinefuronto* 23:7 (July 1998), p. 11.
32. Sakamoto Hiroshi, "1950-nendai ni okeru taishū goraku zasshi no jūyō keii," *The Kyoto Journal of Sociology* 9 (2001), pp. 191–217.
33. *New York Times*, June 27, 1963; *Christian Science Monitor*, July 6, 1963; *Los Angeles Times*, July 20, 1963.
34. *Los Angeles Times*, September 26, 1964, January 11, 1965, March 11 and June 19, 1966, July 22, 1967, September 6, 1968; *New York Times*, November 26, December 6 and 13, 1964, December 16, 1965, December 14, 1970; *Chicago Tribune*, October 19, 1969.

5

Wrestling with Godzilla: Intertextuality, Childish Spectatorship, and the National Body

Aaron Gerow

Godzilla certainly is an intertextual beast. Especially with the 2004 release in the United States of the uncut 1954 original, viewers must be reminded of how that film intersected with many contemporary issues and texts, ranging from the H-bomb testing in the Pacific to *King Kong*, thereby formulating a popular cultural reaction to the atomic bomb, America, World War II, and the cold war. Recalling such original intertexts, however, should not serve to corral and restrict readings of the film and its subsequent series. As a monster stomping over the years through a variety of cultural, political, and social contexts, Godzilla has been intertextual precisely because it has always broken free of attempts to enclose its semiotic wanderings in a single text (or to confine it on Monster Island, for that matter). There have always been other contexts that problematize efforts to fix Godzilla's meaning, and which therefore point to complicated forms of spectatorship that might not only create alternative meanings for the giant lizard, but also celebrate this wandering textuality. Godzilla can offer one window onto what we could call the dual monsters of textuality and spectatorship in Japanese film history, offering an example of the historical struggles over what movies mean and who determines that.

Consider, for instance, the second Godzilla film, *Gojira no gyakushū* (1955), sometimes known in English as *Godzilla Raids Again*. A spiky rendition of Ankylosaurus, Angilas makes his way ashore in Osaka to engage with Godzilla. What ensures is a knockdown dragout with dirt flying and buildings tumbling, but the text that this battle most clearly references, with its handholds and throws, is none other than pro-wrestling. Some cite this work as the beginning of what would be called *kaijū puroresu* (monster pro-wrestling), even though it was the third film, *Kingu Kongu tai Gojira*

(King Kong vs. Godzilla, 1962), that more consciously rendered Godzilla's bouts as an inflated version of a ring battle. This insertion of monster rasslin' into the series may have been part of an effort to elongate the franchise by borrowing the success of pro-wrestling, a sport that, under the deft promotional strategies of the star wrestler Rikidōzan, was one of the most popular media phenomena in Japan from the mid-1950s to the early 1960s. This increased relationship with pro-wrestling is often said to typify the shift in the series away from a serious, though still contradictory effort to deal with traumatic memories of the war and the nuclear age, and toward lighter entertainment aimed at children, in which Godzilla shifts from being a frightening beast to a fatherly hero defending Japan. In tracing a relationship between Godzilla and social reality, many see the work of the 1960s as marking the end of the darker, more troubled and critical cultural milieu of the 1950s, still burdened by memories of the war and the bomb, and the commencement of a lighter, more confident and conservative worldview of a nation enjoying high economic growth. Although fans or scholars describing this shift may admit to finding certain pleasures in the campy implausibilities of the films of the 1960s and 1970s, the rhetoric has mostly made light of these works—and their relationship to pro-wrestling—through such words as "juvenile,"[1] "mere child's play,"[2] "B-movie morass,"[3] or "banalization."[4]

But what is involved in asserting a text "juvenile" or that it is "mere child's play" (*kodomo damashi*)? What assumptions about spectatorship and textuality does it make? While I do not necessarily reject these historical or even aesthetic accounts, I would utilize a reconsideration of Godzilla's relationship to pro-wrestling as a means of complicating their assumptions, especially with regard to the aesthetics of realism versus children's entertainment, all in hopes of sketching an alternative account of the viewer's engagement with the monstrous body. If this sketch does not provide some respect for the oft-denigrated work of the 1960s and 1970s, postulating a joyously physical way of watching Godzilla, I hope it at least forces us to rethink the oppositions between serious and nonserious, realistic and fake that have dominated not only contemporary Godzilla scholarship, but also Japanese film critical discourse since the 1910s and how it has sought to corral spectator behavior. If this discourse has long attempted to contain the monsters of textuality and spectatorship in a project of revitalizing the Japanese national, maybe we can let Godzilla romp around a little more.

*   *   *

Though there seem to be only a few overt echoes between Godzilla and pro-wrestling in *Gojira no gyakushū*, and none in the original Godzilla, there are several texts from the period that specifically make the connection, long before the more obvious *Kingu Kongu tai Gojira*. The first is the two adaptations of the two initial Godzilla films drawn by the manga artist Sugiura Shigeru.[5] Godzilla was a multimedia phenomenon from the start, and especially novelizations and manga versions were published soon after the first

Figure 5.1 Sugiura's wrestler without an opponent: "I'm the strongest in the world!" Sugiura Shigeru, *Sugiura Shigeru mangakan*, vol. 3, *Shōnen SF, ijigen tsuā* (Tokyo: Chikuma Shobō, 1994). © Sugiura Tsutomu.

films appeared. Like Yukawa Hisao's illustrated version of *Gojira no gyakushū*, which appeared in *Shōnen Kurabu* soon after the second film was released, most were rendered with a strongly realist touch. Sugiura's versions, which appeared in March and June 1955, are quite different both in their degree of caricature and in their emphasis on *kaijū puroresu*. The first version is presented as if Godzilla were a wrestler determined to be number one but without an opponent, taking his frustrations out on Tokyo instead (figure 5.1). "Ōabare Tokyo" is pro-wrestling from beginning to end, as the monsters even call their battles matches. Godzilla throws Angilas with a "H-Bomb Throw" and bashes Gyottosu—one of Sugiura's fanciful creations— on the head with a karate chop (figure 5.2).

The karate chop helps us segue to another text connecting Godzilla and pro-wrestling, *Rikidōzan no tetsuwan kyojin*, a film directed by Namiki Kyotarō and released by Shintōhō on December 13, 1954, about five weeks after the first Godzilla film. Rikidōzan was famous for his karate chop, and this is the first of several fiction films in which he starred. His main role is that of a Tarzan-like caveman without command of language who heads off to Tokyo with a boy Tarō in search of a gang that killed his scientist friend and stole a terrible death ray. After he and the boy are thrown into the sea in a train wreck caused by the villainous mob, the film switches to a fish market where we can see not only the catch being unloaded onto the docks, but also a man checking it with a Geiger counter (figure 5.3). Such checks actually occurred in 1954 after the fishing vessel *Daigo Fukuryū Maru (Lucky Dragon No. 5)* was irradiated by an H-bomb test and fears spread of radioactive tuna—an incident also referenced in *Gojira*. When another load is then lifted

Figure 5.2 Godzilla's karate chop! Sugiura Shigeru, *Sugiura Shigeru mangakan*, vol. 3, *Shōnen SF, ijigen tsuā* (Tokyo: Chikuma Shobō, 1994). © Sugiura Tsutomu.

out of the hold of a boat, only to reveal Rikidōzan and the boy in the net (figure 5.4), everyone on the dock scurries for safety when the Geiger counter goes off the scale. Soon the radio is full of reports of a radioactive "monster" (*kaibutsu*) loose in Tokyo.

If Sugiura likens Godzilla to Rikidōzan, *Tetsuwan kyojin* equates Rikidōzan with Godzilla. While it is unlikely, given the short time between their release dates, that *Tetsuwan kyojin* was consciously citing Honda Ishirō's film, the fortuitous textual networks of nuclear discourse in 1954 had Rikidōzan be the "kaibutsu" repeating Godzilla's entry into the metropolis. And make no mistake, an angry Rikidōzan can topple a building if he wants to, as he nearly does to police headquarters when he literally shakes the foundations to get out of jail later in the film. Most likely many in the audience would have enjoyed the parallels drawn between Japan's new pro-wrestling hero and the atomic beast that destroyed Tokyo, but the irreverence may seem disturbing to some. Only months after the *Lucky Dragon* incident, which resulted in the death of one crewman and a massive surge in the Japanese antinuclear movement,[6] the

Figure 5.3 Checking for things radioactive. *Rikidōzan no tetsuwan kyojin* (1954).

Figure 5.4 Another radioactive monster arrives in Tokyo. *Rikidōzan no tetsuwan kyojin* (1954).

nuclear threat is being reduced to a pro-wrestler in a loincloth and a fake beard. The original *Gojira* seemingly dealt with these issues in a much more serious fashion, which is probably one basis for why it, and not *Tetsuwan kyojin*, remains well known.

One reason for the unserious demeanor of these texts, and thus of the connection between Godzilla and pro-wrestling, is likely its audience of children. Sugiura published almost exclusively in children's magazines like *Shōnen Kurabu* and *Omoshiro Bukku*, and *Tetsuwan kyojin* even constructs its story around a child spectator. All the scenes of Rikidōzan the radioactive caveman are narratively the fantasy of a partially paralyzed boy—the boy Tarō—who dreams of becoming friends with his hero, Rikidōzan. This structure of course parallels the most childish of Godzilla films, *Gojira-Minira-Gabara: Ōru kaijū daishingeki* (Godzilla's Revenge, 1969), in which a young boy fantasizes going to Monster Island in order to escape his dreary, bullied existence. Prepubescent involvement is also central to Sugiura's narratives, as it is a child who takes the Oxygen Destroyer to Godzilla—and, of course, does not die—and it is children who best the mob of monsters invading Tokyo in "Ōabare Gojira."

Childishness thus takes away the horrors of nuclear fallout and the tragedy of Godzilla's demise, leading these texts, perhaps, into banalization. But my research on the history of discourses on film spectatorship in Japan makes me suspicious naturalizing certain narrative tones and structures to a child viewership. This was a common tactic in the Pure Film Movement in the 1910s, which complained of the premodernity of Japanese cinema—in particular, the do-good stories of Onoe Matsunosuke and other Nikkatsu films—by in part asserting that it was pandering to a child audience. This was not really a true assertion—Gonda Yasunosuke's audience surveys in the late 1910s show few theaters with a majority adolescent audience[7]—and it was colored by the fact that it also pinned the blame for poor cinema on poor working men and women. The ascription of childishness was less of a description of fact than an effort to naturalize forms of cinema and the interventions necessary to realize them. By tying certain films to spectators considered physically, mentally, and socially immature, reformers not only elevated their own, class-based modernized cinema as mature, but they also marked the cinema of a lower stratum of society as backward in a cinematic teleology, one that then needed benevolent interventions by powerful figures in order to grow up.[8] In researching how child spectators were constructed in order "to produce and place the audience in a certain way," Richard deCordova asks

> What does it mean for us (adults) to understand the child and the moving pictures, to produce a particular image of him or her? In what complex ways and through what processes . . . is that image linked to adult identity? What, in short, is at stake in the system of differences through which our society attempts to constitute a boundary between child and adult?[9]

At least in the case of Japan during much of its cinema history, discourse on child audiences and childlike films was an aesthetic based in class and culture politics, differentiating a culturally acceptable cinema from one that was not. This was a definition of film textuality and reception that was deeply involved in the continued struggle in the prewar—and, I would contend, postwar—years over controlling spectatorship by both children and adults, trying to channel film reception into nationally acceptable forms.

We can turn the tables on this and see Sugiura's manga not as childish renditions of the Godzilla stories, but as strategic efforts to reappropriate the childish by offering a different model of reading these texts. These are, in a

Figure 5.5 They won't let down their guard—or their smiles. Sugiura Shigeru, *Sugiura Shigeru mangakan*, vol. 3, *Shōnen SF, ijigen tsuā* (Tokyo: Chikuma Shobō, 1994). © Sugiura Tsutomu.

sense, an alternative interpretation of Godzilla. It is interesting to note the differences between the originals and Sugiura's manga. The first manga is relatively true to the story surrounding Godzilla, though it drops the love triangle and leaves Dr Serizawa alive at the end. What is most different is the tone of the work. No matter what tragedy seems to be unfolding, Sugiura's characters are not only cheerful, but are also having a great time (figure 5.5). There can be a gleeful anarchy to this cheer, especially when the boys show us wide grins as they exclaim upon seeing Godzilla turn Tokyo into a sea of fire, "Is this the end of Japan?" (figure 5.6). This desire to pursue merriment in any situation spreads to the monsters and literally breaks down the narrative of *Gojira no gyakushū*, making only a few frames of "Ōabare Gojira" resemble its source. The philosophy, if you can call it that, is of *yukai*, pleasure and amusement, pursuing the path as far from seriousness as possible. This can involve not only the abdication of responsibility and the pursuit of infantile consumption—taking advantage of evacuations, for instance, to eat everything in the local bakery—but it can also have a critical edge, with some panels commenting on the ridiculousness of Godzilla attacking Japan when it was America that dropped the bomb, or noting the immediate commodification of this supposedly antiwar beast.

The praxis of *yukai* is essentially the body in free motion, and Sugiura's characters are defined by an excess of movement (figure 5.7). The point is not that they are moving fast or are excessively violent, but that much of their movement is often meaningless and without motivation. Sugiura's characters frequently take poses, lifting their legs and arms, creating signs with their hands that signify nothing, except perhaps that this is a Sugiura manga (figure 5.8). Even Godzilla gets in on the act (figure 5.9). Akatsuka Fujio, Japan's most inventive gag manga artist and a self-acknowledged descendant of Sugiura, inherited this use of poses especially with the "Shē" stance that

Figure 5.6 Grinning at a Japan turned into a sea of fire. Sugiura Shigeru, *Sugiura Shigeru mangakan*, vol. 3, *Shōnen SF, ijigen tsuā* (Tokyo: Chikuma Shobō, 1994). © Sugiura Tsutomu.

Figure 5.7 Sugiura's body in motion: "0 ningen" (1958). Sugiura Shigeru, *Sugiura Shigeru mangakan*, vol. 3, *Shōnen SF, ijigen tsuā* (Tokyo: Chikuma Shobō, 1994). © Sugiura Tsutomu.

Figure 5.8 The hand gesture: "Gojira" (1955). Sugiura Shigeru, *Sugiura Shigeru mangakan*, vol. 3, *Shōnen SF, ijigen tsuā* (Tokyo: Chikuma Shobō, 1994). © Sugiura Tsutomu.

Figure 5.9 Godzilla repeats the gesture: "Ōabare Tokyo" (1955). Sugiura Shigeru, *Sugiura Shigeru mangakan*, vol. 3, *Shōnen SF, ijigen tsuā* (Tokyo: Chikuma Shobō, 1994). © Sugiura Tsutomu.

Iyami started in *Osomatsu-kun*. In our network of texts, it's significant that the movie Godzilla himself assumes this pose later on in *Kaiju daisensō* (Godzilla vs. Monster Zero, 1965).

As an embodiment of *yukai*, this excess of body movement expresses the pure pleasure of kinesis and physicality, celebrating a body unfettered by significance or seriousness, if not physical laws themselves. The epitome of this bodily excess are the many ninja that Sugiura drew, whose movements extend to transforming the very shape of their bodies (figure 5.10). The monster here is not the other, but rather the ideal, the body that is deliriously destructive both because it is powerful and because it escapes the confines of everyday physical definition. It is not hard to understand the attraction *kaijū* held

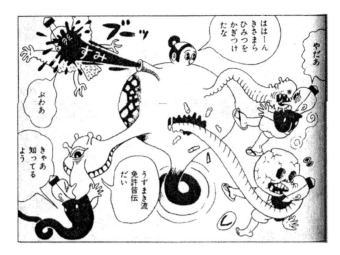

Figure 5.10 The hero's monstrous body: Sugiura Shigeru's "Doron Chibimaru" (1955–1957). *Gyagu manga kessakusen* (Tokyo: Bungei Shunjū, 1988). © Sugiura Tsutomu.

for this mode of viewing. Narratively, what these ninja, and many other Sugiura characters and monsters do, is *abare*—go on a rampage, giving full expression to their body movements, no matter what destruction that might cause. *Abare* in Sugiura most often should not have a point, and so while Godzilla in "Ōabare Gojira" goes on a rampage ostensibly to revenge his younger brother's death, all the rest of the *kaijū* are destroying Tokyo merely for sport, as they themselves say.

One could argue that Sugiura sports with *Gojira* in the same way, rampaging around with the text. This interpretation of Godzilla, one that shifts into its own aesthetics, selectively reads and rewrites the text, eliminating the serious for the amusing, lifting the films out of whatever reality they had to enjoy the willful destruction of any such reality—just as his characters smile and yell out "Awesome!" (*Tende sugoi ya!*) upon seeing devastation. Chaos and disorder are the realms of pleasure, so just as Sugiura's manga rarely follow a linear narrative, often stopping the story for moments of ecstatic ruination, this reading envisions a *Gojira* in which only the scenes of battle and destruction matter, regardless of the narrative. If this sounds a lot like the late 1960s and early 1970s Godzilla films, then perhaps we can imagine some parallels, if not influences, between this mode of spectatorship and the texts themselves.

I would argue that this same form of pleasurable viewing was also used on pro-wrestling. Clearly Sugiura feels a strong attraction for pro-wrestling as *yukai*, not only turning Godzilla into a pro-wrestler, but also citing Rikidōzan in other works (figure 5.11) and even creating a character called Puroresunosuke. The narrative of pro-wrestling in Japan as elsewhere is essentially that of *abare*, as the order enforced by the referee breaks down, and the fight spills outside the ring. *Abare* was an essential element in Rikidōzan's films, as one can see in a later

Figure 5.11 Rikidōzan fighting for the ninja: Sugiura Shigeru's "Doron Chibimaru" (1955–1957). *Gyagu manga kessakusen* (Tokyo: Bungei Shunjū, 1988). © Sugiura Tsutomu.

work entitled *Okore! Rikidōzan* (Get Mad Rikidōzan!), directed by Ozawa Shigehiro and released by Tōei on October 31, 1956, especially in the scene where Rikidōzan thrashes out in a nightclub at some gangsters working for a corrupt politician. Some would argue that this fight is more serious than Sugiura, if not more realistic; Rikidōzan in almost frightening fashion does seem to go wild here, throwing furniture and people as he curses in English. As some, including the novelist and *puroresu* fan Muramatsu Tomomi, argued, pro-wrestling was a serious business and had to be watched "with dead seriousness."[10] This was in part because of the ideological function pro-wrestling was asked to play in the 1950s. The narrative that Rikidōzan offered Japanese audiences was of a Japanese wrestler pummeled by larger American wrestlers, honorably enduring fouls and illegal moves until he finally became furious and defeated his opponent with a barrage of his patented karate chops. As Yoshikuni Igarashi argues, this narrative replicated wartime propaganda stories in a postwar context, offering a suffering body that could expose the operations of the other (America) and memories of the war, as well as exorcise them through a spectacle of violence. For such an ideological narrative to be effective, it had to be taken seriously, a stance that necessarily implies believing in the authenticity of the bouts, of the violence, and of Rikidōzan's Japaneseness[11]—this despite the fact that the matches were mostly rigged and Rikidōzan was actually Korean. What becomes crucial in these accounts of seriousness and belief are the media operations of believability that try to lead spectators away from discovering the falsity of the entire endeavor: a variety of textual and extra-textual devices, ranging from sponsorship by newspaper companies to the blood on Rikidōzan's body, that promised authenticity.[12] By some accounts, the majority of Japanese did in fact believe Rikidōzan's matches were for real.

I don't want to entirely question that assertion or the reality of the media strategies to control audience reception. But I do want to note some problems. First, by seemingly conceiving of spectators as having only a binary choice between believing and not believing, this conception of pro-wrestling's seriousness could end up ignoring alternative forms of reception. Second, focusing so much on the processes of deception could imply, in Frankfurt School fashion, that the reception of popular cultural texts is largely a matter of being fooled. Unfortunately, the fact that Rikidōzan himself targeted children as a significant audience—one continually represented in his films—only seemed to lend evidence to the sense that all those who believed in Rikidōzan's narrative were similarly childlike regardless of their actual age. But in making this argument, those who stress media efforts to make audiences believe fail to focus sufficiently on how these efforts sought to control or eliminate other forms of spectator involvement as well.

Lee Thompson describes one view of pro-wrestling as rigged (*yaocho*) and as a media scholar analyzes the media devices through which such fakery could be concealed.[13] Following Erving Goffman's frame analysis, he offers one model of wrestling as a transformation of the primary framework of fighting, applying publicly accepted rules to what originally is without rules. Pro-wrestling, he argues, then could involve a further shift, adding an adjustment that only a few know about: the fixing. The model Thompson describes represents pro-wrestling defined as an either/or system of belief, but both the sociologist Kobayashi Masayuki and the philosopher Irifuji Motoyoshi say that it is fundamentally flawed, and not because either man argues that pro-wrestling is not fixed.[14] Rather, they both point out that what this describes is rigging in, say, Olympic wrestling, not pro-wrestling, because with the former one can easily conceive of the bout without the fakery. What, however, is pro-wrestling without the fixing? It is certainly not regular wrestling because that rarely involves bloodshed or fighting outside the ring. Moreover, as Irifuji notes, pro-wrestling includes many moves such as the back breaker, piledriver, or the backdrop that simply could not be done without the cooperation of the wrestler receiving that move—without such cooperation, we'd really have some necks and backs broken. Perhaps some spectators cannot understand such facts of physiology, but to argue that is again to contend that pro-wrestling fans, as believers, relate to the sport through ignorance or self-deception. To scholars like Kobayashi and Irifuji, reception of pro-wrestling is based on the full knowledge of such cooperation.

As Irifuji argues, Thompson's model is essentially realist. Irifuji is citing philosophical realism, but we can bring this into the realm of aesthetics. To analyze pro-wrestling through a true-false binary both valorizes the true and assumes that spectators would opt for the real if they had the choice. Even if we admit that Rikidōzan's pro-wrestling is a fictional performance, it is still presumed that it must use its resources to present a convincing illusion of the real. Thus, in the fiction film *Okore! Rikidōzan*, the fight in the nightclub is represented as realistic through such devices as long shots and the sounds of objects being broken. Placing pro-wrestling in a film, however—a performance within a performance, a text within a text—threatens to render ambiguous what the real is that spectators should opt for. The danger is that by presenting this fight, which any spectator would know is part of a fictional narrative, as realistic, an ontological quandary is created when one tries to distinguish this battle first from the match in the ring that concludes the film, and second, from the bouts that millions of Japanese saw on television. Without any visible difference between the match in the film and the match in reality, or between the fight outside the ring in the film (to which pro-wrestling often moves as part of its realist aesthetic), and the bout outside the ring (frame) of the film, all three become equally real—and equally fictional.

Tetsuwan kyojin, in part by denying a realist aesthetic, emphasizes other, nonserious enjoyments divorced from belief in the real. Obviously, Rikidōzan's body in the movie is too excessive to be real, but its constructedness is not merely a matter of fact laid out for the audience to passively see. Rather, the film encourages spectator participation in its construction. Consider a brief series of shots where Rikidōzan and Tarō jump on to a train in which the villains are traveling to Tokyo: first there is an extreme long shot (actually a process shot) showing the two running up to the edge of a cliff overlooking the train seen below; then there is a cut to a long shot low angle of the two beginning to jump; the third shot is of them landing on the roof of the train. This is a classic montage effect: their leap is not shown in a single shot; rather, the cut from the second to the third shot prompts the spectator to make the spatial and narrative connection. This might be a case that turns Andre Bazin's famous discussion of the limitations of montage on its head. Bazin asserts that Charlie Chaplin in *The Circus* is funny because we see him caught in a lion's cage in one shot. Cutting between him and the lion would, through the power of montage to create associations, be sufficient to convey the narrative situation, but it would have no impact because no one would believe the two were in the same cage.[15] Such a reality of space, however, would not work in *Tetsuwan kyojin* because it would contradict the physical incredibility found elsewhere. If Bazin faulted a montage option where the spatial relation between the lion and Charlie would only be mentally constructed, and not visibly evident in one shot, we can say that *Tetsuwan kyojin* opts for the fictional imagining of space because it did not mind acknowledging its fakery. Narratively, this might be justified by the fact that this action is the product of the imagination of a child, but that in some ways is the point. Irifuji argues that in its essence, pro-wrestling is less a transformation of a real fight than a performance that allows the complex imagination of the ultimate—and thus impossible in reality—free-for-all. Based on the firm awareness that it is not a real fight, such imagination—not the actuality of the wrestler's pain—is at the core of pro-wrestling, and this implies that pro-wrestling is fundamentally a product of the spectator's processes of reading and imagination. The narrative frame of *Tetsuwan kyojin* only underlines that.

Gojira-Minira-Gabara: Ōru kaijū daishingeki shows that the Godzilla films of the 1960s and 1970s largely pursued the same spectatorship. The shift toward *kaijū puroresu* is also an aesthetic turn away from realism in conjunction with that spectatorship. This is reflected in not only the move from black and white to color and low- to high-key lighting, but also in a shift in camera angles. The early—and especially the recent—Godzilla movies utilize lower angle shots of the monster in an effort to place spectators in the diegesis, as if they might also be under threat. Those low angles are less evident in the middle-era films as the battles become less of an incident imposing itself on one, than a show to be watched. To borrow Andre Gaudreault's term used for early cinema, this is quite literally a case of monstration, of showing, not narrating, and spectators are encouraged to play with their imaginative reading of the scene.

These issues of style and viewership are not just confined to cinema. Sugiura's manga also offered an aesthetic that was less concerned with realism, one that pursued a different notion of time and space and of textuality itself. As Yomota Inuhiko stresses, Sugiura Shigeru picked up what postwar manga, led by Tezuka Osamu, largely abandoned.[16] In another name to add to our network, Tezuka, three years before *Gojira*, himself told a story of a monster island that, affected by fallout from nuclear tests, produced its own mutated creatures that threatened the human race. *Kitarubeki sekai*, or *Nextworld* as it is known in English, is more like the first *Gojira* in offering a serious story, one of the most narratively complex manga Tezuka ever produced.[17] It was one of the best of his efforts to legitimize the manga medium in the face of continued claims by educators and parents that it corrupted young children. This quest to give manga authority, it should be noted, was coupled with a dual-pronged strategy of consolidating narrative realism in the medium. The form of Tezuka's characters was not necessarily realistic, but in a work like *Tsumi to batsu* (*Crime and Punishment*, 1953), he famously tried, in these elongated panels depicting the murder of the pawnbroker amidst several contiguous spaces (figure 5.12), to create an integrity of space that not only lent realism to the action, but also contributed to Tezuka's fundamental project: the subordination of manga devices to narrative. Crucial to this was centering narrative in character and thus psychology: much within the frame, from the human body to the inanimate background, worked to evoke the complex emotions of the characters. As a basic principle, then, every line was narratively motivated.

This was an aesthetics that Sugiura resolutely resisted. If Tezuka aimed for a depth of space, Sugiura frequently compressed and flattened it, overlapping his characters as if they were just sheets of paper. If Tezuka aimed for the narrativization of a realistic space, Sugiura warped and played with it, inserting unmotivated movements or poses and sometimes even teasing with panel borders by having characters exceed the frame only to go behind that of another panel (figure 5.13). Exposed as a mere flat drawing, space was rendered a realm that could sometimes bear little rhyme or reason. This overt textuality proliferated beyond the frame of Sugiura's manga as he copiously kept scrapbooks, using them to continuously quote, alter, and adapt many popular cultural images and icons. It was his surrealism that helped prompt a revival in interest in Sugiura in the 1970s and 1980s among the alternative manga press. In certain ways, his "childish" manga had significant links with the avant-garde.[18]

*   *   *

If these texts and their viewers are so playful, what then happens to textual narrations of the nation, such as those offered by Rikidōzan? What is clear is

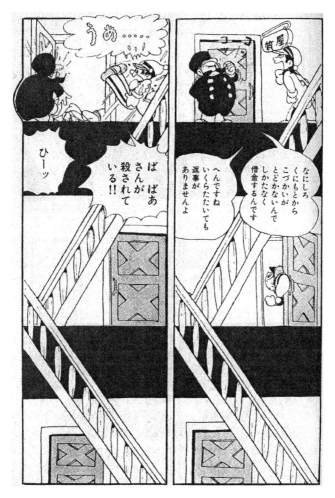

Figure 5.12 Tezuka's spatiallyl integral, narratively motivated manga. Tezuka Osamu, *Tsumi to batsu* (Tokyo: Kadokawa Shoten, 1955). © Tezuka Productions.

that these monstrous stories do complicate any self-evident national division of self and other. As Thompson and others have argued, media discourse on Rikidōzan usually distinguished between his humanity, founded in a strong sense of right and justice, and the monstrous, animal-like foreign wrestlers. As we have seen, however, Rikidōzan in *Tetsuwan kyojin* was also Godzilla, an atomic beast invading Japan from the sea possessing distinct *animal* associations. Igarashi has already noted Rikidōzan's hybrid status, defending Japan, but through American-style wrestling that rejected traditional Japanese martial arts. Rikidōzan as Godzilla had a strong American facet to his persona—recall how he cursed in English as he beat up the gang in *Okore! Rikidōzan*. Igarashi interestingly argues that such hybridity could actually work to suture conflicting terms in postwar memory, allowing for

Figure 5.13 Feet in and out and behind the frame: Sugiura Shigeru's "Sarutobi Sasuke" (1954–1955). *Natsukashi no hīrō manga daizenshū* (Tokyo: Bungei Shunjū, 1987), © Sugiura Tsutomu.

consolidation of the nation. This aligns with the work of Kang Sang-Jung, Jennifer Robertson, and others, who argue that the modern Japanese national body (*kokutai*) is less exclusionary than exhibiting a flexibility of borders that can efficiently absorb others, precisely because the boundaries between self and other are so vague.[19]

It is my argument that this sutured national body could often be knowingly fictional. As Michael Raine has argued, the late 1950s exhibited a fascination with the body as a new basis for emerging forms of cultural identity.[20] We can cite sumō and pro-wrestling as two major factors in this focus on the body, and certainly pleasure in viewing powerful flesh—even if it was just a rubber suit—helps explain the popularity of Godzilla. But one of the main bodies Raine discusses is that of Ishihara Yujirō, brother of Shintarō and arguably the most important male star in the postwar. With long legs—and Japanese often lamented their short legs at the time—his body represented a hope for a new subjectivity founded in physicality. Such a body found a home generically in Nikkatsu Action, which in the years around 1960 offered the imagination of a free, roaming body, an individual agent beholden to no one. The space it roamed, however, was *mukokuseki*, nationless, as it seemed that this new free body could only exist as long as this was not Japan or, more precisely, was a fictional Japan.[21] It is significant that subsequent to this, the two major icons of the nation in Japanese film of the 1960s and 1970s were Tōei's chivalric yakuza and Shōchiku's Tora-san, both outsiders, and both impossible anachronisms.

Especially with our reservations against realism, we can argue that the nationality of Rikidōzan—or of Godzilla, for that matter—was consumed in part because it was fictional. Following Kinoshita Naoyuki's argument that postwar Japan saw a revival in a culture that could enjoy the fake as the fake, after a period in which modern Japanese culture after the Sino-Japanese war no longer allowed such pleasures, Kawamura Taku argues both that the enjoyment of Rikidōzan was based on a cognizance of his constructed performance, and that his status as epitomizing ideal Japaneseness was thus only possible through the fictionality of his nationality.[22] Intense audience interest in Rikidōzan's narrative was fully evident by all accounts, but even if in some cases this involved serious expressions of belief, it was equally likely that this was pleasurable involvement in what was a good story brought to physical presence. If we are to think about the reception of narrations of the nation, we must consider aesthetic models of their narration—realist or not—and how much the suspension of disbelief allows the vicarious experience of the nation without necessarily believing or being interpellated by it.

Perhaps Sugiura can offer us an extreme test case of a virtually carnivalesque disregard for the seriousness of nationality, overturning the national body with elastic ninja monsters that gleefully ignore the boundaries between bodies, if not self and other. I would argue that this active, playful, and self-consciously imaginative spectatorship/aesthetic has a long lineage in Japanese cinema, from Onoe Matsunosuke's 1910s period films to Itō Daisuke's wild camera movements in the late silent period, from Hayafusa Hideto's action films for Daito in the 1930s through to Tōei 1950s *jidaigaki* like the three-part *Shin shokoku monogatari: Fuefuki dōji* (New Tales of the Realm: The Boy with the Flute, dir. Hagiwara Ryō, 1954). Most have, in one form or another, suffered the appellation "childish" or "juvenile" by the arbiters of taste. Given that it was Tōei that ruled the box office during the 1950s, the so-called golden age of Japanese cinema, one can claim that this mode of cinematic experience presented a significant, historical force alongside the critically approved humanist realism of a Kurosawa or a Mizoguchi, but one subject to more discursive restrictions. It is precisely the chaotic nature of this reception that earned the ire of more Fordist conceptions of cinema and spectatorship that especially used the realist model to confine reception to the dutiful understanding of the national truth. Realism has been the dominant discourse on film since the 1910s in both criticism and scholarship, and we should not forget that it has been the main reason Rikidōzan and Godzilla—especially the middle-era Godzilla films—have been second-rung cinematic citizens.

Perhaps because of this, the free body often gets contained. Sugiura's rampaging monsters are finally tamed and confined to a zoo-like structure at the end of "Ōabare Tokyo." And Tarō in *Tetsuwan kyojin* has a special ray-like device for eradicating radioactivity, given by the scientist, which he uses on the caveman. The threat of Rikidōzan the Godzilla—if not Rikidōzan the Korean—is removed and the loin-clothed man at the beginning is gradually transformed into a civilized Japanese, shaved, wearing a suit, and able to understand language. This is one of the charges brought against the late 1960s Godzilla: that it was being assimilated into the national fold by becoming banal. We should note, however, that unlike the Godzilla films, Rikidōzan here, in a sense, is becoming more realistic. It can more often be realism than fantasy that serves to contain anarchic modes of alternative spectatorship, as much as it can promise social significance. We, as scholars, must be careful of where our spectatorship places us in the continuing struggle over control of the meaning of the text. We should be wary of which rays our methodological devices project, less we turn our *kaijū* into manageable objects and miss out on the deliriously unstable pleasure of wandering through the variety of intertexts and wrestling with monsters.

Notes

This essay was first presented at "Global Fantasies: Godzilla in World Culture," held at Columbia University in December 2004. I would like to thank the organizers and the other participants for their support and suggestions.

1. Stuart Galbraith IV, *Monsters Are Attacking Tokyo!* (Venice, CA: Feral House, 1998), p. 32.
2. Satō Kenji, *Gojira to Yamato to bokura no minshū shugi* (Tokyo: Bungei Shunjū, 1992), p. 8.
3. William M. Tsutsui, *Godzilla on My Mind* (New York: Palgrave Macmillan, 2004), p. 21.
4. Yoshikuni Igarashi, *Bodies of Memory* (Princeton, NJ: Princeton University Press, 2000), p. 121.
5. Sugiura is one of Japan's unique manga artists. Trained as a painter but eventually finding work under Tagawa Suihō (*Norakuro*) in the 1930s, his humorously playful work into the 1950s, including the hit *Sarutobi Sasuke*, seemed to be "for children," as opposed to either the more serious themes of Tezuka Osamu or the adult violence and sex of *gekiga*.
6. For more on how this movement built up steam, see James Orr, *The Victim as Hero: Ideologies of Peace and National Identity in Postwar Japan* (Honolulu: University of Hawai'i Press, 2001).
7. See, for instance, Gonda Yasunosuke, *Minshū goraku mondai*, in *Gonda Yasunosuke chosakushu*, vol. 1 (Tokyo: Bunwa Shobō, 1974).
8. Robert Sklar has found similar discourses in the United States. See his *Movie-Made America* (New York: Basic Books, 1975), pp. 122–140.
9. Richard deCordova, "Ethnography and Exhibition: The Child Audience, the Hays Office and Saturday Matinees," *Camera Obscura* 23 (May 1990), p. 94.
10. Muramatsu Tomomi, *Watakushi puroresu no mikata desu* (Tokyo: Chikuma Shobō, 1994), quoted in Igarashi, *Bodies of Memory*, p. 122.
11. This is Lee Thompson's argument in "Rikidōzan to 'Nihonjin' no teiji," in *Rikidōzan to Nihonjin*, ed. Okamura Masashi (Tokyo: Seikyūsha, 2002), pp. 69–98.
12. See Lee Thompson, "Puroresu no furemu bunseki," in *Nihon puroresu-gaku sengen*, ed. Okamura Masashi (Tokyo: Gendai Shokan, 1991), pp. 27–60; and Igarashi, *Bodies of Memory*, pp. 128–129.
13. Thompson, "Puroresu no furemu bunseki."
14. See Irifuji Motoyoshi, " 'Hontō no honmono' no mondai toshite no puroresu," and Kobayashi Masayuki, "Puroresu shakaigaku e no shōtai," both printed in *Puroresu*, a special issue of *Gendai Shisō* 30:3 (February 2002).

15. Andre Bazin, "The Virtues and Limitations of Montage," in *What is Cinema?*, vol. 1 (Berkeley: University of California Press, 1967), pp. 41–52.

16. Yomota Inuhiko, "Kodomotachi no Rabure," in *Sugiura Shigeru, nanjara hoi no sekai ten*, ed. Tomita Tomoko (Mitaka: Mitaka-shi Bijutsu Gyarari, 2002), pp. 9–19.

17. For an analysis of this and other Tezuka manga, see Natsume Fusanosuke, *Tezuka Osamu no bōken* (Tokyo: Shogakukan, 1998).

18. One should note that Sakaki Maki, one of the most artistically radical manga artists of the 1960s, completely dissecting manga into its constituent elements of line and panels, eventually began illustrating children's books in a style that consciously cites Sugiura.

19. See Jennifer Robertson, *Takarazuka* (Berkeley: University of California Press, 1998), and Kang Sang-Jung, *Nashonarizumu* (Tokyo: Iwanami Shoten, 2001).

20. Michael Raine, "Ishihara Yujirō: Youth, Celebrity, and the Male Body in late-1950s Japan," in *Word and Image in Japanese Cinema*, ed. Dennis Washburn and Carole Cavanaugh (Cambridge, UK: Cambridge University Press, 2001), pp. 202–225.

21. For more on Nikkatsu Action, see Watanabe Takenobu, *Nikkatsu akushon no karei na sekai* (Tokyo: Miraisha, 1981–1982).

22. Kawamura Taku, "Enjirareta 'Rikidōzan,' enjirareta 'Nihonjin,' " in *Rikidōzan to Nihonjin*, ed. Okamura Masashi (Tokyo: Seikyūsha, 2002), pp. 37–68. Kawamura refers to Kinoshita Naoyuki's *Yo no tochū kara kakusarete iru koto* (Tokyo: Shōbunsha, 2002).

6

MOTHRA'S GIGANTIC EGG:
CONSUMING THE
SOUTH PACIFIC IN 1960S JAPAN

Yoshikuni Igarashi

WHY DO MONSTERS ALWAYS COME
FROM THE SOUTH?

In an essay originally published in 1992, the cultural critic Nagayama Yasuo raised an intriguing question: why do monsters always come from the South—specifically the South Pacific—in Tōhō monster films?[1] Godzilla's original habitat is in the South Pacific. Mothra—a giant silkworm moth—inhabits the imaginary Infant Island, which is in close proximity to the Polynesian Islands. The equally imaginary Faro Island in the South Pacific is supposed to be the home of King Kong in *King Kong vs. Godzilla* (1962). Monster Island, where monsters congregate, exists somewhere in the South Pacific in *Godzilla's Revenge* (1969). Although Nagayama offers many suggestive answers—such as that the monster comes back to reenact Japan's prewar colonial fantasies—ultimately his argument is less historical than allegorical. His overall argument fails to take into account the evolving cultural roles of the monster—its evolution from foe to friend. Godzilla's blind fury in the 1950s represents a threat to Japan's postwar prosperity, whereas Mothra's egg in the 1960s becomes an emblem of Japan's consumerism. Tōhō monsters are transformed from fearful, destructive entities to lovable creatures amidst the rise of consumer society in Japan.

Nagayama's question might be posed again, but more historically: why do monsters come from the South in the 1960s? If the image of the monster is historically unstable, so too is the trope of the South. Though the South plays the role of innocent past, impervious to social change, in Japan's historical discourse, the particular form this past takes in the 1960s is revealing. The South may take up its typical role in the 1960s—the "other" within the self, the innocent past that Japan can appropriate—yet its role is specific to its cultural moment. In the 1960s, as Japan was experiencing extreme economic and social changes as a result of the postwar boom, the South became a mirror of Japan's desire to escape the effect of its economic success—consumerism. Greed was just another name for conspicuous consumption in popular discourse, while the South retained a child-like innocence that served as an antidote to consumerism. Ironically, the South's countercommercial image was available in the form of consumable objects. Shrouded in exotic and yet nostalgic ambience, commodities from the South began to appear in the Japanese market. Surrounding themselves with these objects, consumers were able to imagine themselves as free from and outside of the nation's specific historical condition. The monster, the South's representative, becomes the largest and most visible (in Mothra's case) of these consumable objects.

In this essay I will examine two films, *Mothra* (1961) and *Godzilla vs. Mothra* (1964), in order to investigate how the South returns to Japanese society in the 1960s. In the first film, Mothra embodies the struggle of Japanese society to manage its own historical moment by escaping to a nostalgic past in an easily packaged and consumable form. In the second film, *Godzilla vs. Mothra*, the same monster becomes an image of Japan, fully incorporated into its consumer society. The transformation of the monster within the few years that separates the two films demonstrates how quickly this drastic social change was accommodated by the cultural expressions of postwar Japan.

Yanagita Kunio and the South

The postwar inquiry into the imaginary construction of the South in Japan's popular culture should start at the point where the native ethnologist Yanagita Kunio ended his scholarly discourse. In 1961, right before his death, Yanagita published his last book, *Kaijō no michi* (Passage on the Sea). Although the essays included in the volume were originally published in the first half of the 1950s, they reached a far larger audience in book form. In these essays, Yanagita attempts to problematize the boundaries of Japan by discussing the shared history of the southern islands and the Japanese mainland. By focusing on the objects that arrived from the South, Yanagita hypothesizes a more general movement of cultures and people from the South. This movement, he intimates, exceeded national boundaries. Perhaps the most memorable passage in the book is one about coconuts that arrived on Japan's shores, carried by sea currents.[2] Much in accordance with his past practices of native ethnology, the objects begin a chain of association that intertwines seemingly disparate cultural symbols in his discussion. Through these associations, Yanagita speculates on the southern origins of the Japanese, postulating the islands as the reservoir of Japan's original cultural forms. The South, in Yanagita's model, lies not outside of Japan but at its heart. The location of Yanagita's discovery had particular significance as well. He found the coconuts at the tip of the Atsumi Peninsula across a narrow straight from Ise, the site where Japan's Shintō traditions had been anchored for centuries. His casual mention of the Ise Shrine is, after all, not so casual.[3] At the heart of Japan's national identity, Yanagita found the coconuts—things that came from the southern islands. Yanagita's interest in the region, an interest that originated in the 1920s, thus resulted in destabilizing Japan's national boundaries.

However, as Yanagita's commentators have argued, his turn to the South as subject in his writings on Okinawa in the 1920s must be examined against the backdrop of Japan's colonial history. Murai Osamu, for example, insists that Yanagita's interest in these regions was far from innocuous. It was motivated by a desire to conceal his own involvement as a bureaucrat in Japan's colonial enterprise in Korea. Cultural readings of the shared history of Okinawa and Japan's mainland were an ideological tool with which to divert attention from the reality of Japan's colonial violence.[4] While not sharing Murai's strongly accusatory tone, Akasaka Norio also notes Yanagita's "reorientation" from the North to the South in his initial writings about Okinawa.[5] His earlier desire to trace the otherness of the Ainu in the northern mountains receded into the background as he increasingly sought to discover the shared origins of the mainland and Okinawa in the 1920s.

However, his postwar articulation in *Kaijō no michi* suggests that there was more at work than a simple diversion of attention from Japan's colonial activities in Yanagita's discussions of Okinawa. He was constructing an imaginary form of Okinawa in order to transcend the tension within his scholarship between his keen awareness of the drastic changes in modern Japanese society and his nostalgic desire to recover a pristine past. The South was for him a way to reconcile this conflict between the reality of historical changes and the unchanging past by locating an idealized past outside of the historical development that mainland Japan had experienced. Yanagita appropriates the cultural difference of the South and offers it for the Japanese audience. The effect of this theoretical move is colonial in that it posits Okinawa as a site that has been always already part of Japan. Yanagita's sustained interest in Okinawa resonates with the prewar Japanese colonial imagination that sought to establish the imaginary connection between Japan and the South.

The way Yanagita appropriated the South to overcome the tension within his scholarship also served as a rehearsal for postwar Japan's rediscovery of the South. In the 1960s, images of the South gained wider circulation in Japan's newly arising consumer society largely to lessen the cultural anxiety stemming from drastic social and economic changes. In the midst of such a thorough transformation, the image of South as an allegorical site outside of Japan circulated to preserve Japan's historical continuity. Although written in the 1950s, the essays in *Kaijō no michi* anticipated the changes that would occur in the status of the South in 1960s Japanese cultural discourse. It should come as no surprise that, after the publication of an extensive collection of his work, Yanagita's native ethnology became a highly sought-after intellectual commodity in 1960s Japan, where change was a social norm.

The ideological ties that Yanagita postulated between Japan and the South through coconuts are a key motif in the 1964 film *Godzilla vs. Mothra*, in which another coconut-shaped, gigantic object mediates the two regions in a similarly problematic way. Mothra's egg is washed out of the ground of a South Pacific island by a typhoon, carried by sea currents, and eventually arrives on Japan's shore. It follows the imaginary passage that seems to connect the South Pacific and Japan and that brings numerous other monsters to Japan. Borrowing from Yanagita, I call this sea passage the "kaijū no michi" (passage of monsters). While Yanagita's "kaijō no michi" conceptually posits the shared history of Japan's mainland and Okinawa, the "kaijū no michi" in the 1960s Tōhō monster films establishes the imaginary connection between Japan and the South Pacific. The narratives of the films work toward the restoration of the primordial indivisibility of the two regions. The 1960s Tōhō monster films discover and appropriate the exotic image of South Pacific islands as a source of a counteridentity to a contemporary society completely corrupted by commercialism. Mothra's egg thus fulfills a function similar to that of Yanagita's coconuts in bringing back nostalgic images in order to counter the historical effect of rapid economic development.

Of course, Mothra's egg and the other Tōhō monsters were not alone in following this imaginary passage. During the 1960s, a steady stream of commodities from the South reached Japanese markets. With its defeat in the Asia Pacific War, Japan's colonial ambition and fantasies were gone. The South Pacific (Nanyō) that had once spurred imperial Japan's colonial imagination swiftly receded from popular consciousness. However, as Japan began to reestablish its economic ties with the region, the South returned to the Japanese imagination in the late 1950s and early 1960s. Although the movement of people was still limited (the restrictions on oversea travel were not completely lifted until April 1964), objects carried back to Japan images of the South along with fragments of Japan's colonial past. Ironically the uncanny, countercommercial images of the South returned as commodities.

The consumption of bananas, for instance, quadrupled within two years of the 1963 lifting of the import restriction on bananas.[6] Except for the dried ones that were available during the war and the immediate postwar years, bananas, which could be easily damaged, had remained exotic fruits until the early 1960s. Pineapples also became more affordable in Japan in the 1960s. However, they were still by and large out of reach and thus exotic for many Japanese consumers in the mid-1960s.[7] The mango (whose shape also resembles Mothra's egg) from Panama also first appeared in the Japanese market in 1961.

Just as tropical fruits were becoming affordable, exotic images of Hawai'i— as an icon of the South Pacific—were also widely consumed in Japan. In 1961, Suntory launched a sales campaign for its product Torys Whisky offering as a prize a trip to Hawai'i. The copy phrase, credited to the writer Yamaguchi Hitomi—"Drink Torys and go to Hawai'i" (*Torisu o nonde Hawaii e ikō*)— took hold in the popular imagination and greatly helped boost Torys' sales. Elvis Presley's film *Blue Hawaii* was a box office hit in 1962. Japanese fabric companies took advantage of the film's popularity by introducing lines of apparel that they named the "Blue Hawaii Look." The Hawai'i Tourist Bureau also launched a promotion campaign in the same year lest it miss this great opportunity.[8] In 1963, Tōhō Studios produced the fourth film in Kayama Yūzō's popular *Wakadaishō* series, key scenes of which take place in Hawai'i. Although it was still out of reach for the majority of Japanese, Hawai'i was fast becoming a desirable tourist destination redolent of the exoticism of the South Pacific: the commercialized South par excellence.

However, objects that originated in Japan better illustrated the transformation of the South's images in postwar consumer society. Takara Co. began merchandizing a vinyl inflatable doll named Dakko-Chan in April 1960 (figure 6.1). Although its initial sales were slow, the doll caught the attention of the market by the summer months, and Takara Co. could not produce enough dolls to meet market demand.[9] The figure of Dakko-Chan with its dark skin and thick lips reproduced the colonial images of the South that the cartoon *Bōken Dankichi* had helped to circulate in the 1930s.[10] In *Bōken Dankichi*, the images of the natives were wiped clean of their historical and geographical associations and rendered as the blank slate on which the Japanese protagonist, Dankichi, could inscribe Japan's colonial aspirations.[11] In the cartoon, Dankichi drifts ashore on a small island in the South where he tames and trains the dark-skinned cannibal natives as well as several exotic animals.[12] As the "white boy" on the island, Dankichi rules as a colonial master who introduces elements of modern (and Japanese) civilization to a population mired in ignorance. Under his tutelage, the islanders build such

Figure 6.1 Dakko-Chan. Used with permission of Mainichi Shinbunsha.

modern institutions as a school, a bank, a Shintō shrine, a palace, a post office, a hospital, railways, and even a military. The natives perform their innate Japanese-ness—they already speak Japanese—while at the same time their difference is constantly marked. That the author, Shimada Keizō, concocted the story completely out of his imagination, without specific knowledge of the South, merely confirms the fantastic nature of the South's image that gained circulation in the prewar period.[13] In the 1960s, the diminutive figure of Dakko-Chan infantilized the natives, reducing the formidable images of the South to a consumable size.[14] The cannibal natives who had populated Japan's colonial imagination were transformed into a safe, adorable doll in the 1960s.[15] The colonial uncanny ceased to be a menacing entity as postwar Japan began to consume/cannibalize the South.

In the two Mothra films, the natives on the island, who were played by Japanese actors with body paint, enact and package Japan's colonial fantasies for easy consumption. That the natives are imprisoned in the infantile stage of human development provides a critical perspective on contemporary international politics. It is no accident that the island from which Mothra emerges is named Infant Island. While living in primitive conditions, the natives are highly critical of the modern powers whose arms race and resultant nuclear testing have destroyed the bulk of their island. The early stage of human civilization found on the island serves as a counteridentity to contemporary society. The islanders are the noble savages who still maintain the humanity that the moderns have long lost. The South offers a way to critique the modern consumer society of postwar Japan. However, this marked difference between the South and Japan does not escape the eroticized gaze of the modern consumer. The South returned to 1960s Japan in forms increasingly reachable to the masses. The natives' nobility is undermined by their savagery, which is offered as an exotic pleasure. The half-naked natives perform their rituals ostensibly to fight against the greed of the moderns, yet their performance easily caters to the sexually charged gaze of modern viewers. Just as in the case of Yanagita's Okinawa, the "innocence" of the South Pacific was easily reified and circulated within the cultural as well as the commercial discourse of 1960s Japan.

MOTHRA AND THE FLOW OF FANTASIES

Even as these films fetishize the South in terms of commodity goods and commodified bodies, they consciously critique capitalist greed as the force that ultimately undermines the welfare of modern society. However, the commodified images that these films project on the screen necessarily end up undermining the films' professed goal of restoring the South's critical status. Already exoticized and consumed by the cinematic gaze, the natives and their habitat not only represent counter-perspective to modern society but also anticipate modern consumerism. Even while Mothra appears in the first film comfortably ensconced in nostalgic images of the South, the monster comes, by the time of the second film, to be identified with Japanese society.

Originally conceived during the height of the 1960 anti-U.S.-Japan-Security-Treaty movement, *Mothra* bears the distinctive marks of cold war international politics. Three renowned literary figures participated in the collective writing project of "Hakkō yōsei to Mosura" ("Glowing fairies and Mothra"), the original story of *Mothra*. The completed story was published in January 1961, and a movie version was released in July of the same year. The three writers—Nakamura Shin'ichirō, Fukunaga Takehiko, and Hotta Yoshie—are reticent about what exactly inspired them to produce the story at this particular juncture of postwar history. Yet the text carries clear marks of the frustration that Japanese intellectuals felt over Japan's subordinate position that the renewal of the U.S.-Japan Security Treaty consolidated. The story amply demonstrates that the three authors intended to give postwar Japan a critical distance from U.S. hegemony by reclaiming the South Pacific.

Although inspired by this anti-U.S. narrative in the original story, the film version of the story directed by Honda Ishirō already operates in the post-anti-Security-Treaty movement paradigm of the 1960s, where the focus on economic growth provided a diversion from Japan's real status as a U.S. client state. Japan's nationhood would be rehabilitated through its economic success, rather than by a forceful political maneuver. The colonial fantasies of the South that returned to postwar Japan were shadows of the political reality of prewar imperial Japan. However, the historical fact that Japan once controlled a large area of the South Pacific never registers in the film. Under the hypereconomic drive of the 1960s, the images of the South in the film are dissociated from actual history, while being quickly tamed and packaged for visual consumption.

The narrative begins with a report about Infant Island in the South Pacific, which the nation of Roshirika recently used as a nuclear testing site. (In the movie version, the name was altered to Rorishika.) Roshirika is a compound of the first two syllables of Roshia (Russia) and the last two syllables of Amerika (America). The U.S.-Russia political tension of the cold war is shifted to the binary structure of Japan and its menace, Roshirika. Although three-quarters of the island has been blown up, shipwrecked Japanese sailors are washed ashore and encounter the natives. To investigate the mystery of the islanders who inhabit the radioactive areas and possess a radiation-fighting concoction, which they have given to the sailors, an academic survey team, which consists of both Japanese and Roshirikans, is dispatched. The narrative clearly marks the island as a mythical site that transcends both the political tension and the resultant destruction of the nuclear testing. As Nagayama Yasuo suggests, Infant Island serves as a synecdoche for the ideal nation that the authors wished Japan to be—a nation that is capable of providing a critical perspective on contemporary international politics from the unique experience of surviving nuclear devastation.

The film also reveals the hegemonic role that the Unites States plays in relation to Japan and Infant Island. The fact-finding team makes a number of fantastic discoveries on the island, the most amazing of which are two women of miniature size (there are four women in the original story). Although the survey team leaves the island undisturbed, one of the members—the sleazy Roshirikan character Peter Nelson—returns there to capture the two women. Despite their supernatural ability to communicate telepathically, the minia- ture women (Shōbijin) are treated not as humans but as cherished objects both by Nelson and by their Japanese protectors. Although they are brought to Japan, the women's singing resonates with the natives' prayer and hatches Mothra's egg on Infant Island. They animate the Thing, yet they are treated as objects, kept like dolls in a carrying case. In the original story, to silence the plea by a Japanese survey team member to release the women, Peter Nelson insists, "[t]hey are not humans. They are things (*mono*), the samples that I collected on Infant Island. They are private property."[16] Nelson's greed—a thinly disguised caricature of American capitalism—easily transforms the supernatural into private property.

His prized possessions—the miniature women, who are copies of each other—show an uncanny resemblance to the objects that began to be mass produced in Japan in 1959 and were imported back to Japan from the United States in the 1960s: Barbie dolls. Although the Shōbijin were as tall as two feet in the original story, they were shrunk to the size of Barbie (30 cm) in the film. By the mid-1960s, the Japanese economy had reached a level where it was possible to merchandize three-dollar dolls, albeit still in a limited number, for prepubescent girls. Nelson claimed his ownership over the miniature women in the same way girls enjoyed their dolls as their very private property. In 1964, Barbie began to shroud herself in exoticism. She began to travel outside of the United States, and several of her destinations included Hawai'i and Japan.[17] The doll in exotic costumes was a prized object for young Japanese female consumers in the mid-1960s.[18] Barbie, like the two Mothra priestesses, embodied the desire for the exotic other that was rendered affordable by Japan's economic success.[19]

Furthermore, like the doll, with her sexually suggestive body, the two miniature-sized women reveal the economy of sexual fantasies among the United States, Japan, and the exotic South. Although their flesh is not as exposed as the natives', the juxtaposition between their singing and the natives' dance/prayer demonstrates the underlying sexual appeal of the two figures. The original story clearly foregrounds the problematic sexuality through Nelson's rather crass comments:

> "Are you claiming that those little creatures are human beings? If they are women of humankind, you should marry one of them."
> A perverse grin appeared on Nelson's face.
> "A Jap and a miniature woman!"[20]

As perverse as Nelson's comments are, they astutely point to the sexual desire that drives the economy of fantasies. The women's miniature size, like Barbie's, is merely a device to disguise the obvious tension between sexual fascination toward the other and its denial under child-like innocence.

Contrary to the original story, the film version is eager to downplay this sexual tension, while foregrounding greed as the mechanism that mercilessly commodifies the exotic. Although critical of U.S. nuclear testing in the South Pacific, the film's rather didactic criticism targets the more generalized subject of human greed. The Roshirikan character Peter Nelson who claims Mothra's priestesses as his "private property" securely places the blame outside Japan, intimating the unnamed party—U.S. capitalism—as the cause of all evils. Motivated by sheer greed for profit, Nelson forces the women to perform on stage in front of a theater full of people. However, his greed eventually brings his own demise. Through their singing, the women telepathically communicate with the Thing, which eventually appears in Tokyo. Although Nelson escapes Japan for Roshirika with the Shōbijin, Mothra, which has metamorphosed into a giant moth, follows their telepathic voices to a Roshirikan city. The story ends when the Roshirikan police kill Peter Nelson (the killer is unidentified in the original story) and the two women are safely reunited with Mothra. Nelson's excessive greed makes him a menace even to his native land. In his forceful escape from the pursuing monster, he fires at Roshirikan police officers, who in return shoot him down. The Monster that has traveled from the South to Japan, and eventually to Roshirika, returns to the South once the Roshirikans take care of their own problem. With the death of Nelson, capitalist greed is safely contained, while being completely evacuated from Japan. Now free of an external, corrupting power of excessive greed, Japan is once again allowed to dream about its uncorrupt primordial ties to the South Pacific. *Mothra* offers a counternarrative to the modus operandi of 1960s Japan—economic growth.

Though the film is eager to present a didactic, anticommercial message, the visual images that it projects on the screen belie its high moral stance. For example, the sequence that involves the two women's stage performance attempts to illuminate the contrast between the corrupt modern world—the United States as well as Japan—and the sacred world of the island. The camerawork, however, ironically reveals the complicit relations of the two worlds: the gaze of modern commercialism already penetrates the natives' identity. The sequence first reveals the two women's mysterious power, which will ultimately undermine Peter Nelson's evil intent to exploit them commercially. After Nelson's brief introduction, the women are brought to center stage in a gilded miniature carriage that descends on a wire from the opposite side of auditorium. Positioning himself in front of the orchestra box, Nelson appears as if he is standing on a boat. The women, who are dressed like fairies wearing crowns, land on a stage set that mimics a tropical island. Once Nelson opens the door of the golden carriage, the women emerge to sing a song. Although the women perform for Nelson's commercial kingdom, they secretly undermine his design through their singing.[21] Two Japanese characters, the journalist and the linguist, who earlier participated in the scientific expedition, come to realize the women's supernatural power during the performance. Right after sharing the information that Nelson secretly financed the entire expedition and hence it has been a capitalist enterprise from the start, they recognize that the women are actually communicating through their singing with Mothra on Infant Island. Close-up shots of their awestruck expressions announce the gravity of their discovery: the women's power to put the modern world in peril. The unearthing of the hidden scheme in the modern world, involving Nelson's financial dealing, leads to the revelation of the mysterious ties that the women possess with the island. The modern world, punctuated by the dark secret of capitalist greed, is contrasted with the mythical underground world of Infant Island, to which the women send a secret message. By digging beneath the capitalist gloss, the linguist and the journalist excavate the pure "natural" meaning of the song.

Despite the film's insistence on the qualitative difference between the two worlds, the sequence also offers visual cues that mark the dominance of the modern commercial gaze. From the close-up shots of the journalist and the linguist, the camera cuts to a full view of Infant Island. A graphic match between the stage scene and the island picture—the water line in the pictorial frame positions the island as if it is a stage set—assures a smooth transition between the stage and the island scenes (figure 6.2). The camera then cuts to the scenes of the cave where Mothra's egg is enshrined. The half-naked natives, their hair unkempt, consume a hideous looking liquid and produce the music to accompany two dancers who engage in a sexually suggestive dance. The natives are there to articulate what the Barbie-sized women merely insinuate—sexual attraction. It is also noteworthy that the camera positions are identical in both the extreme long shots of the stage and those of the cave. In the theater, the camera appears to be set on the top of the balcony section looking down on the stage, while it also assumes an identical high-angle position in relation to the performing natives in the cave (figures 6.3 and 6.4). Despite the change in venues, filmgoers assume the identical position in relation to the performers in each space: the viewers are visually transported to the scene on Infant Island to consume the natives' exotic song and dance. The gaze of the modern viewers is already an integral part of the space of their ritual performance. While undermining Nelson's commercial scheme by awakening Mothra, the performance of the miniature women and natives visually support the capitalistic flow of fantasies by

Figure 6.2   Infant Island, from *Mothra* (1961). Mothra © 1961 Toho Co., Ltd. All Rights Reserved.

Figure 6.3 Stage Scene, from *Mothra* (1961). Mothra © 1961 Toho Co., Ltd. All Rights Reserved.

Figure 6.4 Natives on Infant Island, from *Mothra* (1961). Mothra © 1961 Toho Co., Ltd. All Rights Reserved.

offering visual pleasure to contemporary viewers. As happens at numerous popular tourist sites, the natives in the film perform their exotic selves for modern voyeurs.

In contrast to the literary exercise of "Hakkō yōsei to Mosura," the film version of *Mothra*, as a product of a much larger commercial enterprise, resonated deeper with the commercial transformation that was taking place at the particular moment. While maintaining the anticommercialism of the original story, the film visually represented the "other" as in the form of easily consumable images. Prewar colonial fantasies about the South returned to postwar Japan in the new guise of anticapitalism. But, in the end, these fantasies—turned into commodity form in film—seamlessly flowed into the global movement of commodities and capital in the 1960s.

GODZILLA VS. MOTHRA, OR THE STORY OF A DIFFERENT KIND OF PAST

Mothra returns to Japan in the 1964 film *Godzilla vs. Mothra*. By 1964, Japan's own economic growth policies were securely in place, contributing to the construction of a formidable capitalist system. The success of the 1964

Tokyo Olympics was just one example of the miraculous economic growth of 1960s Japan under the auspices of the Liberal Democratic Party's economic policy. While the South still stands as a counter-entity to the capitalist modern society in *Godzilla vs. Mothra*, there is no longer a Roshirikan character that absolves Japan of capitalist guilt. Instead, Japanese characters here enact greed for the audience, intimating that it is deeply entrenched in Japanese society. The international tension that has led to the nuclear devastation of Infant Island is given secondary treatment. Furthermore, in the three years since the original film, Mothra appears to have grown less hostile to the capitalist world. Although maintaining a critical stance toward Japanese society, the monster never engages in destructive behavior, and, in effect, ends up defending Japan against the menace of Godzilla.

The opening scenes of *Godzilla vs. Mothra* first establish Mothra's affinity to Japan's consumer society. After being washed out of the ground by a typhoon, Mothra's giant egg drifts toward Japan. Once the egg reaches Shizugaura, a fictional location near Nagoya, a Japanese entrepreneur purchases the egg from the local fishermen's organization in order to promote it as a key attraction of his future theme park. (It should be emphasized that Yanagita found his coconuts at the tip of the Atsumi peninsula, in close proximity to the fictional Shizugaura.) The giant egg is given a monetary value of 1,224,560 yen based on the entrepreneur's dubious calculation: the giant egg is as big as 153,820 chicken eggs, and a chicken egg is worth 8 yen (actually the total should be 1,230,560 yen). In the wonderful world of capitalism, even a monster's egg can be purchased for a price.

Although the Mothra priestesses come to Japan to request that the egg be returned to Infant Island, their plea falls on the deaf ears of the entrepreneur and his financial backer. Once they find more sympathetic listeners, the women warn them that, though the Mothra that will hatch from the egg means no harm, as it roams around seeking food, it is bound to hurt innocent people. Meanwhile, Godzilla suddenly awakes from the nearby reclaimed land designated for industrial development. The monster destroys part of the Yokkaichi industrial area, an area known to be the heart of Japan's chemical industries, which were the key sector in Japan's economic growth in the 1960s. Then it single-mindedly heads toward Mothra's egg. In contrast to the carefully prepared story surrounding Mothra, the film offers almost no clues as to why Godzilla appears at this particular moment. Mothra's egg follows the *kaijū no michi* to reach the Japanese coast, while Godzilla is already in Japan waiting literally in the subterrain of industrial development for an opportunity to emerge.

In a desperate search for a way to contain Godzilla, three Japanese visit Infant Island to solicit Mothra's help. When the visitors arrive on the desolate island, they are captured and taken inside a cave by a group of natives. Although the Japanese characters are dressed in protective suits when they land, the scenes inside the cave show what they have worn underneath: spiffy attire. The two men wear a tie and a suit, while the female photographer appears in a fashionable dress and hat.[22] They came to the island dressed in the height of fashion as if they are visiting a trendy resort town. Their attire perhaps anticipates the island's future as a favorite destination for Japanese tourists, along with such islands as Guam, Saipan, and the Hawai'ian islands.

The natives refuse the Japanese visitors' request, citing the selfishness of the modern world that has led to the island's destruction. However, hearing the woman's plea for saving innocent lives, Mothra agrees to fight Godzilla. Mothra turns itself into a defender of Japan who fights against Godzilla's destructive forces. The rivalry between Mothra and Godzilla is motivated by different kinds of attitudes toward the past within 1960s Japan. Mothra—the modern day silk deity—returns to Japan as an embodiment of the idealized past, feeding on the nostalgic desire to recover what is already lost.[23] Infant Island serves as a metaphoric South where the innocent past is preserved for Japanese consumption. Similar to Yanagita's southern islands, Infant Island and its monster provide a symbolic anchor to a nation that has experienced radical historical changes. Mothra decides to fight the monster that threatens Japan's economic prosperity, the condition that has supported this symbolic value of the South.

For his part, Godzilla embodies a different kind of past, not the tamed, commercialized kind, but the past of preindustrial labor conditions that persisted despite the new regime of the high-growth economy. The dark, rough surface of the monster's body resonates with memories of the bodily hardship that was common in rural Japan until the mid-1960s. The 1963 photo by Minami Yoshikazu of a 21-year-old farmwoman's hands vividly testifies to the demands of an agrarian household of the 1960s (figure 6.5). Although the woman married into a farm family in Chichibu well endowed with gifts—things—she herself was turned into a thing in the farm household. One of the sections of Minami's photo essay about the lives of farm-women aptly carries the subtitle "Living Tools."[24] The woman to whom

Figure 6.5 Minami Yoshikazu, "The Hands of a 21-Year-Old Woman" (21-sai no yome no te), 1963. © Minami Yoshikazu.

these hands belonged engaged in sericulture in Chichibu while enjoying the lowest status in her husband's household and the local community. The cracked surface of her hands demonstrates the monstrous reality of 1963 Japan.

This reality survives under the new commercial regime of 1960s Japan. Underneath the glittering surface of consumer goods was cheap manual labor. The two photos by Hanabusa Shinzō from 1963 offer a glimpse into the labor conditions of Japan's electrical goods industry at the time (figures 6.6 and 6.7). As Simon Partner convincingly argues, the nimble hands of female workers, often employed under substandard labor conditions, were essential to Japan's economic growth in the 1950s and 1960s.[25] The visual affinity of the two hand images by Minami and Hanabusa attests to the bodily dimension of industrial production in 1960s Japan. Those hands that had raised silkworms now assembled transistors in a shack in the country. The monster that awakes in 1964 may best be read as one of the last expressions of what Japan's industrialization was eager to conceal: bodies qua things within its labor practices. If silkworms can be monstrous, then bodies

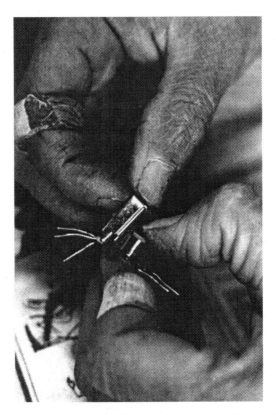

Figure 6.6 The hands qua transister assembling machine. Hanabusa Shinzō, "Rural Electronics Manufacturing, Ina City, Nagano Prefecture" (Nōson denshi kōgyō), 1964. © Hanabusa Shinzō.

Figure 6.7 The site of production. Hanabusa Shinzō, "Rural Electronics Manufacturing, Ina City, Nagano Prefecture" (Nōson denshi kōgyō), 1964. © Hanabusa Shinzō.

in pain—the hands that raise them—must surely be monsters. Rising from his sleep in a subterrain of industrialization, Godzilla is determined to strip Mothra's egg of its commercial glories and reduce it back to a mere thing—a silkworm egg.

Another historical reference made in the film suggests a slightly different meaning for the egg. Learning of the entrepreneur's plot to commercially exploit the giant egg, the photographer Yuri makes a comment: "So he is trying to turn it [the giant egg] into *'kin no tamago'* (a golden egg)." In the early 1960s, the phrase *kin no tamago* widely designated the young job seekers from the countryside who moved to cities right after graduating junior high school. The high-growth economy and the rapidly changing industrial structure created a demand for young, untrained workers in cities. While this condition provided a way out of hard agricultural work (women had gained career choices other than marrying into an agrarian patriarchy), the young recruits had to endure inferior working and living conditions—similar to those of prewar Japan—at family-owned shops and small-scale factories. Though employers may have cherished these young workers as money-bearing golden eggs, there was little golden about their lives in cities. Godzilla perhaps emerges to burst the hyped media image of the young workers.[26]

The fantastic and almost divine images that shroud Mothra sharply contrast with the commercialism and greed that postwar Japan had come to embrace. Yet Mothra's egg is snugly encased in the incubator at the theme park construction site. The nostalgic past that the object embodies is already deeply embedded in Japan's postwar capitalist economy. As an emissary from the dark, declining past, Godzilla challenges the more slick, commercialized images of the past. (This is the last time Godzilla acts as an evil force before his return in the 1984 version of *Godzilla*.) The king of the monsters manages to kill the opportunistic entrepreneur and his backer and destroy the facilities of the theme park, thereby destroying the exchange value of the egg. He even manages to kill the mature Mothra—a Mothra in imago form—that has flown from Infant Island to defend the Japanese people. But Godzilla is unable to crack the giant egg. The monster gets more than what he bargains for: two larvae that emerge from the egg tame Godzilla's fearful force by enwrapping him in their silk thread. In the end, Mothra's larvae transform Godzilla into a thing like themselves—a cocoon. The modern deities of the exotic South summarily defeat the king of the monsters. It turns out, despite the Mothra priestesses' warning, that Mothra's larvae destroy nothing in Japan, while silencing the desperate cry against industrial and commercial development.

Thanks to Mothra, postwar Japan reunites with its own problematic past, albeit in an already commercialized form. Although the monster originates on an island in the South Pacific, it plays a role in a purely domestic drama of 1960s Japan. Godzilla appears from Japan's underground to represent the abject past that haunted Japan's industrialized economy. The story that the giant monster tries to tell is by definition nonsensical: he merely roars. This is a battle that he has no chance of winning. In 1954, Godzilla performed another kind of abject past—that of war memories—and managed to touch the minds of millions. In 1964, Godzilla is relegated to being a sidekick to a giant moth, which happily shrouds itself in nostalgia. The king of the monsters appears in the film only to be ushered out in a humiliating way. In the world outside of the films, Godzilla emerges from his cocoon, so to speak, in the form of vinyl and tin toys to be circulated in 1960s Japan. In the end, what was most monstrous in 1960s Japan turned out to be the flow of capital and commodities that transcended Japan's national boundaries, a flow that easily tamed monsters into kids' toys and eventually into collectables or purveyors of nostalgia.

ALLEGORY OF A MONEY-EATING MONSTER

Godzilla's defeat did not conclude the taming of the monsters in the 1960s. A lovable monster that emerges from his cocoon in a 1966 episode of the acclaimed TV series, *Urutora Q* (Ultra Q) is literally enslaved by consumerism. Kaneda Kaneo, a boy who is obsessed with money, one day finds a fist-sized cocoon that makes the sounds of coins when shaken (since *kane* means money in Japanese, his name embodies his passion for money).[27] At

Kaneo's house, the cocoon grows to fill his room. After being sucked into it, Kaneo emerges from it the next morning as the money-eating monster, Kanegon. Despite his grotesque appearance, the human-sized monster does no harm to other humans. Yet, in order to sustain his life, Kanegon must keep eating money. The register on his chest keeps rolling up as he eats cash, but rolls down when he remains idle. Lest it become zero—he dies when he has no balance—he has to eat money all the time.

Kaneo's personality still remains intact inside Kanegon, who desperately wants to resume his human shape. Whereas the adults in the episode are fearful of consumerism's monstrous effect on humans (his parents warn against it before Kaneo turns into a monster) and shocked to see Kanegon, his young friends treat him nonchalantly just as they did before. They chip in what little they have as his food and try to make him a show attraction to raise money for him. Unlike the adults, the children adapt to the harsh reality of the money economy with no qualms. They are the natives of Japan's consumer society with their own antiheroic monster. Their hangout—habitat—is in a large open space that appears to have been cleared for a large construction project. It is a temporary sanctuary manifested in the midst of Japan's boom economy. The natives in this temporary space are also marked as liminal, transgressive beings—hence they have no fear of Kanegon. Yet their habitat is under a constant threat from the outside adult world. There they encounter their arch nemeses, the two construction workers that constantly harass the children with their monstrous bulldozer. Just as the natives on Infant Island were, the children are threatened by the menacing adult figures, the paragons of economic development.

As the South was consumed by Japanese capitalism's voracious appetite, the exotic exterior from which to critique contemporary Japanese society quietly disappeared from the screen. Such an exterior was eventually sought in outer space, from which many monsters in the *Urutora Q* series and the later Tōhō monster films come. In this particular episode, the children thriving in the interstices of industrializing Japan are substitutes for the "innocent" natives of the South. They are the natives deep within postwar Japanese capitalism, who nonetheless maintain a tie to tradition: for a solution, they consult a diviner who answers that Kaneo will return to his human shape when the leader figure (*higeoyaji*) of their arch nemeses handstands. A slapstick with the two construction workers ensues, and the children gain a minor victory by throwing the man upside down. The children are blessed with the power to reverse the effect of commercialism, and Kaneo returns to his old self. At home, however, he discovers that both his parents have turned into Kanegon despite their own warning. Their metamorphosis signals hypocrisy of the adults' disavowal of the commercial world.

Kanegon is no more than a caricature of postwar Japan's pursuit of prosperity. The monster appears as a human-like figure without any awesome power to reject what goes on in 1960s Japan. The *Urutora Q* episode casts the children and their culture as the last hope against the adult world that fully embraces consumerism. In the end, Kaneo's parents embody consumerist greed, while the children successfully bring Kaneo back to his old self. Yet, despite the fact that they may still be tricksters in consumer society, the world they live in is rapidly being colonized by the consumer economy. The children's friendship is already mediated with money: the price of helping bring Kaneo back to his human shape is bargained between Kaneo and his friend. Kaneo's friends have no qualms about displaying him in order to earn some cash for him. After all, they will grow up to assume monstrous form—do they not belong to the generation that will fully embrace the frenzied, ostentatious consumption of Japan's bubble economy during the late 1980s and early 1990s? In the end, the episode's optimistic message that the children are capable of outmaneuvering the adult economic order is no more sustainable than the image of the South as a counter-identity to 1960s Japan.

The optimistic message was there rather as a commercial scheme to attract young viewers. Monstrous images were offered on television not as serious social commentaries, as was the case in the Godzilla films of the 1950s, but as a magnet for the young audience. In their desperate contest with television, Tōhō Studios emulated this television strategy and began to offer more personable monsters on the screen in the mid-1960s. When the lingering images of the colonial other disappeared from the screen, the natives of a newly rising consumer society found their habitats within the fantasy worlds of television and movies. While monsters may have offered an imaginary path to step out of everyday life in 1960s Japan, they came with high price tags. Kanegon—the natives' antihero—is just more honest about its need for money.

NOTES

I would like to thank Teresa Goddu and Paul Young for their willingness not only to watch and discuss key scenes from *Mothra* with me but also to read and critique drafts of this essay. My gratitude also goes to Beth Harrington for her help in transforming my prose into a more reader-friendly style.

1. Nagayama Yasuo, *Kaijū wa naze Nihon o osou no ka* (Tokyo: Chikuma Shobō, 2002), pp. 7–8.
2. Yanagita Kunio, *Yanagita Kunio zenshū 21* (Tokyo: Chikuma Shobō, 1997), p. 393.
3. Ibid., pp. 392–393.
4. Murai Osamu, *Nantō ideorogi no hassei: Yanagita Kunio to shokuminchi shugi* (Tokyo: Ōtashuppan, 1995), p. 25.
5. Akasaka Norio, *Umino Seishinshi: Yanagita Kunio no hassei* (Tokyo: Shōgakkan, 2000), pp. 241–260.
6. Tsurumi Yoshiyuki, *Banana to Nihonjin* (Tokyo: Iwanami Shoten, 1982), pp. 5–7.
7. A college friend, who was born in Chiba Prefecture in 1961, once told me of his excitement about a pineapple that his father brought home when he was still a child. His family immediately proceeded to gather around the pineapple to take a family photo with it.
8. Shimokawa Kōshi, *Shōwa/Heisei kateishi nenpyō* (Tokyo: Kawade Shobō Shinsha, 1997), p. 315.

9. Although the original price was 180 yen, the dolls could command as much as 800 yen at the peak of the boom. Takara sold 800,000 dolls from July through September 1960 and eventually sold more than 5 million in the next two years, including sales in Southeast Asia, Europe, and the United States. Shimokawa, *Shōwa/Heisei kateishi nenpyo*; Ishikawa Hiroyoshi et al., *Taishū bunka jiten* (Tokyo: Kōbundō, 1994).

10. *Bōken Dankichi* was serialized in *Shōnen Kurabu* from the June 1933 issue through the July 1939 issue.

11. Yano Tōru identifies *Bōken Dankichi* as a pinnacle of the perspective that constructed images of the natives of the South Pacific islands through a series of negative images ("primitive," "inferior," "lazy," "moronic," "unhygienic," etc.). Yano calls this perspective the "*Bōken Dankichi* syndrome." Yano Tōru, *Nihon no nanyō shikan* (Tokyo: Chūō Kōron, 1979), p. 154.

12. Dankichi and his islanders even encounter dinosaurs on an island. Shimada Keizō, *Bōken Dankichi manga zenshū* (Tokyo: Kōdansha, 1967), pp. 261–265.

13. Ibid., pp. ii–iii.

14. In 1959, NHK (Nihon Hōsōkyōkai) aired a puppet show version of *Bōken Dankichi*. Although it is not clear how faithful the NHK version was to the original, the show was evidence of postwar Japan's rediscovery of the South. Ibid., p. 651.

15. The writer Takeyama Michio similarly created the figures of headhunters in writing about Burmese society from his imagination in the postwar. Using the structural correspondence between the "Burmese" headhunters in *Biruma no Tategoto* (Burmese Harp, 1947) and those in *Pocahontas* as a point of departure, Masaki Tsuneo explores the trope of headhunters in the European as well as the Japanese imagination as an important literary devise through which to understand colonial power relations. Masaki Tsuneo, *Shokuminchi gensō* (Tokyo: Misuzu Shobō, 1995), particularly pp. 1–15.

16. Takeda Taijun, Nakamura Shin'ichirō, and Fukunaga Takehiko, "Hakkō yōsei to Mosura," *Gensō Bungaku* 39 (Fall 1993), p. 51.

17. Chino Yukiko, *Bābī kara hajimatta* (Tokyo: Shinchōsha, 2004), p. 63.

18. Mattel designed and merchandized a limited edition of Barbie in kimono for the Japanese market in the 1960s. Ibid., p. 63.

19. Chino Yukiko, who was born in 1955, gives accounts of her own and her contemporaries' encounters with Barbie in the 1960s. Ibid., pp. 51–60.

20. Takeda, Nakamura, and Fukunaga, "Hakkō yōsei to Mosura," p. 45.

21. According to *Gojira daijiten*, the women sing in ancient Malay, asking Mothra to come rescue them and to restore peace. Nomura Kōhei, ed., *Gojira daijiten* (Tokyo: Kasakura Shuppansha, 2004), p. 274.

22. The 1992 version of *Godzilla vs. Mothra* replicates this incongruity between the Japanese characters' attire and the natives' "primitive" appearance on Infant Island.

23. It is important to point out that Yanagita wrote extensively about Oshirasama, the deity of sericulture in Japan's Tōhoku region.

24. Minami Yoshikazu, "Aru sanson no seikatsu—Chichibu," *Taiyō* (July 1967), pp. 174–184.

25. Simon Partner, *Assembled in Japan* (Berkeley: University of California Press, 1999), pp. 193–224.

26. For detailed accounts of the labor and living conditions that the young workers faced in cities, see Kase Kazutoshi, *Shūdan shūshoku no jidai: Kōdoseichō no*

ninaitetachi (Tokyo: Aoki Shoten, 1997); Momose Yoshiko and Yamamoto Tomoo, *Kin no tamago no 40 nen: 1960 nendai "kin no tamago" to yobareta wakamototachiga ita* (Tokyo: Tsukubanesha, 2004).

In light of this interpretation, the revered manga master Tezuka Osamu offers a fascinating reading of *Bōken Dankichi* in his commentary included in *Bōken Dankichi manga zenshū*. He compares Dankichi to the young job seekers from the countryside. The grown-ups in the cities, like the natives on the island, eventually recognize the youth's sincerity and help them out. It turns out that Dankichi was, after all, a golden egg. Tezuka Osamu, "Sutōri manga no sendatsusha," in Shimada, *Bōken Dankichi manga zenshū*, p. 671.

27. *Urutora Q*, episode no. 15, 1966. TBS. Director: Nakagawa Harunosuke. Script: Yamada Masahiro. Special effects: Matoba Tōru.

7

HYBRIDITY AND NEGOTIATED IDENTITY IN JAPANESE POPULAR CULTURE

Joyce E. Boss

On its face, the story of Godzilla's origins, as related in the first film, *Gojira*, seems straightforward. Dr Yamane's theory—which ends up functioning as the standard party line—is that Godzilla is a mutation born of the H-bomb tests. We may well ask, however, a mutation of what? In the earlier scenes on Ōdo Island, Godzilla is spoken of as a destructive monster of ancient legend; clearly, his reputation precedes him.[1] What, then, is the relationship between the Godzilla which had just been created, or animated, within the post–atomic era and the Godzilla of Ōdo Island folklore?

This tension, never fully resolved in the original film, is emblematic of the many ways in which various forms of hybridity mark the totality of the global Godzilla phenomenon. In essence, Godzilla's origins are rooted not just in two different phenomena (the "creature + radiation" formula), but also in two competing narratives. To simply ascribe "hybridity" to Godzilla's nature, however, is almost too easy and potentially meaningless. Though hybridity is a wonderfully utilitarian theoretical trope, its very hyper-applicability limits its usefulness: all texts or genres (or monsters) can be described as "hybrid" in some way. As Jan Nederveen Pieterse states in his essay "Hybridity, So What?" "[h]ybridity is a terminology and sensibility of our time in that boundary and border-crossing mark our times."[2] However, Nederveen Pieterse goes on to suggest a way in which the concept of hybridity might be recouped to allow for analyses that do more than theorize the obvious. First, he connects the idea of hybridity with the mythic-folkloric Trickster figure, which embodies and enacts the hybrid's liminal essence as boundary-crosser: "In this sense, hybridity consciousness represents a return of the Trickster, now at a collective scale."[3] Second, Nederveen Pieterse asserts the function of power in border-crossing:

Acknowledging the contingency of boundaries and the significance and limitations of hybridity as a theme and approach means engaging hybridity

politics. This is where critical hybridity comes in, which involves a new awareness of and new take on the dynamics of group formation and social inequality.
This critical awareness is furthered by acknowledging rather than by suppressing
hybridity.[4]

In other words, recognizable instances of hybridity—in characters, genres,
texts, and such—call our attention to larger unresolved social issues involving
identity and power.

The two hybridity "threads" posited by Nederveen Pieterse—the mythic-
folkloric and the political—can be woven together in reading the Godzilla
films and, more generally, postwar Japanese popular culture. Specifically, the
numerous supernatural and monstrous creatures and characters that appear
in postwar Japanese popular texts might indeed be read as "Trickster at a
collective scale," and clearly one set of boundaries—"the dynamics of group
formation and social inequality"—along which these neo-Tricksters cluster
are those that mark the ambivalent and unresolved postwar relationship
between Japan and the U.S. military. This relationship is precisely analogous
to what Susan Napier identifies as the somewhat "love-hate attitude" that the
Japanese seem to have "toward monsters in the postwar period starting with
Godzilla himself."[5] And this core ambivalence can be seen in the hybrid
identity of two such neo-Trickster figures, one being Godzilla and the other
(one of many possible examples) being the protagonist Saya in *Blood: The
Last Vampire* (a manga-based anime film), who is a human-alien hybrid
working for a shadowy U.S. entity and who tracks vampires on the grounds,
of all places, of Yokota Air Base.

Although the Trickster can be defined and described in myriad ways, a
relatively straightforward definition will suffice here: The Trickster is a
character, often a protagonist who recurs in a cluster of myths or folk tales,
who transgresses and transcends rules, who challenges the order of things,
who is not necessarily evil or villainous, and whose presence and actions
indicate a realm of stress, conflict, tension, ambivalence, or anxiety within a
community (imagined or otherwise). Some of these contested areas include
sexual and family roles, the demarcation between the human and the nonhuman, and the relationship between humans and divinity. Trickster figures
help to explain why, or simply remind us of the fact that, while rules and
boundaries make social order possible, the transgression of rules and boundaries is also necessary for societies to adapt and survive, and further, that rules
and boundaries are themselves sources of conflict in that they reflect and per-
petuate power structures that empower some at the expense of others (or
Others). Indeed, some would say that transgression is, for better or worse, a
core characteristic of human nature. Lewis Hyde, in *Trickster Makes This
World*, offers a wonderfully evocative description:

> We constantly distinguish—right and wrong, sacred and profane, clean and
> dirty, male and female, young and old, living and dead—and in every case
> trickster will cross the line and confuse the distinction. . . . Where someone's

sense of honorable behavior has left him unable to act, trickster will appear to suggest an amoral action, something right/wrong that will get life going again. Trickster is the mythic embodiment of ambiguity and ambivalence, doubleness and duplicity, contradiction and paradox.[6]

Tricksters anger us; they delight us; they anger us; they discomfit us; they terrify us; but to be successful, they must also entertain us.[7]

Japanese myth and folklore is certainly rich in trickster figures. In Shintō mythology, there is Susa-no-o, brother of the sun goddess Amaterasu, who in Hyde's telling "us[es] dirt to disturb the line between heaven and earth and upset[s] the way the cosmos has been differentiated."[8] In folklore, three of the best-known and most recurrent figures are *kitsune*, *tengu*, and *kappa*. *Kitsune*, the fox, is a shape-shifter, often appearing as a female temptress to male humans; the *tengu*, usually associated with mountain regions, is also a shape-shifter prone to malicious trickery. The *kappa* is a particularly intriguing figure; he is dangerous and bloodthirsty, he not only lures children and animals to their deaths by drowning, but he is also responsible for bestowing upon humans the skills and techniques of bonesetting.[9] Several scholars have demonstrated the persistence of these folkloric archetypes into the modern era, albeit often in less dangerous and much more *kawaii* or kid-friendly form.[10]

Given this context, we might say that Godzilla—and the monster figures of *kaijū eiga* generally—is in many ways an exemplar of the enduring Tricksteresque figures of Japanese folklore as rendered in contemporary popular culture. In many ways, Godzilla is associated with *kami*-like qualities, especially evident in the scenes that herald his arrival. Beginning with the original *Gojira*, and in subsequent films, Godzilla's approach is signaled by shaking earth (the thuds causing dishes to rattle on shelves, books and household items to fall, and eventually the walls and roof to cave in) and often also by a howling storm of wind and water—in other words, earthquakes and typhoons, which enjoy a deeply traditional association with *kami*. Steve Ryfle, in his summary of some key scenes in the original Japanese film that were cut in the American version, recounts a scene on Ōdo Island in which an elderly man states that the misfortunes befalling the islanders must be the work of Godzilla. Ryfle observes that this scene, which was not included in the American release *Godzilla, King of the Monsters*, "helps establish the Godzilla mythos, the sense that this monster is a force of nature that has struck before, and will again."[11] The Godzilla of the Ōdo Island legend is a terrifying and unpredictable force who wreaks havoc in his wake, and whose powers indicate the living dynamic forces at work in this world just beyond mundane everyday reality.

The ocean is another powerful natural entity that figures prominently in the films; indeed, the opening shot in *Gojira* is of the ocean surface, and the first few scenes depict the unexplained loss or destruction of ships at sea. However, in 1954 these scenes also recalled the *Lucky Dragon* incident, in which a Japanese fishing vessel had inadvertently strayed into the Bikini H-bomb fallout area, with horrifying consequences for its crew. Indeed the press coverage and resulting public outrage fueled Tanaka Tomoyuki's original inspiration for a radioactive monster film. So in *Gojira* there are depictions or echoes of the H-bomb, of nuclear radiation, of cities in flames: in 1954, nine years after Hiroshima and Nagasaki—and just as many years into the American occupation—audiences in Japan did not have to reach too far to "get it." As William Tsutsui asserts, Godzilla evoked not only "long-standing Japanese fears," especially "a deeply rooted vulnerability to the awesome and erratic forces of nature," but also "more immediate and agonizing memories of man-made destruction": "The specters of Hiroshima and Nagasaki, though repressed formally and informally by Japanese society, the Japanese government, and the U.S. occupation forces, were particularly vivid, harrowing, and unresolved in 1950s Japan."[12] Yet in the backdrop there still is the earlier Ōdo Island legend, which is never explicitly rejected as superstitious or unscientific. So we have in Godzilla an entity that is simultaneously associated with "authentic" Japanese tradition and "alien" U.S. military might.

The latter association is perhaps more evident. There are many films that feature some appearance by, or appeal to, the U.S. military in some way, but in reading such features some attention must be paid to the ways in which such scenes or footage were inserted, enhanced, or edited specifically for U.S. release and never seen by Japanese audiences.[13] But even if there were no explicit depictions of U.S. warcraft or soldiers, the presence of the U.S. military is signaled obliquely by other cues, ostensibly associated with Godzilla: the endlessly repeated scenes of cities and towns being evacuated; families literally carting their possessions away, apparently on a moment's notice; the valiant but ineffectual response of the Japanese military (in the postwar world, the Self Defense Forces); the raid sirens blaring as the thunderous footsteps approach. To Japanese of a certain generation, not only to those who were in Hiroshima or Nagasaki during the war but also in Tokyo and Yokohama, these signs—which recur, in some form, in the entire Godzilla oeuvre—may well be just as explicit in their signification even in films without a single U.S. American character, belatedly inserted or otherwise.[14]

It should be noted that in addition to the U.S. military, there are non-American foreign elements and threats in a number of the films. These foreign elements are most often associated with the cold war, and occur in films from the height of that era. For example, in *Godzilla vs. the Sea Monster* (1966), the terrorist group identified in the Japanese version as the "Red Bamboo" can, according to Ryfle, be seen as "an apparent stand-in for the People's Republic of China and its nuclear proliferation,"[15] and the Red Bamboo fighter jets that attack Godzilla are Soviet-made aircraft; this scene is recycled in *Godzilla's Revenge* (1969). Perhaps the most memorable cold war scenario depicted in the films occurs in *Godzilla 1985* (1984), in which the Japanese prime minister is caught between the two superpowers, the United States and the Soviet Union, both of which urge the use of nuclear weapons to destroy Godzilla.[16]

In the post–cold war era, two films in particular have revisited the Pacific War in provocative ways. The first of these, *Godzilla vs. King Ghidorah* (1991), includes flashback scenes in which "Godzillasaurus"—that is, the dinosaur that is later exposed to H-bomb radiation and becomes Godzilla— helps defend an island-bound group of Japanese soldiers against an invading U.S. force during World War II. These scenes were the source of some controversy in the United States, where the film itself was not released theatrically, and provided the first depiction of Godzilla (or, more accurately, the proto-Godzilla) as an erstwhile defender specifically of the Japanese nation, or at least the national interest as present outside the national boundaries, not simply a kinetic-frenetic distraction for would-be alien invaders or as a some-what vague protector of human beings against a generalized menace (e.g., the threat of pollution, as in *Godzilla vs. Hedorah* [1971]).

The *kaijū*-as-defender conceit finds its most dramatic expression in *Godzilla, Mothra, and King Ghidorah: Giant Monsters All-Out Attack* (2001, usually referred to in fan parlance as *GMK*), but the defender here is not Godzilla. This film, eliding all of the previous "sequels," presents a Godzilla that has come back to life as a result of possession by the restless and angry spirits of the war dead. His attack on Japan will be met, a prophecy states, by the "Yamato Defenders," three ancient forces—Barugon, King Ghidorah, and Mothra—who will awaken to protect Japan. The fulfillment of this prophecy (which is related by a sage-like elderly man) accounts for most of the film's subsequent action.

The presentation of this prophecy is notable, first, for its direct invocation of a thoroughly fictionalized yet completely recognizable *kami* tradition, and second for its association with the legacy of the war. The spirits that pos-sess Godzilla include both the Japanese soldiers who died in the war as well as their non-Japanese victims; yet because the victims' souls outnumber those of the Japanese, it is they who (in a surprisingly straightforward mathematical calculation, given that we are dealing with the spirit realm) control this otherwise hybrid Godzilla and who wish vengeance, thereby giving Godzilla his motivation for yet again attacking Japan. Given the current status of the ongoing debate between Japan and its Asian neighbors, as well as among Japanese themselves, regarding the symbolism of the visits to Yasukuni Shrine by the prime minister and other officials, *GMK* is remarkable in that it simultaneously recognizes the victim status of other Asian nations *and* affirms the necessity of paying respect to the Japanese soldiers, who are also presented as victims in the sense that their unhappy souls are now entrapped in Godzilla.

Part of the subtext here is the way in which this legacy has been dealt with, or rather not been dealt with, in postwar Japan. As Marilyn Ivy suggests in *Discourses of the Vanishing: Modernity, Phantasm, Japan*, this history is an ongoing source of ambivalence and anxiety:

> [As with Germany,] World War II also left Japanese with an enormity of mourning tasks, but they have never been as unambiguously recognized (even by way of

denial) as the German ones. Japan's invasion of Asia, the massacres perpetrated there, and the oppression of minorities within Japan have not attained the status of the Holocaust. . . . Yet, the metatrope for loss in Japan, as in Germany, is World War II.[17]

In *GMK*, this quasi-acknowledgment takes the form of the fictional depiction of disembodied spirits, which are never distinctly visualized, possessing a rampaging monster.

Yet *GMK* does not simply stop at reflecting on the losses of the war; its narrative recoups the possibility of loss transformed into victory and honor regained. In the end, the *kaijū* triumvirate who are the Yamato Defenders are unsuccessful in overcoming Godzilla. Ultimately, it is a valiant Japanese naval commander, Admiral Tachibana, who destroys Godzilla (for the time being), solo-piloting a heavily armed submersible craft. In effect, Japan is saved by a reinvigorated military spirit embodied by the character of Tachibana; indeed, the two subsequent films, *Godzilla Against Mechagodzilla* (2002) and *Godzilla: Tokyo SOS* (2003), both depict a fictionalized Japanese hyper-military force charged with containing Godzilla by deploying all manner of (science-fictional) new-tech weaponry. In this sense, Japan is more assertively depicted in the more recent films as assuming the mantle of an effective and innovative military power. Yet the modern Japanese military can be depicted as an aggressive force in the postwar era only in fantasy films, and Godzilla himself remains beholden to a legacy in which Japan was defeated not by the countries it dominated but by the United States. This ambivalence is still negotiated through the figure of Godzilla, 50 years after his first screen appearance.

Finally, it might be instructive to consider Godzilla within the larger context of postwar Japanese popular culture where a plethora of quasimilitary imagery can be found in contemporary manga and anime. One intriguing example of a recent anime film in which the U.S. military appears explicitly as an oppressive and manipulative force is *Blood: The Last Vampire* (2000), based on a manga by Tamaoki Benkyō.[18] The protagonist, Saya, is one of many vampire-hunter characters that populate present-day manga and anime; like many young female anime protagonists, she wears a standard sailor-suit school uniform while wielding serious weaponry—in this case, a samurai sword—in a visual conceit that juxtaposes dissonant signs. Further, she is hybrid in a more literal way: she herself is part kin to the vampiric aliens she hunts, which she is compelled to do by shadowy American agents responsible for her creation. The "little America" culture of base life as depicted in the film is clearly a world in which the Japanese characters—particularly Saya—are most definitely not "at home," besieged by monstrous-looking Americans and aliens alike.

Saya serves the interests of the United States, but only because she has no choice, and the film depicts the power dynamics at work here with little ambiguity. She can therefore be read as standing in for any number of anxieties in a postwar Japan whose relationship to the United States, particularly the military, is still unresolved, and her battle takes place on what is literally contested ground, a U.S. military base. The bases remain a very visible (and, for some, a very emotionally charged) reminder of Japan's defeat at the hands of the United States some 60 years ago. In the symbolic topography of postwar Japan, places such as Yokota (where *Blood* takes place), Okinawa, and Yokosuka are sometimes seen—and spoken of—as territories that would be reincorporated into the Yamato of the imaginary, and that must be defended or reclaimed.[19]

Popular culture characters such as Godzilla and Saya (and many others) have origins and genealogies inflected by paradox. As Tricksters, they are examples of figures whose hybrid quality and multifaceted identity mark the ongoing social ambivalence in Japan regarding the complex role the U.S. military has played in the evolution of its national and cultural identity.[20]

NOTES

Many thanks to all in the G-fandom community for the inspiration they continue to provide, and particularly to the many G-Tour 2004 participants who shared conversation and feedback. Special thanks to Peter Brothers for his own work and for his encouragement.

1. Following the lead of many Godzilla scholars, in this essay Godzilla is assumed to be male. William M. Tsutsui articulates the reasons why in *Godzilla on My Mind: Fifty Years of the King of Monsters* (New York: Palgrave Macmillan, 2004), pp. 11–12. Except for *Gojira*, the film titles given are those of the U.S. releases, either theatrical or DVD. Specifics regarding titles and release dates are taken from J.D. Lees and Marc Cerasini, *The Official Godzilla Compendium* (New York: Random House, 1998), and J.D. Lees, "The Unofficial Godzilla Addendum," *G-FAN* 68 (Summer 2004), pp. 35–50.

2. Jan Nederveen Pieterse, "Hybridity: So What?: The Anti-Hybridity Backlash and the Riddles of Recognition," *Theory, Culture & Society* 18:2–3 (2001), pp. 219–245. Online text accessed through EBSCO.

3. Ibid., p. 239.

4. Ibid.

5. Susan Napier, "Panic Sites: The Japanese Imagination of Disaster from *Godzilla* to *Akira*," *Journal of Japanese Studies* 19:2 (Summer 1993), p. 349. Online text accessed through JSTOR.

6. Lewis Hyde, *Trickster Makes This World* (New York: North Point Press, 1998), p. 7.

7. See Paul Radin, *The Trickster: A Study in American Indian Mythology* (New York: Schocken Books, 1956) and Robert D. Pelton, *The Trickster in West Africa: A Study of Mythic Irony and Sacred Delight* (Berkeley: University of California Press, 1980).

8. Hyde, *Trickster Makes This World*, p. 177.

9. See Richard M. Dorson, *The Legends of Japan* (Rutland, VT, and Tokyo: Charles E. Tuttle Company, 1962).

10. See, for example, Michael Dylan Foster, "The Metamorphosis of the Kappa: Transformation of Folklore to Folklorism in Japan," *Asian Folklore Studies* 57:1 (1998), pp. 1–24; Noriko Reider, "Transformation of the Oni," *Asian Folklore Studies* 62:1 (2003), pp. 133–157. An exhilaratingly detailed analysis of the color

taxonomy of the Power Rangers can be found in Tom Gill, "Transformational Magic: Some Japanese Super-Heroes and Monsters," in *The Worlds of Japanese Popular Culture*, ed. D.P. Martinez (Cambridge, UK: Cambridge University Press, 1998), pp. 33–55.

11. Steve Ryfle, *Japan's Favorite Mon-Star: The Unauthorized Biography of the "Big G"* (Toronto: ECW Press, 1998), p. 56.

12. Tsutsui, *Godzilla on My Mind*, pp. 16–19.

13. See, for example, the account regarding *Godzilla vs. the Thing* (1964) in David Kalat, *A Critical History and Filmography of Toho's Godzilla Series* (Jefferson, NC: McFarland & Co., 1997), p. 22.

14. One film that features an especially prominent American character is *Godzilla vs. Monster Zero* (1965) in which "Astronaut Glenn" (played by Nick Adams) is the U.S. sidekick to "Astronaut Fuji" (Takarada Akira). Given the association between the U.S. space program and the U.S. military, Glenn might be read as (and has often struck me as behaving like) a "stereotypical American military guy" stationed in Japan, even taking up with a somewhat shady local woman (Miss Namikawa, who turns out to be an alien agent from Planet X).

15. Ryfle, *Japan's Favorite Mon-Star*, p. 135.

16. Steve Ryfle recounts the way in which the U.S. release deliberately mistranslated the original dialogue in order to vilify the Soviets. Ibid., p. 241.

17. Marilyn Ivy, *Discourses of the Vanishing: Modernity, Phantasm, Japan* (Chicago: University of Chicago Press, 1995), p. 14.

18. Benkyō Tamaoki, *Blood: The Last Vampire 2002*, English adaptation by Carl Gustav Horn (San Francisco: Viz Communications, Inc., 2002).

19. The tensions over the U.S. military bases on Okinawa are of course made even more complex by the history of relations between the Japanese and Ryūkyūans and the legacy of Japanese imperialism.

20. This ambivalence has only become heightened in the wake of the resurgence of nationalist sentiment in Japan. See Howard W. French, "Specter of a Rearmed Japan Stirs Its Wartime Generation," *New York Times*, June 20, 2001; accessed online through the New York Times Premium Archive. Of special interest are the quotations from Mizuki Shigeru, the war veteran turned manga artist who is best known for his *GeGeGe no Kitaro* series.

8

Teaching Godzilla: Classroom Encounters with a Cultural Icon

Joanne Bernardi

If we pay attention to them, monsters do have something to reveal. They show us the reality of the impossible, or of those things that we label impossible; they point out that the world we think we live in, and the world we actually inhabit, may not be the same place at all.

John Michael Greer, Monsters: An Investigator's Guide, pp. 3–4

Never before have so many known so little about a subject so big and important.

U.S. Army film, The Atomic Café

The second quote, above, from a cold war period U.S. Army film clip in *The Atomic Café* (1984)[1] segues into an explication of the "atomic explosions" of the nuclear devices that achieved military and political trump card status during that era. It is not too much of a stretch to say that they could also be describing—pun included—Honda Ishirō's elusive original (uncut and undubbed) 1954 film *Gojira*. Although hardly a life and death matter in comparison, this source for the 1956 *Godzilla, King of the Monsters* was not commercially released in the United States until 2004, a mind-boggling 50 years after it was made. This was the Godzilla that I first encountered sometime in July or August 1982, when Honda's 1954 version of the film was included in the Public Theater's *Summer in Japan* series in New York City. An eclectic mix of titles, the series marked Tōhō's fiftieth anniversary. Then I knew nothing about Tōhō's apparent penchant to screen *Gojira* only on such commemorative occasions. I went because, come to think of it, I couldn't recall having seen a performance by the titular character, ever. At the time I was already working toward a career in Japanese and film studies, but in my conventionally insular, graduate student's frame of mind, Godzilla had never registered as "Japanese." The experience left me deeply impressed and more than a bit shaken. Why was this "cheese"? Where was Raymond Burr? As I remember it, the entire audience seemed to be in a trance. There was a chuckle or two when a child one row down broke the oppressive silence with a faint, bewildered wail in high-pitched Japanese: "Daddy . . . Tokyo . . . *crushed!*" After that, the 1954 *Gojira* virtually disappeared. It wasn't until I tried to talk about this experience with others that I realized screenings of this seminal incarnation of Godzilla were rare.

It has never been hard to find people willing to talk about Godzilla the monster (particularly his goofy years), but in general their knowledge comes from the later dubbed, often recut films in the series, the television syndication prints that are routinely broadcast in the United States. Nothing is more frustrating than to have seen an incredible film that you then are unable to share. When *Godzilla, King of the Monsters* was eventually released on DVD, I realized that there had to be at least a video copy of *Gojira* somewhere. I wanted to include both films as course material for my students for several reasons, beginning with each of the films' remarkably different views (United States and Japanese) of nuclear history and the postwar period.[2] Email, the internet, and the good fortune of similarly thinking minds finally made "teaching Godzilla" a possibility rather than a dream. I started predictably with a course on popular genre film, an opportunity to incorporate the general phenomenon of the Godzilla series as well as both versions (1954, 1956) of the first film. Casting my net wider, I watched more films and/or their alternate versions: the original Japanese language version, when available, and the dubbed and routinely "rearranged" U.S. release (all ostensibly in preparation for class, of course). I was fascinated by how increasingly difficult it soon was to pin down "which" or "whose" Godzilla I encountered onscreen. Class discussions compounded the mix with the inevitable "what?" "when?" "where?" and, to a much lesser degree than generally might be expected, "why?"

Why teach Godzilla? In an article covering the events of *Gojira*'s fiftieth anniversary year, the definitive Godzilla fanzine, *G-FAN*, noted that the "In Godzilla's Footsteps" conference at the University of Kansas in Lawrence "unquestionably garnered the most media coverage."[3] "Leaping Lizards! Godzilla Enters the Academy" exclaimed the title of one such report in *The New York Sun*. This newspaper article describes the conference as an investigation of the ways in which (in addition, of course, to being "just plain fun") "Godzilla ties together issues of cultural and historical significance—including nuclear war, environmentalism, [and] Japanese-American relations." But the article also mentions that Godzilla's newly found "toe-hold in the classroom" (a result of "increased attention to the quotidian") meets with "reluctance from certain corners." A case in point: Roger Kimball's remark that such studies "make parody virtually impossible."[4] I assume he is alluding to the popular notion of "academic" as four syllables for a (politically correct) "wet blanket." But if *Gojira* merely cashed in on the contemporary monster craze without documenting an important moment in the history of the atomic age, would such a radically new version as *Godzilla, King of the Monsters* have been concocted for the popcorn-loving American audience? A comparison between the Japanese and U.S. release versions of most films in the Godzilla series, beginning with the original and its "remake," presents its own unique lesson in parody.

The ubiquitous presence of the dubbed U.S. version of any given Godzilla film has resulted in the popularization over time of a generic Godzilla that is undeniably fun, but also all too familiar. In Cynthia Erb's study of King Kong, Godzilla's American-bred counterpart, she describes the icon's repeated exposure throughout popular culture as a "trivialization" and "a kind of censorship," a pitfall on the path to understanding its "use value in contemporary culture."[5] This is no less true for Godzilla. "Since Godzilla," Osugi Hiroshi's 2002 exhibition at the Tarō Okamoto Museum of Art in Kawasaki drew attention for his unorthodox choice of a sociological rather than entertainment context. Even so, while the title of one review warned, "Take heed: Scaly monster born of nuclear blast still relevant," another marveled at Godzilla's journey "from Kitsch to High Art," citing one fan's reaction to the exhibit as "a little embarrassing."[6] Now that the original film is becoming widely available in the form the director intended it to be seen, we can decide for ourselves just how educational the erstwhile familiar Godzilla can be.

In the following essay I outline a basic approach to "teaching Godzilla"—metacultural monster, icon, phenomenon in toto—that, in my experience, students have been keen on pursuing. For clarity, I have limited my parameters here: the college undergraduate is the intended target audience, although these ideas are amenable to tweaking for a much wider range; also, my focus is Godzilla onscreen. The fundamental concept of Godzilla begins with and continually draws on *Gojira* and *Godzilla, King of the Monsters,* and they receive the most attention here. Nevertheless when possible I make suggestions for a study of Godzilla that is more comprehensive and phenomenon-wide. I have used a variety of titles from the "Godzilla film" world, including other Tōhō-produced *kaijū eiga* (monster films) featuring monsters that have shared the screen with Godzilla, such as Rodan and Mothra. These *kaijū eiga* are monster/creature films that share kinship with science fiction films, a topic that I say more about later on.

A LOGISTICAL APPROACH

Cynthia Erb's study of King Kong, a figure who plays a part in Godzilla's conception, provides a basic battle plan that makes sense for us to follow in approaching the subject of Godzilla. She supplements a historical and reception study approach with both textual analysis and contextual issues of race and global importance. In effect, she strategically builds on Barbara Klinger's similarly integrated schema for working toward a "total history" (at least as a working goal) that provides for and makes manifest a historical synthesis of synchronic and diachronic change, acknowledging the constantly changing contexts in which a single film is seen.[7] This is a key starting point for taking on the complexities of such popular icons as King Kong and Godzilla, figures with a cultural resonance that has grown (and been transformed) by accretion as they age. In 1954, *Gojira*'s creation was prompted by 1950s cold war anxiety and the escalation of egregiously secretive nuclear testing. The figure of Godzilla has been recurrently reactivated in subsequent films in the series, and a plethora of altered versions, TV broadcasts, and rereleases, both onscreen (such as the 1982 Tōhō retrospective and *Gojira*'s 2004 U.S. theatrical release) and in the newer formats designed for the ever-increasing parameters of home consumption. Recurrent reactivation asks changing generations to renegotiate, as well as question, the dynamics of Godzilla's meaning and place in the postwar, cold war contexts.

In terms of choosing the contextual resources to study within this shifting and layered, interactive framework, Erb, much like Klinger, starts with those materials "closest" to the film at hand (beginning with basic cinematic practices of production, distribution, exhibition, changing media) and working outward, as Erb puts it, "toward increasingly distant domains" (other relevant or associated industries, media, art; social and historical contexts; cross-cultural reception, retrospectives, and rereleases).[8] In the classroom a consideration of such a wide range of references and resources (from material generated by processes of film planning and production to mass media coverage of a film, industry or other interrelated historical moments and social processes), will inevitably be uneven, contingent on the particulars or purpose of the course. As a working strategy, however, this approach cultivates the frame of mind necessary in avoiding the inherent trap of selective focus: that bogeyman of teaching, the single monolithic reading.

A complete "Godzilla primer" would include both series-related and film-specific topics for mining meaning from Godzilla's "textual encrustations,"[9] the interconnected and interactive build up of cumulative Godzilla-relevant events, contexts, and materials. I can only mention these here. A study of Godzilla iconography and narrative convention begins, in my mind, with a discussion of how we interpret cultural artifacts and icons as somehow representing Japan. Next we must acknowledge the variety of directions the Godzilla series takes over its half-century track record. From somber beginnings, it has made its way through the space age, self-referential parody, its own awkward adolescence (the Tsuburaya child-friendly years), and a number of highly entertaining scenarios that comment on contemporary attitudes toward the military, the media, government, corporate culture, popular perceptions of science (and science fiction), environmental issues, a changing global world order, terrorism, and nuclear catastrophe.

There are specific clusters of ideas throughout the Godzilla series that are either preserved, altered (for better or for worse), or subverted. The elemental appearance and participation of the military, for example, has in more recent years branched out into a new motif of a core group of increasingly elite and variably gendered special units, with acronyms on caps, uniforms, and special powers that add more layers to an already complex system of signs and symbols. The media has been another important piece of the formula, beginning with *Gojira*. Television sets play a prominent part in the mise en scène and in motivating the story (NHK broadcasts began about a year before the original version of the film was made). Some motifs are uncannily resilient: the United Nations as a viable guarantor of global order; specific framing techniques (a single close-up of Godzilla's eye, for example); the familiar "remote island" establishing shot that is seemingly a legacy of *King Kong*'s Skull Island. In order to study a figure that has been the focus of so many layers of accumulated readings, it is useful at this point to impose structure in the form of genre analysis and genre-related considerations. The process of situating Godzilla in the context of our understanding of how genres function further clears the air of any falsely familiar traces.

GENRE AND IDENTITY

Even though it is commonly recognizable, science fiction is something of an equal opportunity genre accommodating the likes of monsters, robots, aliens, creatures, clones, beasts, mutants, extraterrestrial phenomena, any combination of the above, *and* humans. In Vivian Sobchack's engaging analysis, *Screening Space: The American Science Fiction Film*, she begins her inquiry with an analysis of the nature of the central beast (or creature, monster or alien) of science fiction film as a general category onscreen. This enables her to sort through nuanced generic variations in 1950s science fiction in a way that helps us comprehend differences between the creature film's creature and the monster of horror.[10] Godzilla commonly falls under the rubric of the 1950s creature film that, as Sobchack points out, shares elements of both science fiction and horror. If we judge according to Sobchack's criteria, the pathos of Godzilla's twentieth-century reactivation arguably renders him less impersonal than science fiction's creature, but still lacking an interior presence comparable to that of the quasi-sympathetic monster that belongs to horror. Godzilla's wide arc of transformations throughout the entire series of films and all the many variations calls for a dexterity of judgment on a film-by-film basis. Still, the process of locating any given onscreen manifestation of Godzilla on this generic spectrum is a point of departure for unraveling the internal logic in each individual film.

What is the function of film genre, and what is genre film? The complex provenance of genre theory in film studies would be a lengthy detour here. Briefly, film genre is (in definition and function) a key mechanism in the integrated processes of production, distribution and exhibition, and consumption. Rick Altman has persuasively argued that film genres are hybrid and dynamic, effectively challenging traditional notions of them as finite, clear, and stable. Altman's own definition of film genre is that it is a "multivalent term multiplied and variously valorized by diverse user groups."[11] In *Film/Genre*, he prefaces his argument by summarizing, point by point, prominent positions on and common assumptions about genre and film. He describes these positions "in as straightforward a manner as possible" in order to establish a foundational context for his own position that follows.[12] The succinct way in which Altman summarizes each point tempts us to flip them into questions that lead into a discussion about the function, meaning, and significance of genre in the context of onscreen Godzilla.

For example, if film genres (such as science fiction and horror) are universally recognized public categories defined by the film industry and recognized by the mass audience, how does that process of public recognition "come about"?[13] If the process of generic reception depends on texts whose genres are "immediately and transparently recognizable," why are we drawn to those films that are, in this respect, "mysterious and complex"?[14] Subsequently, if we acknowledge that some films embrace characteristics of multiple genres, does their reception change over time? Are genres transhistorical? Do genres undergo predictable development? Do they age like living beings (a process in which they can be seen "to develop, to react, to become self-conscious, and to self-destruct"), or evolve biologically through "unpredictable mutation"?[15] If genre films share fundamental characteristics and depend on the cumulative effect of repetition, does the "pleasure of genre film spectatorship" derive "more from reaffirmation than from novelty"?[16] Does genre have a ritual or ideological function, or perhaps both? These questions help students think about where (or whether or why) Godzilla films "fit" any given description or function of genre. Such a critical perspective also enlists their detailed attention to iconography, characterization, language and narrative form, structure, and visual style. How do such constitutive elements work to define Godzilla films at the level of production? How are they recognized by the audience, and what are the audience's expectations? To what extent are individual films products of a specific time and place, or are they in flux, changing along with the times?

One of many (often radioactively enlarged) mutant creatures inhabiting the general category of 1950s onscreen science fiction, Godzilla is the product of a hybrid film genealogy although he subsequently becomes an original generic influence in his own right. The figure was first ingeniously marketed in the United States as the "King of the Monsters," a position that he has admirably defended. In Dave Elliot's recent, tongue-in-cheek *A Field Guide to Monsters*, Godzilla is the single identified-by-name entry presented centerfold style, and in the handy "Monster Size Comparison Chart" in the appendix, he towers above all but the antennae of the Deadly Mantis, his compatriot Mothra's giant wingspan, and (a monster more in the category of the inane) *Ghostbusters'* Stay Puft Marshmallow Man.[17] Godzilla's globally popular and long-running series is a world in itself, a cycle of 28 feature films that has morphed in many directions through the decades by a process of often highly creative self-feeding. Godzilla's bodily alterations and subjective transformations are now commonly read as gauging crosscurrents of change in Japan as a nation. Not bad for "just" a monster, routinely called a "cheesy" one at that.

Who is Godzilla and where did he come from? Is this a monster with, as a student once claimed, "the depth of the cardboard buildings that he lays to waste"? Or is he more of a complex creation, an errant golem, a manifestation of the perils of the atomic age? Is he an ancient god of lore, or a symbol for the Bomb, the United States, nuclear holocaust, the souls of dead soldiers, bomb victims, or even a vengeful Mother Nature? Or is he just a person in a silly rubber suit? Sobchack points out that although science fiction in film predates World War II, "it only emerged as a *critically* recognized film genre *after* Hiroshima."[18] But the "creature feature"—Godzilla's apparent niche—that became so popular during this period has received the critical brush-off by science fiction and horror purists alike. Science fiction relegates the creature/bomb films to the realm of pseudo-science, as evidenced by Sobchack's quote from one purist who sees radioactively charged creatures like Godzilla as "bugaboos dressed up in atomic hats."[19] Similarly, it can be argued that Godzilla films fall short as horror because Godzilla (as monster) is not necessarily always any given film's most central figure (although this varies from film to film). There is some truth to this view. Referring to the hospital sequence showing the results of Godzilla's rage, a student once observed that "[these] images evoke a feeling of despair that cannot be attributed solely to the monster Gojira." Particularly in the original *Gojira*, Godzilla's destructive force is challenged as the core emotional catalyst by Dr Serizawa's anguish and eventual sacrifice. This subtle connection between Godzilla and Dr Serizawa is not as clear in the U.S. version, where the focus is deflected by Raymond Burr's American star reporter, Steve Martin.

In discussions of Godzilla, it is always hard to know exactly which Godzilla is the subject at hand, the dreaded yet strangely compelling "Gojira," or the more supporting-role type "King of the Monsters" and his dubbed-version descendents. Even Cynthia Erb, who makes a convincing case that Godzilla mobilizes "the mythic King Kong story to allegorize national traumas characteristic of postwar Japan," remarks that to consider Godzilla an allegory about the anxieties of the atomic age "has become something of a cliché."[20] This is true in the sense that the familiar Godzilla as a pop culture icon has become so trivialized that by rote we jokingly associate the figure with "atomic breath." It would never have occurred to the 1954 Japanese audience of *Gojira* to draw a connection between "nuclear devastation" and "cliché."

A key obstacle to discussing the cultural value of Godzilla is that, as Chon Noriega points out, Godzilla films are commonly not judged historically but "aesthetically according to Hollywood standards."[21] One remedy is to sort through the contextual tangle that produced Godzilla; we can begin by looking up Godzilla's onscreen "family." This puts us in a position to understand better the visual (and material) history of the origins of the atomic age in the late 1940s and early 1950s. We can then deepen our comprehension of the period through the specific visual legacy of atomic bomb testing, especially the Bikini "Operation Castle" Bravo shot that radioactively contaminated the *Daigo Fukuryū Maru (Lucky Dragon No. 5)*, a Japanese tuna trawler. This incident is alluded to in the opening sequence of *Gojira*, and it strongly influenced Honda in the direction he chose to take Godzilla's story.

A FILM BEAST GENEALOGY

Film as a medium affects its cultural environment just as this context has its own reciprocal role to play. Vivian Sobchack's critical acknowledgement of the 1950s creature film facilitates a careful investigation of *Gojira*, *Godzilla King of the Monsters*, and the creature Godzilla's filmic family tree. Additionally, Cynthia Erb's study of King Kong provides a template suitable to Godzilla that takes us beyond surface similarities between films to an analysis of the dynamic process of exchange between a film and the historical, sociological, and cultural climate at the time of release (or rerelease or reviewing). This line of inquiry can take myriad directions. I begin with a basic line up of 1950s releases that clearly correlate to the plot, iconography, and visual style of *Gojira*, and subsequently tinkered-with *Godzilla, King of the Monsters*. To a degree, these contemporary 1950s films are also important to the continuum that has become the iconography and narrative conventions of the Godzilla film series. None of these films are Japanese, because in Japan Godzilla gave birth to his own original genre.

First a caveat: I can suggest titles that are guaranteed to provoke discussion, but familiarity with the closest screen "relatives" of the original *Gojira* illuminates its contemporaneity in ways I cannot do full justice to here. A basic genealogical search best begins by dividing relevant films into two groups of titles. In the first group are films primarily informed by the travel documentary and jungle adventure traditions, featuring the stop-motion animation special effects pioneered by Willis O'Brien. The second group comprises the cold war creature films of the 1950s. The first group can be dated back to O'Brien's earliest work in the mid-1910s, but *The Lost World* (1925, released in a restored version in 1997) and *King Kong* (1933, rereleased in 1952 in the United States and 1953 in Japan) are the two most influential titles. The silent *The Lost World*, based on a novel by Sir Arthur Conan Doyle and probably the lesser known of the two films for a student audience, features several conventions that trickle down, through *King Kong*'s 1952 rerelease, to the general creature film formula that characterizes *Gojira*. The most significant of these is the central image of a captured (displaced) prehistoric (primitive) beast "bigger than ten elephants"[22] who is put on display, escapes, and terrorizes an urban center (London) on a destructive rampage. There is also a central romance here involving the requisite "beast magnet" and a young reporter. The supporting cast is led by an eccentric scientist/explorer (Professor Challenger), and the narrative turns on the elemental incongruence of urban (human-made) "civilization" and primitive, uncharted territory (here, an isolated plateau in an Amazonian jungle "greater than all Europe"[23]). In addition to battling, prehistoric monsters and terrified, fleeing masses, there are other iconographic elements that will eventually become familiar. The climax at the end of the film, for example, features the beast ("Bronty" in promotional material) crashing through London's emblematic Tower Bridge before swimming out to sea.

Merian C. Cooper and Ernest Schoedsack, *King Kong*'s creators, were established names in the travel documentary/jungle adventure genre, the context in which the film would have been received by its original audience. Kong, a figure of "monstrous hybridity [that] manages to absorb most of the binary structures characteristic of Western thought—East/West, black/

white, female/male, primitive/modern,"[24] is subsequently reconfigured, as Erb illustrates, in an entirely new context upon its 1950s rerelease. *King Kong* is rereleased the year after *The Thing from Another World* (1951), an early example of what Sobchack isolates as the 1950s creature films' characteristic, precarious balance between science fiction and horror.[25] In the wake of *The Thing*, the central opposition between the imaginary and the real in the *King Kong* story readily slips into that of the alien and the familiar. I mention here as examples at least two of the iconographic embellishments that *King Kong* adds to the "lost world" formula in 1933 that in turn make their way as elemental features via Kong into Godzilla iconography. These are the use of a primitive, isolated South Sea island as Nature's mother lode in all its mystery, and the introduction of would-be pilot heroes who battle the beast. There is also good reason to argue that Godzilla, particularly in his original appearance, embodies a transference of Kong's beastly savagery, majesty, and pity.

This brings us to the second group of films relevant to Godzilla, the creature films that become a phenomenon in the 1950s. There are already subtle premonitions of the cold war/creature film nuclear theme in *The Thing from Another World*, which was released in Japan in 1952. Dr Carrington, a former "Bikini scientist," has the insufferable arrogance to claim that "knowledge is more important than life," and he is dispatched for this transgression in the end.[26] In addition to including the elemental reporter, the cast of characters is marked by a clear conflict of interest between the military (heroes here) and science. Subsequent creature films share an even closer and historically more interactive relationship with Godzilla. *Them!* (1954) has mutant ants that are a by-product of the first atomic bomb tests at Alamogordo, and a paleontologist who, in contrast to *Gojira*'s Dr Yamane, helps to destroy the titular creatures. But, like Yamane, he has been given the final ominous word of warning. The displaced and rampaging dinosaurs of Eugene Lourié's films also have much in common with Godzilla (*Gorgo* features Godzilla's trademark "suitmation" and was originally planned to be set in Japan, where it premiered in 1960). Lourié's *The Beast from 20,000 Fathoms* (1953), which opens with a flash-to-mushroom cloud sequence of an atomic bomb test ("Operation Experiment," stock footage of the Crossroads Baker shot) is most often cited as having been influential in the making of *Gojira*.

In an early scene in *The Beast*, the scientist-hero who eventually brings about the destruction of the primordial Beast-Rhedosaurus, soberly follows a remark on the magnitude of the "X-day" explosion with the observation, "what the cumulative effects of all these tests and explosions will be, only time can tell." Later, lamenting plans to kill the beast, his paleontologist counterpart sighs, "What a loss to science."[27] Just as Godzilla is killed by the Oxygen Destroyer (with its unmistakable resemblance to the two fissile half spheres of an atomic weapon), the radioactively regenerated Beast is felled by a radioactive isotope shot from a weapon. There is, however, something notably different about the Beast's final climax in comparison, as he dies in dramatic anguish framed against the giant roller coaster at Coney Island. This ending recalls Kong's death dive from atop the Empire State Building, after his suspenseful looming over Manhattan atop the Empire State Building with the precariously perched Faye Wray. The deaths of King Kong and the Beast are to some extent shown with (varying degrees of) emotion, but they are primarily spectacular, like Godzilla's death in the more recent *Godzilla vs. Destoroyah* (1995). In *Gojira*, Ifukube Akira's elegiac music plays sparsely in the background as the monster is undramatically (and a bit implausibly) pinpointed by a single Geiger counter held to the surface of the water, and he is seemingly come upon while sleeping. This was meant to be his end, for all we know, and in place of the more formulaic spectacle, the noble sacrifice of Dr Serizawa gives these final moments a resonance and emotional weight.

MONSTER OF THE HOUR

This brings us to the complicated question of Godzilla's cultural currency at his point of origin in *Gojira*. Where did Godzilla stand in the context of cold war films and the contemporary culture's persistent nuclear preoccupations? How does this translate into the context of current culture and today's historical situation? Today, film roles are still available for nuclear energy to play. The 2005 Review Conference of the parties to the Nuclear Non-Proliferation Treaty, held at the United Nations this past May, had a quiet repercussion in physics and engineering professional society publications. Among the articles that appeared on the history, current status, and speculative future of the nuclear battlefield, *The Bulletin of the Atomic Scientists* featured a profile of the changing face of onscreen fictional nuclear catastrophe, weapon disarmament, and detonation. The article ultimately gives a dim assessment of popular culture's potential as a medium for public change, but it provides a contrast between contemporary film disaster scenarios and the "cultural time capsules" of cold war films that is thought provoking. During the "duck-and-cover era" of the 1950s, the public preoccupation was a nuclear Armageddon; today, biological terrorism is the greatest public fear. There is a sidebar to this article that both demystifies and dismisses the nuclear-related plotlines of the recent films mentioned, including the titles in the quote below (the "Insultingly Stupid Movie Physics" web site is one critical source cited). This sidebar throws cold water on the idea of any *real life*, "Our Friend the Atom," Walt Disney ending to these fictions, but the article itself draws our attention to how much the public perception of apocalypse has changed:

> Today we've entered the era of the friendly, functional cinematic nukes. These nuclear weapons aren't the proverbial "destroyer of worlds," but the saviors of humanity. They possess utility and a higher purpose. Twice they've thwarted a giant asteroid from slamming into the Earth (*Deep Impact* and *Armageddon*) and once they helped reset the rotation of its core (*The Core*).[28]

In *Nuclear Fear: A History of Images*, Spencer R. Weart describes 1950s public attitudes toward visual images of nuclear devastation that are important to Godzilla's beginnings. Most importantly, the unleashing of nuclear weapons on Japan, followed by repeated atomic testing and radioactive fallout-related incidents well into the 1950s fueled sentiment that nuclear energy grossly violated the order of nature. This happened because it was the perfect point "historically, psychologically, and socially" for linking nuclear energy (able to take on a "wealth of ambiguous associations") with the fear of contamination, an age-old fundamental and "primitive" human theme. In time this association grew larger to embrace the concept of transmutation, the idea of individual and social life cycles as processes of death, destruction, and rebirth. A sanitized version of *Operation Ivy* (a film documenting the October 31, 1952 Ivy Mike shot, the first full-scale H-bomb) was televised in the United States on April 2, 1954 and subsequently worldwide, but generally speaking there were no detailed, easily accessible images of the actual effects of nuclear detonations up until then. There was even something perfunctory about the still and moving images of Hiroshima and Nagasaki that were eventually made available to the public. Usually, the horrific destruction was shot with minimal, visual evidence of human casualties and, as Weart puts it, "from an Olympian distance." The convergence of such factors at this point in time fostered an optimal tabula rasa for conjuring up radioactive screen monsters. In this context, a figure like Godzilla could easily become a popular symbol of "myth [made] ferociously visible," a central image with a visual impact too forceful for any tidy-resolution ending to eclipse.[29]

The contrast between the Japanese and U.S. versions of the first Godzilla film is a topic rich with implications in terms of the two countries' divergent attitudes toward each other and their national self-images. Both films appeared at a moment of critical remove from World War II and the recently ended American occupation. In this sense, the difference in the beginning and ending of each film is particularly revealing. In order to accommodate the new narrative perspective of Steve Martin, *King of the Monsters* begins with a full five minutes dominated by this character and his expository narration. The first image on screen is the pan of "Tokyo" after Godzilla's devastation, but other than the few footsteps and roar behind the opening title, we have no way of associating the monster with this scene. Burr also has the last lines at the film's end, "The menace was gone but so was a great man. But the whole world could wake up and live again."[30] In comparison, the original Japanese version begins with lengthy, rolling opening credits, accompanied by Godzilla's repeated stomp and deep, throaty roar. The first sequence, as described earlier, is an indirect but unmistakable reference to the *Lucky Dragon* incident that took place eight months prior to the film's release. At the end of the original version, Yamane has the final word. Unable to believe that Godzilla is the only one of his kind, Yamane wonders aloud what would happen if the nuclear incidents that awakened the fury of Godzilla failed to come to an absolute end.

In addition to savoring "Raymond Burrisms" ("Well, it's big and terrible"), students will want to know the extent of the U.S. nuclear testing program in the Pacific before 1954, and familiarity with this history and its visual impact is critical to a full appreciation of Godzilla.[31] Operation Castle, which included the Bravo shot that contaminated the *Lucky Dragon*, was the fifth series of Marshall Island detonations. The first, Operation Crossroads, took place 11 months after Hiroshima and Nagasaki, and required the evacuation (the first of many for the Marshall Islanders) of 167 Bikini Islanders to Rongerik Atoll, 125 miles away. The first Crossroads shot, Able, was dropped from a B-29, but the subsequent Baker (July 25, 1946) was a stupendous underwater detonation designed to measure weapon-effects on livestock and a World War II ghost fleet. According to the U.S. Department of Energy, "Two million tons of water were contained in the eruption, and two million yards of sediment were removed from the lagoon floor."[32] The large degree of fallout was unforeseen, and a planned third shot (Charlie) was canceled. Crossroads was followed by Pacific Testing Grounds Operations Sandstone (1948) and Greenhouse (1951) with results that affected the design of future weapons, lightening their load and improving their perform-ance. Operation Ivy, the fourth series in the Marshall Islands, included Ivy Mike (October 31, 1952), the first full-scale H-bomb. It vaporized the island of Eluklab, the detonation site. From the initiation of the atomic weapons testing program, the United States had a vested interest in its photographic documentation, and the Ivy Mike film (*Operation Ivy*) was screened at the White House in June 1953 for a group including the Cabinet and the Joint Chiefs of Staff. Not only could they see Eluklab vanish into a crater, but the fireball's size was also made clear by a superimposed, dwarfed silhouette of New York City's skyline.[33] There were televised broadcasts of testing at the Nevada Proving Grounds that same year. But at the time of the Bravo incident (March 1, 1954), the general public had been given little access to graphic visuals of what the magnitude of such detonations could be, little by way of information about actual effects, and much publicity about "fall out" and "death ash." The situation was idea for cultivating free-floating anxiety.

The details of Castle Bravo, the most powerful hydrogen bomb ever tested by the United States, and its effect on the *Lucky Dragon* are well known. Because of a miscalculation, the force of Bravo's blast (a yield of 15 mega-tons) exceeded expectations by 2.5 times the planned calculations. It was not just a change in wind patterns that caused the *Lucky Dragon*'s contamination, resulting in the eventual death of the ship's radio operator and a "hot tuna" scare (500 tons of radiation-polluted tuna was discarded) that subsequently paralyzed Japan. The islands of Rongelap, Rongerik, and Uterik were also in the path of radioactive fallout contamination, and islanders and U.S. military and civilian personnel also received large doses of radiation. In all, according to the Embassy of the Republic of the Marshall Islands, between 1946 and 1958, "the U.S. detonated 67 nuclear bombs in and around the land, air, and water of the Marshall Islands." The total yield was over 7,200 times more powerful than the bombs of Hiroshima and Nagasaki.[34]

In the transformation of *Gojira* into *Godzilla, King of the Monsters*, the original version's references to atomic testing and World War II urban devastation (from both saturation bombing and nuclear detonation) are famously removed, rendered incoherent or untranslated. In an interesting case of inversion, a scrambled mix of stock footage clips of several U.S. atomic test preparations and detonations are added as an opening sequence in *Rodan, The Flying Monster*, the August 1957 U.S. release of Tōhō's *Sora no daikaijū Radon* (1956). Honda's *Radon* isn't really about nuclear tests and ends with a tinge of sadness for the pterodactyls that die together rather than survive without each other. The U.S. version begins with two atomic explosions, the first ("Mission Gigantic") taking place "in the faraway Pacific, on a tiny island atoll, miles away from inhabited land . . . [observed from] a battleship in the remote Pacific from which all shipping has been banned." After the second test is completed ("On target! The kill is complete!"), the narration turns somber: "But what have these tests done to Mother Earth? Can the human race continue to deliver these staggering blows without arousing somewhere in the depths of Earth a reaction, a counter attack, a horror still undreamed of? There are persons in the Japanese islands who believe that the horror has already been seen."[35]

Why teach Godzilla? In addition to marking the sixtieth anniversary of Hiroshima and Nagasaki, 2005 is the "World Year of Physics," a United Nations endorsed, international celebration of this branch of science. This is in commemoration of Albert Einstein's banner year, 1905, in which he proved, among many things, that atoms are real. How nuclear history has been regarded since then varies for different cultures and individuals. In the United States, you can visit (once a year) the Trinity Site where an atom bomb was first exploded, or visit one or two "atomic museums." The Nevada Test Site has the dubious distinction of being the world's most bombed placed ever. Japan has peace memorials and museums at Hiroshima and Nagasaki. In the Marshall Islands, three islands no longer exist, having been vaporized by atomic testing. At the time of this writing, the Marshall Islands ERUB (the Enewetak, Rongelap, Utrik and Bikini Atolls Survivors Group) members hope to be included when Congress is presented with the latest version of the Republic of the Marshall Islands Changed Circumstances Petition, which requests additional compensation from the United States appropriate to new information on "a wider extent of radioactive fallout than previously known or disclosed and more recent radiation protection standards."[36] Bert the Turtle of *Duck and Cover* fame and *The Thing from Another World* are now ensconced in the Library of Congress's National Film Registry. The "duck-and-cover" days are in the past, but we will always have nuclear energy. And as long as we do, there will always be a place, and perhaps even a purpose, for new imaginings of Godzilla.

NOTES

1. *The Atomic Café*, dir. Kevin Rafferty, Jayne Loader, Pierce Rafferty, 1982. DVD. New Video Group, 2002.
2. For a discussion of the U.S.-Japan "nuclear dialectic" in the specific context of cold war politics, see Chon Noriega, "Godzilla and the Japanese Nightmare: When *Them!* is U.S.," *Cinema Journal* 27:1 (Fall 1987), pp. 65–69.

3. Armand Vaquer and Brett Homenick, "Godzilla's 50th Anniversary," *G-FAN 71* (Spring 2005), p. 39.

4. Gary Shapiro, "Leaping Lizards! Godzilla Enters the Academy," *The New York Sun*, October 29, 2004.

5. Cynthia Erb, *Tracking King Kong: A Hollywood Icon in World Culture* (Detroit, MI: Wayne State University Press, 1998), p. 13.

6. Ayako Karino, "Exhibition: Take heed! Scaly monster born of nuclear blast still relevant!" Asahi.com, October 8, 2002, http://www.asahi.com/english/national/K2002 061700423.html; "Godzilla goes from kitsch to high art," CNN.com, June 10, 2002, http://www.cnn.com/2002/TRAVEL/NEWS/06/10.

7. Barbara Klinger, "Film History Terminable and Interminable: Recovering the Past in Reception Studies," *Screen* 38:2 (Summer 1997), p. 107.

8. Erb, *Tracking King Kong*, p. 19.

9. Ibid.

10. See chapter 1 ("The Limits of the Genre: Definitions and Themes") in Vivian Sobchack's, *Screening Space: The American Science Fiction Film*, 3rd ed. (New Brunswick, NJ: Rutgers University Press, 1999), particularly pp. 26–55.

11. Rick Altman, *Film/Genre* (London: British Film Institute, 1999), p. 214.

12. Ibid., pp. 13–14.

13. Ibid., p. 15.

14. Ibid., p. 16.

15. Ibid., pp. 21–22.

16. Ibid., p. 25.

17. Dave Elliot, *A Field Guide to Monsters* (New York: Hylas, 2004), pp. 32–33, 182–185.

18. Sobchack, *Screening Space*, p. 21. Emphasis in the original.

19. Ibid., p. 49; Sobchack quotes Frank Hauser, "Science Fiction Films," in *International Film Annual*, ed. William Whitebait (New York: Doubleday, 1958), p. 89.

20. Erb, *Tracking King Kong*, pp. 151, 28.

21. Noriega, "Godzilla and the Japanese Nightmare," p. 74.

22. *The Lost World*, dir. Harry O. Hoyt, 1925 (restored and remastered version). Reproduction of original souvenir program, n.p., DVD. Image Entertainment, 2000.

23. Ibid.

24. Erb, *Tracking King Kong*, p. 17.

25. See Sobchack, *Screening Space*, pp. 17–55 for her argument on the generic relationships among science fiction, the creature film, and horror. Erb cites Bill Warren's explanation for the reason why King Kong became associated with a recycling of 1930s and 1940s horror films during the 1950s. Erb, *Tracking King Kong*, p. 142. See Bill Warren, *Keep Watching the Skies! American Science Fiction Movies of the Fifties (1950–57)*, vol. 1 (Jefferson, NC: McFarland, 1982), p. xiv.

26. *The Thing from Another World*, dir. Christian Nyby (prod. Howard Hawkes), 1951. DVD. Warner Video, 2003.

27. *The Beast from 20,000 Fathoms*, dir. Eugene Lourié, 1953. DVD. Warner Video, 2003.

28. Josh Schollmeyer, "Lights, Camera, Armageddon," *Bulletin of the Atomic Scientists*, 61:3 (May/June 2005), pp. 42–50. Other reflections on the history of nuclear testing include "Working (and Not Working) on Weapons," a personal

narrative by former H-bomb physicist Kenneth W. Ford, and "Physics and Ethics," in *Radiations* 11:1 (Spring 2005), pp. 5–7; "The Hidden Atomic Fortress that Time Forgot," *IEEE Spectrum* 42:4 (April 2005), pp. 12–14, on the still-surviving Hanford B reactor, the world's first full-scale nuclear reactor; and "On Display: The Unthinkable," a review of The National Atomic Museum in Albuquerque, NM, in *Technology Review* 108:7 (July 2005), p. 82. This attention to nuclear history can also be attributed to the commemoration of 2005 as "The World Year of Physics," marking 100 years since Albert Einstein produced the photon paper, his dissertation on atomic sizes, the Brownian motion paper, the first paper on Special Relativity, and $E = mc^2$.

29. Spencer R. Weart, *Nuclear Fear: A History of Images* (Cambridge, MA: Harvard University Press, 1988), pp. 187–188, 421–426, 157, 183–184, 246–247, 191–195.

30. *Godzilla, King of the Monsters*, dir. Honda Ishirō and Terry Morse, 1956. DVD. Simitar Entertainment, 1998.

31. The two primary sources for the following information are the U.S. Department of Energy's *Albuquerque Operations Office Film Declassification Project Video Tape Fact Sheets* (Nevada Operations Office, June 1998) and Peter Kuran's digital restorations of declassified nuclear testing footage. To date Kuran has directed five documentaries on nuclear testing that are available on VHS and DVD through his company, Visual Concepts Entertainment and other venues. The most important of these is *Trinity and Beyond: The Atomic Bomb Movie*, dir. Peter Kuran, 1995. DVD. Goldhil, 1999. The declassified archival footage that Kuran digitally restored for his work is also available (unrestored) for purchase or download from the Nevada Site Office, http://www.nv.doe.gov/news&pubs/ photos&films/testfilms.htm.

32. *Film Declassification Project*, p. 9. The impressive Baker shot explosion is a favorite visual "atom bomb test" citation.

33. Weart, *Nuclear Fear*, p. 157.

34. "The Republic of the Marshall Islands and the United States: A Strategic Partnership," Embassy of the Republic of the Marshall Islands, Washington, DC, http://www.rmiembassyus.org/Exhib%20Intro.htm.

35. *Rodan*, dir. Honda Ishirō, 1956 (U.S. release version). DVD. Sony Music Entertainment, 2002.

36. "Republic of the Marshall Islands Changed Circumstances Petition to Congress," May 16, 2005, *Congressional Research Service Reports*, accessed through the *National Library for the Environment*, http://www.ncseonline. org/NLE/CRS/abstract.cfm?NLEid=64160.

9

"Our First Kiss Had a Radioactive Taste": Ohashi Yasuhiko's *Gojira* in Japan and Canada

Kevin J. Wetmore, Jr.

A young woman appears alone on stage. She speaks:

It was like I was all wrapped up in the faint scent of camellias. He said nothing, just looked deep into my eyes, as gentle as a spring day that goes on forever. . . .

I'm just an ordinary girl. All I want is to sit in some trendy café over a cup of coffee, nattering on about myself and trying to impress him; or squeeze his hand, pretending to be afraid at some boring horror flick; or cuddle up on a sandy beach at night and, swept away by the sweet waves and the salty breeze, give myself up to his mad kisses. I know it's banal, but still, I want dates like that. But I can't. Why, you ask? Because, well, after all, he's . . . Godzilla. . . .

He was such a late bloomer and our dates were always so platonic. But then one day—we'd been talking about family, where we grew up, whatever was on our minds, and then there was a lull in the conversation—he stuck his palm out, urged me to climb up, and brought me right up to his mouth. . . . It was our first kiss. It had a radioactive taste.[1]

So begins Ohashi Yasuhiko's *Gojira*, a romantic satire with giant monsters. The play is a love story about an 80-meter tall lizard and Yayoi, the teenaged "ordinary girl" who loves him. Yayoi brings Godzilla home to meet her family, who reject him as an unsuitable suitor, and Godzilla's family is not happy with the match either. After a fantasy sequence in which their wedding is interrupted by Tsuburaya Eiji, the two must decide whether or not to remain together. It is, as one reviewer of a Canadian production put it, "*Guess Who's Coming to Dinner* remade by Tōhō Pictures."[2] In this essay I will argue that Godzilla is as much the product of traditional Japanese theater as other, already acknowledged sources, and then explore Ohashi's play *Gojira* in Japan and Canada—there have been no American productions to date—and how the different productions have used the character of Godzilla to symbolize different things.

Godzilla has inherent roots in the traditional theater of Japan in two ways. First is through the use of traditional performance in the original film. In 1954's *Gojira*, three masked dancers perform a *kagura* dance to the accompaniment of flute and drum music. *Kagura* is a contraction of *kami gura* (seat of the gods) and is an indigenous performance tradition that grows out of Shintō and is traditionally performed at Shintō shrines. Beginning in the seventh century, *kagura* is performed music, dance, and pantomime that consists of two parts. The first is ritual preparation for the arrival of the *kami* (gods) and the second is "entertaining the illustrious divine guest" as well as the human audience.[3] In *Gojira*, the masked dance is presumably to entertain Godzilla and the gathered villagers. The ritual in the film, the audience is told, has replaced human sacrifices to Gojira. In other words, rather than offering up the sons and daughters of the village to appease the monster, the villagers now simply entertain him.

An old man explains to the reporter in the original version that the *kagura* piece is "all that we have left" of the memory of Gojira. Interestingly, in the American version with Raymond Burr, Burr's character attends the same performance, and is told by his interpreter that what he is witnessing is "a rare ceremony, one that is all but forgotten," which is simply not true.

The second way in which Godzilla is the child of the theater is that movie monsters grow out of their culture's stage traditions. In the West, for example, the film *Dracula* and its title character grew out of the stage play *Dracula*, based on Bram Stoker's novel, and its representation of the title character. Bela Lugosi had enormous success on stage before playing the count on film. In fact, the character of Dracula is based on Henry Irving, Bram Stoker's boss and the greatest actor at the turn of the century in England. Characters such as Dr Jekyll and Mr Hyde, Frankenstein's monster, and Dracula are all outgrowths of the theatrical naturalism of the late nineteenth century. They are all human monsters, so to speak, that are played realistically in keeping with modern Western theatrical tradition.

Godzilla, on the other hand, grows out of the kabuki tradition of giant monsters on stage, often played by actors in elaborate costumes. In plays such as *Tsuchigumo* by Kawatake Mokuami (1816–1893), based on a Noh play of the same name, a giant spider menaces the hero. In the dance play *Musume Dojoji*, a beautiful young woman is revealed to be a giant serpent. There are all sorts of large monsters in kabuki—giant octopi, giant snakes, and giant toads among others.[4] In *Tenjiku Tokubei Ikoku-Banashi* (The Tale of Tokubei from India, 1804), Tokubei the magician summons a giant fire-breathing toad to destroy the house of his enemy Sōkan. The stage direction reads:

> A toad of monstrous size crashes through the golden doors at the rear of the room, smoke billowing around it. . . . The toad raises its head, opens its mouth, props its front legs on the top step and breathes fire.[5]

Sōkan's soldiers attack the toad. The stage directions read, "The toad's eyes open and flames rush from its mouth, forcing the soldiers to retreat."[6] These stage directions echo a scene often repeated in Godzilla films, in which soldiers attack a giant monster, but are forced to retreat under the attack of fire breath, or sonic boom, or tremendous wind, or a cocooning silk stream, or some other supernatural power. The toad continues to breathe fire as it destroys the mansion, the curtain closing to reopen on a destroyed set and the bloody head of Sōkan in the toad's mouth. The toad is attacked again several times by the soldiers, but it is invulnerable to all attacks: "Victorious, the toad waddles confidently [stage] right and poses." Tokubei's toad is Godzilla's father, for his son often will, upon defeating his enemies, pose, almost *mie*-like, asserting his victory.[7]

Similarly, in *Masakado* (1836), Takiyashi, the daughter of an assassinated usurper, avenges her father by attacking the true emperor's troops with a giant toad that she summons. Takiyashi's toad attacks the palace and Mitsukuni, the leader of the troops sent by the emperor.[8] While, as William Tsutsui observes in *Godzilla on My Mind*, there were large monsters in the Western cinema that also influenced *Gojira*, most notably *King Kong* and *The Beast from 20,000 Fathoms*, these monsters were achieved through stop-motion animation, not through costumed actors.[9] More recently, in such plays as *Yashagaike* (Demon Pond), a *shimpa* play by Izumi Kyoka subsequently made into a film in 1979 by Shinoda Masahiro, men in costume represent animals and supernatural creatures.[10] In short, in Japanese theater there is a tradition of representing giant monsters and spirits by men in masks, makeup, and costume. *Kaijū* cinema is the direct descendant of these plays.

It seems only fair that if Godzilla begins in the theater he should return there, and return he did in 1987, courtesy of Ohashi Yasuhiko (b. 1956), one of the fourth generation of postwar angura playwrights, emerging in the mid-1980s.[11] Ohashi is strongly influenced by Tsuka Kōhei, the "foremost representative of the second generation" who "forged a playwriting style remarkable for its humorous, absurdist slant on the serious problems of youth," according to John Gillespie.[12] Ohashi did not train as a playwright, actor, or director, however, coming to theater by studying electrical engineering at Musashi Institute of Technology. As a result of this technical background, Ohashi "has created remarkable properties and designed bold stage sets . . . terrible winds blow, rough waters surge, burning red lava flows, or the living room suddenly transforms into a mountain of rubble filling the whole stage."[13] This penchant for technical spectacle and a desire to engage Japanese popular culture in new and imaginative ways makes *Gojira* an emblematic play for both Ohashi and 1980s Japanese theater. In 1983, Ohashi, Itō Yumiko, and others formed the Gekidan Riburesen (Freedom Boat Company). Its name is the combination of the Spanish word *libre* (freedom) with the Japanese *sen* (boat), and spelled with the characters for "separation," "wind," and "spirit."[14] The name is meant to suggest the sort of imaginative leaps that occur in plays like *Gojira*. In 1987, the company presented the play, Ohashi's fifth (he now has approximately 40) and it has been revived in Tokyo and has toured Japan so often that an estimated 100,000 people have seen the play at least once.

The plot is simple, although the references and stage effects are both complex. After the opening monologue with which I began this essay, Yayoi asks Godzilla to meet her family. The audience learns that when Yayoi was wandering on Mount Mihara she came across a sleeping Godzilla, and it was love at first sight. Meanwhile, Yayoi's family is rehearsing their first meeting with a potential spouse, though they are unaware of her current boyfriend. Father states, "I'll be the one who picks out the man my daughter will marry: somebody who stands out and fits in."[15] The audience is shown how Yayoi's family is superficial, obsessed with status, "theatrically self-conscious" in its behavior, shallow and judgmental, and living in the bubble economy of the late 1980s, seeks only material wealth and social status with no regard to culture or values.[16]

The audience is also introduced to Hayata, a policeman in love with Yayoi who is concerned she might now be seeing someone else. An on-stage reporter then announces that Godzilla is walking very carefully from Mihara to Oshima Motomachi, carefully avoiding stepping on houses. Then, Godzilla and Yayoi arrive at the house, marking the first time Godzilla is seen on stage. With "scrunching noises underfoot," Godzilla announces "Good evening everybody."[17] As they scream, he introduces himself, "You must be Yayoi's father. I'm really pleased to meet you. I'm Godzilla."[18]

The family then raises a series of objections to the relationship when Godzilla asks for Yayoi's hand in marriage. The first of these objections is religion, with which Godzilla counters that he is "non-sectarian, so shrine or church, either is fine with me." Hayata asks about children, and grand-mother, whose first love was a tadpole that then turned into a female frog, reveals that Godzilla already has a son. Mother and Father then state that marriage is therefore out of the question, and Godzilla rages, breathing fire.

Grandmother calls Mothra, here Godzilla's brother, who also disapproves of the couple. He argues that Godzilla's acting career with Tōhō is going nowhere and Godzilla should get a real job. (Mothra, by the way, is now a manufacturer of fine cocoons, and Gamera, we learn, has turned himself into a floating hotel!) Mothra's wife, Pigmon, also disapproves of the couple, and the scene segues into a wedding fantasy, which ends when Tsuburaya Eiji, the "father of the groom," throws the bouquet into Godzilla's face. He agrees with Yayoi's family and demands that Godzilla apologize. Godzilla rages again and the family joins Hayata and the defense forces in attacking Godzilla. Hayata is transformed into Ultraman and fights Godzilla, who finally announces that he is breaking off the engagement. He returns to Mount Mihara and the play comes full circle, ending with Yayoi alone on stage as the mountain erupts, revealing the whole thing to be Yayoi's fantasy—but she escapes the mountain and her family with a young man who looks like Godzilla.

The play won the prestigious Kishida Kunio Playwriting Award in 1987 and has been revived many times since. The critics as well delighted in the play. Watanabe Tamotsu, who has a reputation for being highly critical, wrote in *Shingeki* magazine, "It is a perfect play. A perfect narrative."[19] Senda

Akihiko, the drama critic of the *Asahi Shinbun* and leading authority on modern Japanese theater, heaped praises on the initial production, calling it "charming and original," "very exciting," "inspired silliness," and "a powerful and wholly successful production."[20] He relates, "on few occasions have I laughed as heartily as I did watching this delightful play."[21] High schools and college drama societies now perform the play regularly as well.

The play also read as a strong satire of values in Japan in the mid-1980s. The family carries out the traditional tea ceremony with bowls with cartoon characters on them. They value fame, fortune, and status, and not tradition, history, or love. The family is superficial. Japan's great prosperity has resulted in citizens who are "superficial, vulgar, greedy and hypocritical."[22] There is a "huge gap" between the stated value placed on propriety, tradition, and status and the actual behavior of the members of the family.[23] Yayoi's family is, in short, "a parody of everything that contemporary Japanese society has become."[24]

In contrast to the family, of course, is the figure of Godzilla. Respectful, polite, gentle, loving, and traditional, he is everything the family is not. The irony of the play is that Godzilla does not attack Japan, instead Godzilla represents everything that Japan has lost due to the same forces that arguably produced him. It is the family who are the monsters. Godzilla is simple, honorable, and, well, traditionally Japanese.

The play is emblematic of shōgekijo/angura theater of the 1980s. There are four major characteristics of 1980s theater in Japan that are also present in *Gojira*. The first is the sense of carnival: the 1980s modern theater in Japan was fun, playful, and treated serious subjects less seriously. In addition, it was also youth-oriented: the plays were created by and for young people and were meant to appeal to young audiences. The second characteristic is metatheatricality: the plays themselves were very much self-aware of themselves as theater and often referenced life as a kind of theater.[25] In *Gojira*, for example, the family "rehearses" the tea ceremony that will happen when Yayoi brings home a suitor. Grandmother objects to the props, arguing that the bowl they use for the ceremony was bought in a supermarket and has a picture of Doraemon the cartoon cat on it. "We've got to inject some realism into this scene," exclaims Father, to which a knowing Grandmother responds, "Who gives a shit about realism?"[26] Later, when the family discusses reasons for declining a suitor, an exasperated Grandmother asks, "Where's the drama, then? You gotta have drama!"[27] Not only is the family dramatically aware, but by extension the play also is as well.

In a related sense, the play is also aware of the mediatized existence of modern Japan. The Reporter, for example, asks the family to "make it more interesting" as he worries that the audience will change the channel if their conversation with Godzilla is boring. Likewise, the progress of Godzilla as he makes his way to Yayoi's house is constantly updated by a media driven as much by commercial needs as by truth or facts. Even news must be entertaining.

Third, the theater of the 1980s is intertextual and referential.[28] The very title *Gojira* automatically links the play to an entire world of popular culture outside of the theater. The play is highly referential to *kaijū eiga*: Mothra is Godzilla's brother and the best man at his fantasy wedding, Pigmon is Mothra's wife, Ultraman makes an appearance, and nearly all of the major monsters are referenced, as is Tsuburaya Eiji, the special effects maestro of the 1954 film *Gojira*, who puts in an appearance as "Father of the Groom." Yayoi's younger sisters become The Peanuts at one point, the pop music duo that appeared in *Mothra*, and sing the nonsense "Mothra Song" from that movie. The play is, in that sense, a cult play, one in which the audience must be aware of the references in order to understand their meanings. Senda also argues that the play forms an intertext with Tsuka Kōhei's plays, especially *Shuppatsu* (Departure, 1974) and *Shogai* (Life, 1975), as both are family dramas rooted in comedy and irony. *Gojira* is a conscious imitation of Tsuka; Senda notes that "the play quotes Tsuka's plays with the same reverence that it quotes monster movies."[29]

A related fourth and final characteristic is that 1980s plays engage Japanese popular culture on its own terms, seeking to reproduce other forms and genres in theatrical form. Uchino Tadashi states that 1980s theater in Japan "had a strong affinity to other subcultural genres."[30] For example, Kokami Shoji's *Asahi no yo no Yuhi o Tsurete* (A Sunset Like Dawn, 1981) is set in a toy factory and engages computer games, and Kawamura Takeshi's *Nippon Wars* (1984), which concerns warrior androids who are given emotions, plays very much like early anime, manga, or video games.[31]

In a lecture given at the Japan Foundation in Toronto for the opening of the Crow's Theatre production, Senda posits that "one might say that [*Gojira*] typifies the modern drama of the eighties in Japan."[32] Senda argues that there are two major characteristics in *Gojira*. The first is that even though the play is based on a spectacular film, "there is no reliance on elaborate effects and extensive stage devices."[33] Instead, as he argues, "the play depends on the audience's imagination to make invisible things visible."[34] The second is that the enormous monsters of *kaijū* films are shrunk down to "normal" size, which reflects the cultural background of the 1980s: things that used to be huge, important, and perhaps even powerfully frightening are "shrunk down" and made commonplace and small. This reduction also inherently results in an inspired, if silly, comedy that focuses on a small Godzilla that symbolizes the shrinkage of Japan and its values.

It is this humor that served as the bridge by which a play that is ultimately highly referential to Japanese popular culture and at heart a satire of Japanese values in the mid-1980s was able to cross the Pacific to be produced in translation in North America. *Gojira* was first translated into English by John Gillespie as part of the Japan Playwrights Association's *Half a Century of Japanese Theater* project. It was this version, revised and with additional translation by Aoyagi Toshi and Susan Doyon, that was used in a staged reading by Toronto's Crow's Theatre in January 2002 at the Japan Foundation in Toronto. The staged readings "performed to a full house and

[were] enthusiastically received by the audience," resulting in a commitment to a full staging of the work by Crow's Theatre.[35] The positive response also convinced Ohashi to allow a full production of his play. Grant money was received to create a new, stageworthy translation, provided the translator was Canadian. Enter Professor M. Cody Poulton of the University of Victoria in British Columbia, who had extensive experience in translating both modern and traditional Japanese dramas.

Jim Millan states that despite the inherent Japaneseness of the piece, the "absurdist style and the fame of the character" would prove a draw.[36] The larger challenge to playwright, translator, and director, however, was to bridge the cultural gap between 1987 Japan and Canada a decade and a half later. "There's a whole slew of culturally loaded concepts and ideas," explained Poulton.[37] A decision was also made to create two versions of the play, one for performance by Crow's Theatre and one for publication. Ohashi flew to Toronto in the summer of 2002 to work with Poulton, Millan, Doyon, and Aoyagi, going over the script line by line to ensure both accuracy of translation as well as theatrical effectiveness.

In order to contextualize the play for North American audiences, the original intention was to connect the text to the 1950s mentality in America, as director Millan put it, "the 'keep up with the Joneses' middle class" mind-set, combined with the crisis engendered when the daughter asserts her own independence of father, family, and fiancé.

Poulton also sees as the major theme of the work an allegory of "other-ness": a protagonist who wants to be accepted for himself by the mainstream culture and who is rejected for his differences. Toronto, he observes, is a multicultural city (over 50 percent non-Caucasian), and the cast was multi-ethnic, including Korean, Chinese, Irish, African American, and Euro-Canadian performers. The focus of the production would be on interracial attraction and the conflict that it creates within families and within society. "The little references to Japanese pop culture were not so important."[38] The Crow's Theatre production featured John O'Callaghan in the title role. O'Callaghan, an Irish actor, played Godzilla as a lounge lizard. O'Callaghan's monster was shy and reserved, wishing only to be liked and accepted by his fiancée's family.

Overall, the reviews were mixed.[39] Some praised the theatricality of the production. *NOW Toronto* singled out the strength of the performers as the anchor of the show and spoke very highly of the designs, but felt that the "stylistic shifts" were awkward, as was the translation.[40] The *National Post* called the production "a thin slice of camp whose only gesture toward social comment is the suggestion that Japanese families have become very like American ones, or at least like American ones on TV" and in the title of the review referred to the play as "cultish camp."[41] Several reviewers focused on their own ignorance of Japanese popular culture and Japan, arguing that those aspects of the play made it difficult to penetrate as a Canadian audience member.

Subsequently, Mob Hit Productions, called "one of Calgary's more dynamic and interesting young theatre companies," under the direction of

Lawrence Leong produced the play in May 2004.[42] Leong wanted to "create a human representation of a monster to Yayoi's conservative parents."[43] Taking inspiration from a Learning Channel special on circus freaks, the Mob Hit Godzilla was played as "a tattooed punk/death metal guy," played by Dan Perrott with simulated tattoos of lizard scales and fire, allowing him "to be a 'monster' when he needed to be, and a human when he needed to be one, too."[44]

Like Ohashi, Leong relied upon technology to enhance the experience and draw a greater connection to both the cinematic heritage of Godzilla and the popular culture of Japan of which it is a part. Both pre-recorded and live projected video were used, including a video credit sequence, simulating the opening of a *kaijū eiga*. "I wanted to give the audience a theatrical cinematic experience—both cinema and theater at the same time."[45] One reviewer acknowledged that "the video element seems especially apt in a play whose main character is trapped between seeing himself as human and being seen by others as simply a monstrous creation of film come to life."[46] In this sense, the Calgary production is perhaps close to both the North American conception of Godzilla as "wacky movies" and Ohashi's theater of elaborate technological effects blended with simplicity of staging. Unlike the Toronto production, which focused on the human drama, the Calgary production was deemed a success by both the company and the local critics.[47]

Interestingly, given the connection between 1980s theater in Japan and manga, both productions openly referenced anime, connecting one older Japanese pop culture phenomenon with a more recent one. The Calgary production incorporated anime into the production. Crow's Theatre's poster for the production puts Godzilla as a silhouette in the background. Foregrounded is an anime-style young girl (Yayoi). As the Toronto poster indicates, the play should be read not necessarily in terms of *kaijū eiga* but rather in terms of contemporary Japanese popular culture, especially anime and video games, continuing the trend from the 1980s of linking the theater to other subcultural forms.

In this case, however, "anime" and "manga" become synecdoches for all things Japanese. The Canadian audiences experience the play as yet another unfathomable Japanese narrative in which characters transform into monsters, costumed warriors, or other "weird things," deep emotions give way to heightened proclamations of one's inner feelings, and the inevitable climax is a showdown between two supernatural beings. Manga and anime are both way in and distancing effect.

As almost everyone involved in either production freely admits, neither the audiences nor even the artists knew the Japanese cultural references in the play. One reviewer even suggested that no knowledge of Japanese culture was necessary as the comedy carried the play.[48] Another proudly stated that he "could not have told [Godzilla] and King Kong apart."[49] From Tsuka to Ultraman, the cultural background of the play was not a significant part of either Canadian production. While both casts did research into both the films and Japanese marital customs, neither of the directors were fans or even familiar with the Godzilla canon.[50] Many in both casts knew "Godzilla" without ever having seen any of the films. It is not necessary to have seen a single Godzilla film to "get" Godzilla, as he is a cultural presence in North America. But what one "gets" is not Godzilla, but the epiphenomena and not an authentic Godzilla. The result is a Godzilla that is more a North American conception of Godzilla than the Japanese monster. As Leong says, "we told the story from our own cultural references."[51] The Toronto production had a lobby display to aid audience members under 30 or who were not Godzilla fans, but all of the intertextuality of the original in Japan in the late 1980s is lost in the move across the ocean. In other words, Ohashi's play's original meanings and references were irrelevant in the Canadian productions. In Canada, Ohashi's referencing of Gojira is not the referencing of a canon of films known to the audience; it is, instead, the referencing the epiphenomenal Godzilla, the pop Godzilla.

Interestingly, many reviewers of both productions identified the Japan of Ohashi's play with North America, especially the United States, of the 1980s. As Kamal Al-Solaylee writes, "it isn't all that different . . . material wealth is prized above all else, trashy TV rules the land."[52] It is the interspecies love affair, the concern with otherness, the condemnation of shallowness, and the indictment of the media that become the focus, effectively changing a social satire into a romantic comedy with the occasional social comment.

Millan states that the Japanese original is almost irrelevant, as the production was a Canadian production for a Canadian audience through which "we hope to see our own circumstances more clearly." Yet he also acknowledges that the audience did not see themselves in the play: "it was exotic and funny but a curiosity piece."[53] Ironically, despite the erasure of much of what was truly Japanese in the play in order to make it accessible to Canadian audiences, the play still seemed "Japanese," and Japanese culture remains a distant Other, even when linked with the familiar.

Perhaps an apt metaphor for Canadian productions (and future productions in the United States) of Gojira is what happened to the 1954 film version of Gojira. The Japanese version was seen by Hollywood producers as being incomprehensible to Westerners when taken on its own terms, so it was edited, had footage added, and "Westernized," therefore setting an image of Japan different than that of the Japanese original. Yet, despite the attempt to make it "familiar," the film remains distanced and Othered. Godzilla became a synecdoche for Japan. Just as the Godzilla films would be changed, sometimes radically, by the move across the Pacific, so, too, does this Gojira see itself changed for North American audiences, both in terms of meaning and in terms of the Japan represented to that audience. Cushman laments that "Hollywood has added to America's imperialist record by appropriating the character, but deleting the social comment."[54] Arguably, North American productions of Gojira are in danger of doing the same thing.

Uchino Tadashi, in his survey of Japan's 1980s theater culture, notes that "under the guise of postmodern universality, contemporary Japanese theatre was able to be unselfconsciously xenophobic."[55] Perhaps the same holds true in *Gojira* as well. Just as Yayoi's family thinks they know Godzilla and because of what they think they know they fear and reject him, in much the same way we think we know Godzilla and can see in him the worst of Japan. But Godzilla is so much more than the worst things he's done and the best things he's done. He may have a human heart, but in the end, he is still Godzilla.

NOTES

I would like to thank M. Cody Poulton, John Gillespie, Senda Akihiko, Samuel L. Leiter, Lawrence Leong, and Jim Millan for their time, insights, materials, and willingness to be interviewed on the subject of Godzilla. I would also like to thank Yamamoto Takahiro for his assistance with translations from Japanese. This essay would have been impossible without their many kindnesses.

1. Ohashi Yasuhiko, *Godzilla*, trans. M. Cody Poulton (Winnipeg: Scirocco, 2002), pp. 19–20. The play was originally published in Japan: Ohashi Yasuhiko, *Gojira* (Tokyo: Hakusuisha, 1988). It was originally translated into English as Ohashi Yasuhiko, *Godzilla*, in *Half a Century of Japanese Theater III: 1980s, Part 1*, trans. John Gillespie, ed. Japan Playwrights Association (Tokyo: Kinokuniya, 2001).

2. Martin Morrow, "Godzilla vs. the Parents," *Ffwd Weekly* 9:21 (April 29, 2004), n.p.

3. Benito Ortolani, *The Japanese Theatre: From Shamanistic Ritual to Contemporary Plurality*, rev. ed. (Princeton, NJ: Princeton University Press, 1995), p. 14.

4. I am grateful to Samuel L. Leiter for confirming this in an email dated May 17, 2004. In one recently revived play, Ichikawa Enosuke III "battl[es] the creature underwater, even stuffing one of its tentacles back into itself."

5. Tsuruyu Nanboku IV, *Tenjiku Tokubei Ikoku-Banashi* (The Tale of Tokubei from India), in *Kabuki Plays on Stage, Volume 3: Darkness and Desire, 1804–1864*, trans. Paul B. Kennelly, ed. James R. Brandon and Samuel L. Leiter (Honolulu: University of Hawai'i Press, 2002), p. 46.

6. Ibid.

7. Ibid., p. 48. Mie is "[a] picturesque and striking pose taken by an actor at a climactic moment in a play in order to make a powerful impression on the audience. The movements made in assuming the pose culminate in a rhythmic snapping of the head, as the actor produces a glaring expression with his eyes." Samuel L. Leiter, *Kabuki Encyclopedia: An English Language Version of Kabuki Jiten* (Westport, CT: Greenwood, 1979), p. 232.

8. For an English language version, see Takarada Jusuke et al., *Masakado*, in *Kabuki Plays on Stage, Volume 3*, trans. Leonard L. Pronko.

9. William M. Tsutsui, *Godzilla on My Mind* (New York: Palgrave Macmillan, 2004), pp. 19–20.

10. Interestingly, *Demon Pond* was also translated into English by *Gojira* translator M. Cody Poulton, who has also written the only full-length study of Izumi in English: *Spirits of Another Sort* (Ann Arbor: University of Michigan Center for Japanese Studies, 2001). The film version used men in costume to play the creatures of the demon pond and starred famous kabuki actor Bandō Tamasaburō. More recently, film director Miike Takashi directed *Yashagaike*, his first stage production, at the Parco Theatre in Shibuya, Tokyo in the fall of 2004.

Shimpa is "New school drama, a form of theatre which developed after the Meiji Restoration as an attempt to modernize and Westernize Japan's drama independently from the kabuki tradition." Ortolani, *The Japanese Theatre*, p. 318.

11. Senda Akihiko identifies the generations of angura playwrights as being first (1960s), second (early 1970s), third (late 1970s and early 1980s), and fourth (mid-1980s on). Senda Akihiko, "Artistic Profile," in *The World Encyclopedia of Contemporary Theatre Volume 5: Asia/Pacific*, ed. Don Rubin, Chua Soo Pong, Ravi Chaturvedi, Ramendu Majumdar, Minoru Tanokura, and Katherine Brisbane (London: Routledge, 1998), p. 229.

12. See John K. Gillespie, "Ohashi Yasuhiko" in *Encyclopedia of Modern Drama*, ed. Gabrielle Cody and Evert Sprinchorn (Danbury, CT: Grolier, forthcoming).

13. Okano Hirofumi "Introduction," in *Half a Century of Japanese Theater III: 1980s, Part 1*, trans. Mari Boyd, p. 133.

14. Information on Ohashi is taken from Gillespie "Ohashi," Senda, "Artistic Profile" in Senda Akihiko, *The Voyage of Contemporary Japanese Theatre*, trans. J. Thomas Rimer, (Honolulu: University of Hawai'i Press, 1997), and Senda Akihiko "Lecture: *Godzilla's* Perspective, Japanese Theatre from the Eighties Onward (A Summary)" ("Kōen: '*Gojira*' kara mita 1980 nendai ikō no Nihon no engeki (yōshi)"), Japan Foundation, Toronto, Canada, September 23, 2002.

15. Ohashi, *Godzilla*, trans. Poulton, p. 24.

16. Senda, *Voyage*, p. 268.

17. Ohashi, *Godzilla*, trans. Poulton, p. 34.

18. Ibid., p. 36.

19. Quoted in Uchida Yōichi, "The 1980s in the Context of Japanese Theater History," in *Half a Century of Japanese Theater III: 1980s, Part 1*, trans. Mari Boyd, p. 9.

20. Senda, *Voyage*, pp. 266, 268, 269.

21. Ibid., p. 268.

22. M. Cody Poulton, "Translator's Introduction," in Ohashi, *Godzilla*, trans. Poulton, p. 15.

23. Ibid.

24. Ibid.

25. Senda, *Voyage*, pp. 10–11.

26. Ohashi, *Godzilla*, trans. Poulton, p. 5.

27. Ibid., p. 27.

28. Senda, *Voyage*, p. 10.

29. Ibid., p. 268.

30. Uchino Tadashi, "Images of Armageddon: Japan's 1980's Theatre Culture," *The Drama Review* 44:1 (2000), p. 88.

31. Senda, "Artistic Profile," p. 237.

32. Senda's lecture was written in Japanese and was translated for him in Toronto. He was kind enough to send me a copy of the original, and the translations in this article are my own.

33. Senda, "Artistic Profile," p. 237.

34. Ibid.

35. "Godzilla Storms Stage at Factory Theatre Studio Café," *Insight* 22 (Autumn 2002), p. 4.

36. Jim Millan, email to author, June 23, 2004.

37. Quoted in Sue Balint, "Monster Mash," *The Eye*, http://www.eye.net/eye/issue_09.12.02/arts/godzilla.html, September 12, 2002. Accessed November 11, 2002.

38. M. Cody Poulton, email to author, 2003.

39. In addition to the reviews cited below, see also Sid Adilman, "Godzilla: Not Your Average Love Story," *Toronto Star*, September 14, 2002, p. H2; Steven Berketo, "Monster Madness," *Toronto Stage.com*, http://www.torontostage.com/reviews/ godzilla.html. Accessed September 30, 2002; Bruce Raymond, "A Very Likable Godzilla," *Tandem*, http://www.tandemnews.com/viewstory.php?storyid=1811. Accessed September 30, 2002.

40. Jon Kaplan, "Theatre Review: Monster Ball," *NOW Toronto*, http://www.nowtoronto.com/issues/2002–09–26/stage_theatrereviews2.php, September 26–October 2, 2002. Accessed September 30, 2002.

41. Robert Cushman, "Godzilla versus Mother-in-Law Falls Flat as Cultish Camp," *National Post*, September 23, 2002, p. AL4.

42. Bob Clark, "Discovering the Kinder, Gentler Side of Godzilla," *Calgary Herald*, May 7, 2004, p. D9.

43. Lawrence Leong, email to author, October 5, 2004.

44. Ibid.

45. Quoted in Morrow, "Godzilla," n.p.

46. Clark, "Discovering," p. D9.

47. See Clark "Discovering"; Morrow, "Godzilla"; Bob Clark, "Godzilla: A Film Within a Play," *Calgary Herald*, May 5, 2004, p. C5; and Graeme Morton, "Can Girl, Giant Lizard find true love?" *Calgary Herald*, May 6, 2004, p. N1.

48. Kaplan, "Monster Ball."

49. Cushman, "Godzilla," p. AL4.

50. Jim Millan, email to the author, June 23, 2004; Lawrence Leong, email to the author, October 5, 2004; and Morton, "Giant Lizard," p. N1.

51. Leong, email.

52. Kamal Al-Solaylee, "On Stage: Godzilla," *The Eye*, September 26, 2002, http://www.eye.net/eye/issue/issue_09.26.02/arts/onstage.html. Accessed September 30, 2002.

53. Millan, email.

54. Cushman, "Godzilla," p. AL4.

55. Uchino, "Images," p. 86.

10

Godzilla Meets Super Kyōgen, or How a Dinosaur Saved the World

Eric C. Rath

As someone who has written about the lives of performers and their theories of acting, I like to imagine that the man wearing the Godzilla suit in the first movie was an actor who worried about his character's "motivation" as he smashed small models of buildings and roared at airplanes. If he was feeling philosophical, he may have even considered how his character's action could be interpreted as a warning about nuclear fallout or environmental degradation, or as a critique of modernity. Whether the movie *Godzilla* embodies these qualities is something other chapters in this book examine, but these themes are certainly present in a different story about a man in a lizard outfit, the so-called super kyōgen *(sūpā kyōgen)* play "The King and the Dinosaur" *(Osama to kyōryū)* which premiered on April 8, 2003.

Kyōgen is a theatrical form with six centuries of history but it still retains its humor. Kyōgen's usual spotlight is on ordinary people as they contend with each other. Husbands arguing with wives, masters tricked by their servants, shills, and shysters—these are the people who populate the kyōgen stage and make it a real comic relief for audiences who have sat through several hours of the mysterious grace of Noh drama that precedes performances of kyōgen.

Just as the appearance of a man in a Godzilla suit meant something new for Japanese cinema 50 years ago, the appearance of a dinosaur signals something new to the classical world of kyōgen. Kyōgen is a "traditional" art as defined by its codified gestures, classical language, and set repertoire of several hundred plays that are several hundred years old. Kyōgen's dinosaur challenges these traditions in many ways, the most important of which being the play's critique of U.S. foreign policy. In contrast to plays in the classical repertoire that merely suggest social defiance when the servant tricks his master or in the buffoonery of feudal lords, kyōgen's "super" dinosaur carries specific warnings about nuclear warfare and globalization as it strikes a one-two punch of social satire. "The King and the Dinosaur" was written on the eve of the American invasion of Iraq and it premiered two weeks after that invasion took place; moreover, it was intended to be an indictment of U.S. policy. The king is a caricature of George W. Bush who is depicted as a dictator garbed in the robes of democracy, whereas the dinosaur has not come as a destroyer but as a philosopher who ultimately abandons appeals to reason to use magic to avert global catastrophe.

This chapter begins with an overview of "The King and the Dinosaur"; then, it introduces its controversial author Umehara Takeshi (b. 1925). Before he became a playwright, Umehara made his reputation as a reader of Western philosophy and as a prolific scholar of Japanese studies, becoming a very public intellectual in the process. Unlike the classical kyōgen plays in the modern repertoire whose authorship is uncertain—most of these plays are anonymous and probably the work of many creators—Umehara's "super kyōgen" is as much about the author's philosophy as it is about the conflict between a king and a dinosaur. Consequently, the second part of this chapter explores Umehara's play in the context of his ideas. My goal in drawing out the subtext in kyōgen's dinosaur is to cast light on the social and political readings of this creature on stage, and I hope that this will facilitate interpretations of the dinosaur's grandfather on the silver screen.

THE KING, THE DINOSAUR, AND PRESIDENT BUSH

Wearing a costume that is a collision of American patriotic iconography with the garb of classical Japanese drama, King Tottarā, the protagonist in "The King and the Dinosaur," is the ruler of Sunland. Sunland is one of several nations named for planets that are in a loose coalition, and it is the most powerful of these, as King Tottarā explains:

> My Sunland is biggest, the broadest nation in the whole of the world. Sunland is the strongest. It has never ever lost a war in the past. The biggest in the world, the strongest in the world is Sunland, and I am its king. Because of all that, I am the grandest person in the world, the person who is closest to being a god. Well, wait a minute, maybe I am a god. Ha ha ha.[1]

The king summons his "greatest love," the character Money, who wears a U.S. dollar sign for a hat. Money calls his own followers with a magic spell: "Come here. Come here. Hey guys. Come. Globalization, globalization, globalization. . . ."

After the monies arrive, the king welcomes them; but then he declares:

> Money alone won't let me rule the world. For that I need a strong army. If I have an army, I also need weapons. Airplanes and battleships and H-Bombs are also necessary. Hey Money, summon those for me.[2]

Money summons Army, Battleship, Airplane, and H-Bomb who appear. The king greets each one, but shows special affection for the H-Bomb. H-Bomb returns his love, stating:

> I was born in your majesty's country. And now, I have a thousand or ten thousand times the power as when I was born. Your majesty, don't worry. I am your majesty's loyal servant forever. By your majesty's command I will go anywhere. At your command I can always annihilate a city, a country, or even the entire world.[3]

Once he has all of these forces assembled, the king is convinced of his power, but he also knows that something is missing from his arsenal, namely Justice. He declares:

> No matter how much money there is and even if we have an H-Bomb, without Justice, Sunland will not gain the respect of all of the countries of the world. No, without Justice, money and military force become evils instead. Indeed, I wonder what's the best way to get Justice?[4]

A mysterious Crow wielding a scythe appears and tells the king that he can obtain Justice easily because "might makes right." Crow explains: "If you have a lot of money and you have a powerful military force, then you will win the war and Justice will naturally be the outcome."[5] Crow suggests that the king summon Justice with money, and if that does not work, then he should use force. With the help of H-Bomb, Justice is cajoled and threatened into bowing before the king.

At this point, the king is ready to call it a day, but then his Prime Minister and a conniving capitalist named Big Businessman Mokusuke appear. They convince the king to put his stockpile of weapons to use by invading the Land of the Vengeful Spirits (onryō no kuni). The minister and the businessman explain the economic benefits of a war. However, reasons of national security are what really grab the king's attention. Big Businessman warns:

> The Land of the Vengeful Spirits bears a grudge toward Sunland and so they are murdering the people of Sunland all over. This is all the work of the king of the Land of the Vengeful Spirits. In order to preserve the peace of Sunland, you must wage war on the Land of the Vengeful Spirits.[6]

Hearing rumors of war, the allies of Sunland, the Kings of Earthland, Moonland, and Saturnland, enter. King Tottarā tells the other kings that he has decided on war no matter what and that Sunland will act unilaterally if it must. The King of Earthland quickly joins the coalition, Saturnland's king wavers and questions the necessity for war; ultimately, he decides to remain neutral in the war but promises to help in the reconstruction. The King of Moonland relies on a flair for ambiguity to remain allied with King Tottarā and at the same time not taking a clear stand for or against the invasion.

Before proceeding further, it might be insightful in understanding Umehara's message to stop the play and examine the characters who have already appeared. Playwright Umehara has commented that he intended his play as a critique of President Bush's invasion of Iraq.[7] When Umehara wrote the play, this invasion had yet to take place, but as the play entered into rehearsals, the prospect that the invasion would actually take place was very much on the minds of the crew and cast. The original posters and program cover art for the performance at the National Noh Theater by the artist Yokō Tadanori contained a written appeal for peace. One of the actors, Shigeyama Dōji (b. 1983) who played the role of the Airplane, explained in an interview: "This kyōgen was made just before the decision to invade Iraq. Watching the daily news gave me a lot to think about."[8] By the time the play opened, the invasion of Iraq was in its second week.

Umehara explains that President Bush was the inspiration for the character of King Tottarā, but the name also rings of the word "totalitarianism." Umehara indicates that the name itself is a combination of the names of Japan's infamous wartime general Tōjō Hideki and Adolph Hitler.[9] To make these associations clearer, artist Yokō Tadanori who created the costumes for the play, added a Hitler-mustache for the king and decorated his throne with swastikas and human bones.[10] A reference to Charlie Chaplin's movie *The Great Dictator* appears in the form of a globe suspended over the stage that makes a dramatic discharge at the end of the play.[11]

If Sunland is America, then its ally Earthland is England. Saturnland, where "stubbornness" is a tradition might be France but it is probably Germany since it is a land that once had its own dictator and suffered from war. The ambiguous Moonland is Japan: it was once called Sunland (i.e., the land of the rising sun), but after a war it lost the title to the new Sunland of King Tottarā. The King of Moonland explains, "I am the king whose country once battled Sunland, was defeated and gave up the name of Sunland to the [new] land of the sun. However, thanks to the [new] Sunland, after the war we experienced tremendous economic growth."[12] In light of this debt, the King of Moonland pledges to keep his mouth shut in the event of war, explaining that not expressing an opinion is a long spiritual tradition of his people. Money, the Crow, Big Businessman and the Prime Minster are the unidentified characters haunting the Bush White House. Justice, it should be noted, wears capes and tights in a design reminiscent of Superman except that instead of a letter "S," Justice's uniform is emblazoned with the Chinese character *sei* from the word *seigi*, meaning justice.

Returning now to the plot of the play, King Tottarā's coalition force departs to prepare for the invasion, but the king's rest is soon interrupted by his wife the queen and his daughters. The women have learned of the king's infatuation with Money and weapons, and they beat the king. Here, Umehara acknowledges borrowing a page from the ancient Greek playwright Aristophanes's *Lysistrata* when he has the queen threaten to divorce the king if he goes to war.[13] Though fearful of his wife and daughters, the king is still poised to go to battle.

Enter the dinosaur who introduces himself to the king as Tottarāzaurus. King Tottarā is astonished at the similarity of their names. The dinosaur responds that he is in fact the King's ancestor who has miniaturized himself 20 times in order not to frighten him. The king admits that the dinosaur resembles his younger brother—which is an inside joke since the actors playing these roles, Shigeyama Sensaku (b. 1919) and Sennojō (b. 1923) are actually brothers.

Although the dinosaur looks ferocious with claws that could kill creatures tens of times his size, the dinosaur explains that humans are much more deadly: "Human hands make bows and make guns and have killed many creatures haven't they? Not only that they can kill many of their own kind."[14] However, the dinosaur has not come to devour the king, but to convince him of the destructive nature of mankind despite its pretensions of "civilization." He does this by telling the king the story of the fall of the dinosaurs who fought with each other endlessly until a meteor destroyed them all. While the other dinosaurs were busy killing each other, the ancestors of Tottarāzaurus hid in a cave behind the king's castle where they dwelled peacefully for centuries. Like Godzilla, Tottarāzaurus was awakened by man as a warning of humanity's hubris and destructive nature.

Tottarāzaurus tells his story in dance and song that makes the king faint. Seizing this opportunity, the dinosaur possesses the king's mind and commands him to drop a bomb of excrement instead of a nuclear one. Though the king is at first embarrassed and deserted by his advisors when the poop hits the world, his decision to avoid war garners him the "No-Hell" (nōheru) Prize and the loving admiration of his wife, daughters, and humanity.

HOW KYŌGEN BECAME SŪPĀ

"The King and the Dinosaur" is Umehara Takeshi's third "super kyōgen" play. His first play, "Mudskippers" (Mutsugorō) debuted in December 2001 and tackles themes of environmental degradation: the ghosts of mudskippers and other creatures deride a businessman and priest playing golf on their former swamp-home. Umehara's second play, "Human Clone Namashima" (Kurōn ningen Namashima) that debuted in April 2002 tells the story of a fictional Japanese baseball team, the Gaigants (jyaigantsu), and their attempts to overcome the loss of their strongest players to the American major leagues by cloning their famous star player Namashima. The character Namashima is based on Tokyo Giants manager Nagashima Shigeo and the play comments on what has been called the "brawn drain" of Japanese baseball players such as Hideo Nomo, Ichirō Suzuki, and Hideki "Godzilla" Matsui to the Seattle Mariners, New York Yankees, and other teams in the United States.[15]

These three "super kyōgen" are predated by several "super kabuki" plays Umehara wrote, and the term "super"—sūpā in Japanese—was first used in this genre by the acclaimed kabuki actor Ichikawa Ennosuke III (b. 1939) who coined it. Ennosuke apparently admired Umehara's research and requested that he write a play with "the depth of Shakespeare" and "the scale of Wagner." The kabuki actor dubbed the finished work a "super kabuki" as an indication of his admiration for it and because the accepted term for new kabuki plays, *shin kabuki*, was too weak in Ennosuke's view.[16] The script for this play, titled "Yamato Takeru," needed considerable work before it could be performed. Ennosuke comments that he had to cut out more than half of the dialogue. Yet, Umehara's story about the first loser-hero in Japanese history, Yamato Takeru, which he adapted from the eighth-century chronicle *Kojiki*, proved to be a winning formula when combined with Ennosuke's flamboyant staging and acrobatics for which he is famous. When it debuted in 1986, the play ran for six months, which is a phenomenal feat in the world of kabuki where plays change monthly. Adding to the play's appeal were its use of modern, as opposed to early modern language, its spectacular staging, a recorded musical score of one hundred instruments, and the costumes designed by Mōri Tomio, one of Issey Miyake's leading designers. In 1991, Ennosuke's company performed Umehara's second "super kabuki" "Oguri" about the fictional hero Oguri Hangon. Umehara's third "super kabuki" "Ōkuninushi" debuted in 1997, and Ennosuke had performed other "super kabuki" by different authors. The successes of these plays beginning with "Yamato Takeru" have ensured that Ennosuke has the financial support of Shōchiku, the most important production company for kabuki in Japan, for any play he wishes to perform in the future.[17] It should be noted that although these "super" plays broke some artistic conventions in the conservative kabuki world, they were still acted by an all-male cast of hereditary kabuki actors.[18] Given the commercial success of "super kabuki," it is easy to understand why Shigeyama Sennojō asked Umehara to try his hand at writing a "super kyōgen."

While "super kabuki" is characterized by the energetic stunt work of Ichikawa Ennosuke, much of the interest generated by Umehara's "super kyōgen" stems from a sense of anachronism when classical theater is made to comment on current events. For instance, in "Human Clone Namashima," Yokō Tadanori added baseballs to the painting of the pine tree—an icon that adorns every Noh stage—and he produced kyōgen versions of baseball hats, bats, and gloves. Regular audiences to Noh and kyōgen are aware of the art's conventions and laugh when they are broken as when National Living Treasure Shigeyama Sensaku appears with a golf club at the beginning of the play "Mutsugorō" and later cries "hole in one."[19]

These innovations and the associations with successful kabuki productions warrant the use of the term "super" as a contrast with classical kyōgen and modern *(shinsaku)* kyōgen. The Shigeyama family of kyōgen actors who commissioned and performed in all three "super kyōgen" plays have created several *shinsaku* kyōgen including a play about UFOs, "The Fox and the Spaceman" *(Kitsune to ūchūjin)*, in 1979. Umehara's plays differ on several accounts from these modern works. Umehara wrote all three plays in modern Japanese, and it was up to the Shigeyama family, particularly Director

Sennojō, to adapt Umehara's words into the classical language of kyōgen. Yet, as Sennojō explained, it was precisely Umehara's lack of familiarity with kyōgen conventions that made his plays successful.[20] Umehara appears to have been a quick study of the genre for he recognized the power of kyōgen's abstract, rather than realistic, style of representation that enables personifications like hydrogen bombs to take life on stage.[21] In his contribution to the program notes, an essay entitled "Say, Kyōgen is Certainly a Useful Drama" (*Kyōgen tte hontō ni benri na shibai desu ne*), Sennojō confirmed that with the exception of radio drama and Japanese anime, only kyōgen theater could produce "The King and the Dinosaur."[22]

Another defining feature of "super kyōgen" is the large cast of performers involved, as Shigeyama Sensaku noted.[23] The debut performance of "The King and the Dinosaur" had a cast of 13 actors not including the musicians and stage assistants (*kōken*); 11 of these performers were members of the Shigeyama family, and the remaining 2 were professional disciples of the Shigeyamas who regularly performed with them. The Shigeyamas, who are Ōkura school actors living in Kyoto, are fortunate in the male-dominated world of Noh and kyōgen theater to have a large family of sons (in contrast to the leadership of the Izumi school where the former leader's two daughters face considerable discrimination), and that their family gets along well together (unlike the feuding Nomura brothers of the Izumi school). A large family of actors who live in close proximity and play well together provides the theatrical requisite for mounting "super kyōgen" plays, making for a feat that the Shigeyama's rivals would have great difficulty duplicating. Like Ichikawa Ennosuke of kabuki, long before "super kyōgen," the Shigeyamas have established a reputation since the 1950s as theatrical rule-breakers by performing kyōgen adaptations of folk plays, collaborating with performers from other backgrounds including the all-female Takarazuka Revue Theater and ancient court music (*gagaku*), and most recently appearing in television commercials. For their innovations, the Shigeyamas were almost expelled from the kyōgen world in 1963. However, as kyōgen specialist Jonah Salz writes, they "stood their ground . . . and their subsequent publicity gained them supporters for their 'democratic' reforms."[24]

"Super kyōgen" plays may address current affairs, but Umehara considers his kyōgen to be revivals of the original spirit of kyōgen when they were first created in the Muromachi period (1336–1473). Muromachi Japan, he asserts, allowed for more social mobility and criticism that are reflected in classical kyōgen plays. According to his periodization, the subsequent Tokugawa government (1600–1868) prohibited social criticism, and it is his view that parody (*fūshi*), which is entirely absent in Noh drama, disappeared from kyōgen and Japanese comedy entirely.[25] To revive this spirit of parody, Umehara drew upon the works of Western satirists including Aristophanes, Jonathan Swift, and Charlie Chaplin even as he criticized Western values. Audiences with a background in Umehara's thought will realize better how deep his criticism of the West runs in his plays.

Umeharaology

Umehara Takeshi has authored several dozen books on subjects ranging from archaeology to art history and philosophy. In the late 1990s, Umehara wrote in an introduction to English readers that his scholarship had developed according to four phases. When he entered graduate studies at Kyoto University shortly after World War II, he focused on Western philosophy, but he found Western thought too pessimistic. Consequently, in the early 1960s, he switched to the study of Japanese culture, paying particular attention to the influence of Buddhism on literature and aesthetics. Asked to identify his seminal work, Umehara might point as he did in 1996 to a 1967 work *The Concept of Hell (Jigoku no shisō)*.[26] Umehara compares the place of this book in the development of his thought to the *Birth of Tragedy* in the philosophy of Friedreich Nietzsche. Umehara wrote that just as Nietzsche offered a new interpretation of Greek culture in his book, Umehara's study of hell served as a similar point of departure for his own theories about the enduring spiritual substructure of Japanese civilization.[27]

In the 1970s, Umehara turned his attention to the seventh and eighth centuries, writing on one of Japan's earliest temples and statesmen Prince Shōtoku (d. 622) in *The Hidden Cross: A Study of Hōryūji (Kakusareta jūjika*, 1972).[28] He also explored the earliest written texts in Japanese, producing a modern translation of the early eighth-century *Records of Ancient Matters (Kojiki)* and a 1973 study *Songs from the Depths (Minasoko no uta)* in which he contends that poet Kakinomoto no Hitomaru (ca. seventh to eighth centuries) compiled the eighth-century collection of poems, *Collection of Myriad Leaves (Man'yōshū)*.[29] What he calls the "Umehara thesis" is his assertion that the pacification of "vengeful spirits" *(onryō)* has been a running theme in Japanese civilization; he has developed that idea in his interpretations of the *Man'yōshū*, the construction of Hōryūji temple, and many of the tales in *Kojiki*.[30] Umehara himself perpetuates the theme of the pacification of vengeful spirits in his plays. In "The King and the Dinosaur" King Tottarā contemplates the subjugation of the "Land of the Vengeful Spirits" *(onryō no kuni)*, while the mudskippers in his first "super kyōgen" are themselves *onryō*.

Since the 1980s, Umehara has taken an interest in prehistory, especially the Jōmon (10,000–300 BC) and Yayoi (300 BC–300 AD) periods as exemplified by works such as *The Japan Adventure (Nihon bōken*, 1988–89) and *Are You a Yayoi or Jōmon? (Kimi wa Yayoijin ka Jōmonjin ka*, 1984).[31] In this field too, he developed new "Umehara theses," arguing first that modern Japanese retain traits of the Jōmon and Yayoi worldviews in their beliefs about death and that the purest descendants of these native beliefs are to be found in the indigenous cultures of the Ainu of Hokkaidō and the Ryūkyū Islanders of Okinawa. He writes that these people on the geographic outskirts of Japanese society "have preserved the Jōmon strain in its purest form," that is to say, they preserve the "pure" view of the afterworld, which is pre-Buddhist and pre-Yayoi.[32] Japanese culture, according to Umehara, is a combination of the hunter-gather Jōmon culture with the agricultural Yayoi culture. "On the one hand, the

Japanese are an active and adventurous people as embodied by the Jōmon spirit. On the other hand, they are a very quiet people, able to endure simple labor, as embodied by the Yayoi spirit."[33] Part of his intellectual project is to document and recover this Jōmon worldview. One of the subthemes of his first "super kabuki" play "Yamato Takeru" is the tragic oppression of the hunter-gatherer Jōmon society by the agricultural Yayoi society.[34]

Journalists have labeled Umehara's work "Umehara Japanology" and "Umehara Ancient History," both of which might be seen as derogatory except that Umehara himself enjoys repeating these terms.[35] Umehara has been criticized less for his self-promotion than for his views of Japanese culture. The scholar of Japanese religions, Ian Reader, has critiqued Umehara's portrait of Shintō as "nationalistic, [and] anti-Western" since it "glorifies Japanese culture as environmentally pristine and denigrates other (i.e., Western) cultures as destructive."[36] Umehara's efforts to document continuities between the Jōmon period and modern Japanese society have been critiqued as reductionistic.[37]

Umehara locates the destructive nature of modern society in the prominence given to reason in Western thought. He argues that belief in the power of reason, which has been the core of Western philosophy since Plato, has "created a marvelous situation in which humans jeopardize other creatures, animals, plant life, and the global environment."[38] Though Western philosophy has changed since Plato, the West's egocentrism and anthropocentrism have endured. The results have been disastrous according to Umehara: "The rational liberalism of the West wholly embraces the Cartesian worldview that made the individual—the thinking self—absolute, endorsed man's total mastery over nature, and recognized only the existence of mind and nature. Nonhuman life was left entirely out of the picture."[39] According to Umehara, societies that are built upon a rational, monotheistic, and modernist intellectual foundation are destined to collapse and "liberalism will be the next domino to fall."[40]

Umehara proclaims that Japan offers an alternative ancient wisdom he dubs "the civilization of the forest" (mori no bunmei) that will counteract the environmental and spiritual devastation of modernity that foretells the decline of the West. Just like the lone dinosaur in the play who has preserved ancient wisdom in his cave and emerges to save mankind from destruction, Umehara philosophizes that Japan maintains a stone-age philosophy that was once universal but has become virtually extinct elsewhere. "If Japan's civilization has any value," Umehara glows, "it rests in the fact that it retains the strong imprint of the forest civilization of its origins, the civilization of hunting and gathering."[41] When questioned by an American reporter whether his notion of a civilization of the forest runs counter to the reality of Japan's economic growth and record of environmental pollution, Umehara admitted that reality did not yet correspond to his vision for it, stating in an interview published in 1996:

> Unfortunately, my opinion is a minority view in Japan. I ask you to wait ten years. By then, I believe my opinion will be the majority view. Until that time,

I will repeat my ideas again and again, whenever and wherever I have the opportunity to do so.[42]

These words are worth remembering when considering Umehara's "super kyōgen" plays.

However, before reviewing his "super" plays in light of his ideas, it is hard to depart from a discussion of Umehara's thought without considering his scholarly methods. Umehara considers himself to be a philosopher who writes for a general public; he is not a historian, so perhaps his discipline (or at least his interpretation of it) allows for a discussion of ideas without the need to ground them thoroughly in a historical context. This type of intellectual project aims for an analysis of themes such as the concepts of hell, the afterlife, and vengeful ghosts in the writings of authors across the centuries. However, this approach leads him to ignore historical data he disagrees with, as is evident in his view of same-sex relationships in Japan. Umehara contends that homosexuality:

> runs rampant in Western societies, where it has contributed to the spread of AIDS. For some reason, however, it is relatively uncommon in Japan. No doubt the great majority of Japanese feel that homosexuality goes against the natural order of things in the same sense that castration and foot binding do.[43]

Whether Umehara's dismissal of the long history of same-sex relationships in Japan is due to ignorance or guile, it reveals that his references to history are selective and driven by his own idiosyncratic agenda.[44] Umehara's thought betrays a fondness for such sweeping generalizations, as also seen in his assertion that the modern Japanese love for sashimi is "a survival of a hunting and gathering lifestyle" from prehistoric times.[45] Umehara does have a flair for taking a strong stand on contemporary issues; and, by repeating his ideas "again and again, whenever and wherever [he has] the opportunity to do so," he has gained international recognition and the support of the Japanese government for the founding of an International Research Center for Japanese Studies in Kyoto where he worked as director general for many years. This notoriety brought immediate attention to his super kabuki and kyōgen plays and helped to sell out performances.

THE SOCIAL SCIENTIST AND THE MONSTER

The connections between Umehara's ideas and his "super kyōgen" plays that have been touched upon deserve a few more words in light of what has been understood of his thought. All three kyōgen plays demonstrate Umehara's concern for the environment. The inspiration for the first play, "Mutsugorō," came after a trip he made to Isahaya Bay near Nagasaki as president of the Japan PEN Club to survey the destruction of native habitat when the bay was drained. When a mudskipper gasped his last breath in front of him, Umehara felt compelled to write a novel *I am a Mudskipper*

(Wagahai mutsugorō de aru), which became the basis for the kyōgen play.[46] The second play, "Kurōn ningen Namashima," is as much a critique of human cloning as it is an ode to Japan's greatest baseball player Nagashima Shigeo. It was written in the wake of new stories about the Dolly the Sheep and claims in December 2002 by Clonaid—a cloning company founded by the Raëlian "UFO religion"—to have successfully cloned a girl named Baby Eve.[47]

In "Mutsugorō" and "The King and the Dinosaur," humanity learns of the problems of environmental destruction and the perils of nuclear war from animals. By using animals as his spokes-creatures, Umehara challenges Western anthropocentrism and the Cartesian notion of a separation of man from nature, which he asserts motivated environmental destruction in the first place. Animals are not only the creatures most adversely affected by pollution and the rest of humanity's problems, but they are also the beings— apart from the Ainu and Ryūkyū Islanders—who would most closely embody the "hunter gatherer philosophy" of living at one with nature that Umehara seeks to promote.

Significantly, the mudskippers and the dinosaur are also restless spirits *(onryō)* that need to be pacified.[48] The mudskippers appear as ghosts in the play while Umehara's script for "The King and the Dinosaur" contained a chorus of five dinosaurs that director Shigeyama Sennojō had to cut out to make the play more manageable. In these plays Umehara indicates that the ghosts of animals will seek revenge on a humanity that is too ignorant to know how to live with these creatures when they are alive or placate them when they are dead. This supposedly "ancient" view that animals will become ghosts and haunt humans is something Umehara has sought to argue in his research.[49]

Though Umehara derived his ideas in part from his study of Japanese religion, his plays are not didactic in that sense. The programs for these productions contain scientific discussions of mudskippers, cloning, and dinosaurs, respectively; Buddhism receives its share of satire in the form of a golfing-priest in "Mutsugorō." Umehara positions his ideas as antimodern but in harmony with science. He writes, "Over the past century or so it has become clear that living creatures were not created one after another by an anthropomorphic god, as the Old Testament claims, but emerged from one vast evolutionary flow, and furthermore that life is inextricably bound up with the movement of the universe as a whole." Animism, in other words, the prototypical view of nature as divine and of man connected with it that Umehara believes the Japanese have preserved since ancient times, is confirmed by modern science in his thought.[50] "Modern science," he writes, "has demonstrated that all life is basically one, and it has shown that living things and their physical surroundings are all part of a single ecosystem."[51]

Umehara's "final thesis" that all life is intertwined and that the environment should be protected informs his recent writings, including his plays. His conclusion is laudatory but not the road he took to reach it, which is marked by a naive primitivism about the origin of Japanese civilization, a reductionistic view of history, and a scapegoating of the West for Japan's own failings.

In comparison, the notion of a dinosaur saving the world may be just as tenuous, but the dinosaur at least proves to be benign in the end.

NOTES

The author owes a debt of thanks to Jonah Salz for providing source materials, drafts of his own research on super kyōgen, and for his comments on this essay. He also thanks Junko Habu for information about the reception of Umehara's ideas in the field of archeology.

1. Umehara, *Osama to kyōryū: Sūpā kyōgen no tanjō* (Tokyo: Shūeisha, 2003), p. 11. Unless otherwise noted, all translations are mine. The play is available on DVD: Japan Victor Foundation, *Sūpā kyōgen Osama to kyōryū* DVD (Tokyo: Japan Victor Foundation, 2004).
2. Ibid., p. 14.
3. Ibid., p. 17.
4. Ibid., p. 18.
5. Ibid., p. 19.
6. Ibid., p. 26.
7. Umehara's comments in Setouchi Jakuchō, Yokō Tadanori, Shigeyama Sennojō, and Umehara Takeshi, "Warai o!, fūshi o!, tetsugaku o!: Kore ga sūpā kyōgen da," in ibid., p. 183.
8. Shigeyama Dōji's comments in Shigeyama Dōji et al., " 'Osama to kyōryū' ni tsuite, enshutsusha intabyū," in *Sūpā kyōgen Osama to kyōryū* DVD.
9. Umehara Takeshi, "Sensō to kyōgen," in *Osama to kyōryū*, ed. Kokuritsu Nōgakudo Jigyōka (theater program for performance at the National Noh Theater, April 11 and 12, 2003) (Tokyo: Nihon Geijutsu Bunka Shinkōkai, 2003), p. 11.
10. Yokō Tadanori, " 'Osama to kyōryū' isoku to bijutsu," in *Osama to kyōryū*, ed. Kokuritsu Nōgakudo Jigyōka, p. 13.
11. Shigeyama Sennojō's comment in Setouchi et al., "Warai o!," p. 190.
12. Umehara, *Osama to kyōryū*, p. 30.
13. Umehara, "Sensō to kyōgen," p. 11.
14. Umehara, *Osama to kyōryū*, p. 41.
15. "Brawn drain" is Salz's term; a summary of these plays can be found in Jonah Salz, "Anti-Tradition, Anti-Modern: Umehara Takeshi's 'Super-Kyōgen,' " in *Towards a Modern Japanese Theatre Revisited*, ed. Keiko McDonald, David Jortner, and Kevin Wetmore (Lanham, MD: Lexington Books, forthcoming).
16. Umehara Takeshi and Ichikawa Ennosuke, "Taidan: Yomigaeru Yamato Takeru," in Umehara Takeshi, *Yamato Takeru* (Tokyo: Kodansha, 1986), p. 286.
17. Laurence R. Kominz, *The Stars Who Created Kabuki: Their Lives, Loves and Legacies* (New York: Kodansha International, 1997), pp. 244–248.
18. Faith Bach, "New Directions in Kabuki," *Asian Theatre Journal* 6:1 (1989), pp. 80–83, 88.
19. Umehara in Setouchi et al., "Warai o!," p. 205.
20. Shigeyama Sennojō in Shigeyama Dōji et al., " 'Osama to kyōryū' ni tsuite, enshutsusha intabyū."
21. Umehara, "Sensō to kyōgen," p. 11.
22. Shigeyama Sennojō, "Kyōgen tte hontō ni benri na shibai desu ne," in *Osama to kyōryū*, ed. Kokuritsu Nōgakudo Jigyōka, p. 12.

23. Shigeyama Sensaku in Shigeyama Dōji et al., " 'Osama to kyōryū' ni tsuite, enshutsusha intabyū."

24. Jonah Salz, "Roles of Passage: Coming of Age as a Japanese Kyōgen Actor," Ph.D. Dissertation (New York University, 1997), pp. 274–275.

25. Umehara Takeshi, *The Concept of Hell*, trans. Robert Wargo (Tokyo: Shūeisha, 1996), p. 150; Umehara Takeshi, "Kyōgen to fūshi," in Umehara, *Osama to kyōryū*, p. 177; Umehara in Setouchi et al., "Warai o!," p. 194.

26. Umehara Takeshi, *Jigoku no shisō: Nihon seishin no ichi keifu* (Tokyo: Chūō Kōronsha, 1967).

27. Umehara, *The Concept of Hell*, p. 13.

28. Umehara Takeshi, *Kakusareta jūjika: Hōryūji ron* (Tokyo: Shinchosha, 1972).

29. Umehara Takeshi, *Minasoko no uta: Kakinomoto Hitomaro ron* (Tokyo: Shinchosha, 1973).

30. Umehara, *The Concept of Hell*, p. 16.

31. Ibid., pp. 7–8; Umehara Takeshi, *Nihon bōken* (Tokyo: Shōgakkan, 2001); Umehara Takeshi and Nakagami Kenji, *Kimi wa Yayoijin ka Jōmonjin ka: Nihongaku kōgi* (Tokyo: Asahi Shuppansha, 1984).

32. Umehara Takeshi, "The Japanese View of the Hereafter," *Japan Echo* 16:3 (1989), p. 73.

33. Umehara Takeshi, "Japan's Elliptical Tradition: Classical Thought and Modernization," in *Blind Partners: American and Japanese Responses to an Unknown Future*, ed. Ronald A. Morse and Shigenobu Yoshida (Lanham, MD: University Press of America, 1985), p. 17.

34. Comment by Umehara in Umehara and Ichikawa, "Taidan," p. 289.

35. Umehara, "Japan's Elliptical Tradition," p. 13.

36. Ian Reader, "Studies of Japan, Area Studies, and the Challenges of Social Theory," *Monumenta Nipponica* 53:2 (1998), p. 248.

37. Mark J. Hudson, "Foragers as Fetish in Modern Japan," in *Hunter-Gathers of the North Pacific Rim*, ed. Junko Habu et al., special issue of *Senri Ethnological Studies* 63 (Osaka: National Museum of Ethnology, 2003), pp. 263–274.

38. Umehara, "Japan's Elliptical Tradition," p. 18.

39. Umehara Takeshi, "The Civilization of the Forest: Ancient Japan Shows Postmodernism the Way," in *At Century's End: Great Minds Reflect on Our Times*, ed. Nathan P. Gardels (La Jolla, CA: Alti Publishing, 1995), p. 189.

40. Umehara, "Civilization of the Forest," p. 189.

41. Ibid., pp. 180–181.

42. Ibid., p. 196.

43. Umehara Takeshi, "A Buddhist Approach to Organ Transplants," *Japan Echo* 16:4 (1989), pp. 79–80.

44. See, for example, Paul Schalow, "Male Love in Early Modern Japan: A Literary Depiction of the Youth," in *Hidden from History: Reclaiming the Gay and Lesbian Past*, ed. Martin Duberman, Martha Vincus, and George Chauncey (NY: Meridian Books, 1990), pp. 118–128, and Greg Pflugfelder, *Cartographies of Desire: Male-Male Sexuality in Japanese Discourse, 1600–1950* (Berkeley: University of California Press, 1999).

45. Umehara Takeshi, "Japan's Pride," in *Japan and Europe: Changing Contexts and Perspectives*, ed. Claude A. Marbaix (Belgium: Seiko Epson Corporation, 1989), p. 106.

46. The novel remains unfinished. Umehara Takeshi, "Fūshi no fukkatsu," in *Mutsugorō*, ed. Kokuritsu Nōgakudo Jigyōka (theater program for performances

at the National Noh Theater, December 22 and 23, 2000) (Tokyo: Nihon Geijutsu Bunka Shinkōkai, 2000), p. 6; Umehara, "Kyōgen to fūshi," p. 175.

47. Salz, "Anti-Tradition, Anti-Modern," p. 11; Susan Palmer, "The Raëlian Movement: Concocting Controversy, Seeking Social Legitimacy," in *Controversial New Religions*, ed. James R. Lewis and Jesper Aagaard Petersen (New York: Oxford University Press, 2005), pp. 371–385.

48. In explaining the salient points of the prototypical Japanese view of death, Umehara writes, "Not only humans but all living creatures have a soul which, after death, leaves the body and goes to the other world. In particular, living creatures which are important to humans must be sent off carefully to the other world." Umehara Takeshi, "The Japanese View of the 'Other World': Japanese Religion in World Perspective," trans. Royall Tyler, *Japan Review* 2 (1991), p. 166.

49. Umehara in Setouchi et al., "Warai o!," p. 203.

50. Umehara, "The Japanese View of the Hereafter," p. 81.

51. Umehara, "Civilization of the Forest," p. 187.

11

Monstering the Japanese Cute: Pink Globalization and Its Critics Abroad

Christine R. Yano

The year 2004 marked significant anniversaries for two of Japan's prominent global icons: the fiftieth of the monster Godzilla and the thirtieth of Sanrio's Hello Kitty. The two, posed side by side as monumental phenomena on a global stage, provide intriguing contrasts. Godzilla stands tall as a Japanese creature on (primarily) Japanese soil; Hello Kitty sits small as a Brit (full name Kitty White, birthplace London) on turf that can only be described as nebulously global. Whereas the Godzilla of postwar Japan makes his mark through gigantism on the big screen, Hello Kitty of the economic bubble era creates a consumer niche based in the symbolic and actual miniature, her blank face adorning school bags, lunch boxes, and coin purses. Godzilla occupies a public adult world of superheroes and supermonsters. He threatens, destroys, and wages fierce battles. Kitti-chan—as she is affectionately known in Japan using the diminutive term of endearment "chan"—occupies a private world of gingham check, apple pies, and twinkling stars. She comforts and cheers by simply being there. The one subscribes to extraordinary masculinist domination, whereas the other creeps her way in to everyday feminine passivity. Godzilla roars as Kitti-chan silently stares. Consider their mouths: Godzilla expresses himself through a gaping mouth from which radioactive breath acts as a major destructive force; Hello Kitty expresses herself through disarming, benign mouthlessness. Their names provide subtle contrasts: both use the English language, but Godzilla's is a ponderous, newly coined recombinant, whereas Hello Kitty's is straightforward, playful Japlish. Behold their bodies. Godzilla's is dark, reptilian, scaly, and oversized; Hello Kitty's is white, mammalian, furry, and undersized. Both of these figures have become iconic of not only Japan on a global stage, but a particular kind (or kinds) of camp/cool that define that stage in the twenty-first century.

These icons and their camp/cool are, of course, a product of their times. In the two decades after Godzilla's birth in 1954, Japan transformed itself to occupy a far different global niche, moving from postwar reconstruction to international economic and technological giant. At the same time, Japanese domestic focus shifted from production to consumption, from salaryman occupying center stage to a new spotlight on housewife, OL ("office ladies," female clerical workers), and young teen female consumers. In the wake of these dramatic shifts, the development of *kawaii* (cute) culture for domestic sales and its export to the United States and elsewhere suggest a broadening of Japanese popular culture global flows from the monstrous threat that Godzilla presents to now embrace the seemingly benign attractions of cute. Hello Kitty leads the way in this, representing not just herself, but a wave of cute products from Japan, generating what I call "pink globalization"—that is, the transnational trek of *kawaii* goods from Japan to other parts of the world. I invoke the color pink in its various meanings in twentieth and twenty-first century Japan as well as other Euro-American countries: feminine, cute, and sexual.

Japan's pink globalization of which Hello Kitty is a part is saturated with the cultural odor/fragrance of a new order: not the highly aestheticized world of cherry blossoms and kimono, but a youth-oriented, consumerist hipness that has been dubbed "Japan's Gross National Cool" by journalist Douglas McGray. McGray notes that since the 1990s, Japan has gained cultural cachet as the site of global coolness through the popularity of such exports as manga and anime, as well as the high art, manga-inspired, high-fashion linked movement known as "Super Flat" with its proponents Murakami Takashi and Nara Yoshitomo.[1] Hello Kitty contributes to Japan's "Gross National Cool" by way of its pink globalization.

Hello Kitty's global trek began two short years after her birth with her exportation to the United States in 1976, followed by Europe in 1980, and other countries of Asia in 1990. In this chapter I focus on the American portion of that journey, examining Kitty-led pink globalization in two ways: (1) as an almost monstrously widespread phenomenon and (2) as a phenomenon that has been "monstered" by its critics abroad. I base this analysis on interviews conducted at Sanrio headquarters in Tokyo, the company's American headquarters in South San Francisco, at various Sanrio stores in the United States, and on-line websites.

KITTY HERE, THERE, ALMOST EVERYWHERE

Bill Hensley, official spokesman for Sanrio Inc. (the subsidiary in charge of Sanrio products in North and South America) explains, "[o]ur biggest market for her [Kitty] is still Japan and Asia, but our big push going forward is the Western Hemisphere, primarily the U.S. market."[2] In the United States alone in 2002, Kitty goods earned $100 million from branded products and an additional $400 million in licensing fees. Hensley continues, "Clearly, the U.S. is our No. 1 growth market and we're looking to expand."[3] Expansion Sanrio-style, however, strategically avoids the boom-then-bust approach of a passing fad. Instead, the company officially prefers slow and steady sales relying on word of mouth rather than overt advertising or endorsement.

That being said, the company is not above tweaking the processes of word of mouth to expand the word and increase the number of mouths that speak it. The tools of expansion include monthly release of approximately 400 new products so that there is always something new to buy, and contracting with a company whose purpose is to secure product placement in films and television. Sanrio also engages in a strategic "celebrity outreach," a quarterly giveaway of products to celebrities in show business, sports, and other fields. Hensley characterizes celebrity outreach as a bit "like prospecting" in the sense of expending efforts to search for celebrity consumers and then subtly utilizing them once they are found. In an interview at Sanrio Inc. he explains that

> [w]e cover celebrity outreach, and we do send products to—every quarter it's fifty or seventy different celebrities generally . . . But it's kind of like prospecting . . . . We get nice letters back. . . . The challenge is, we can't then broadcast email saying "Oh, she's a Hello Kitty fan." But we kind of build friends [through celebrity outreach] and then let someone else discover the story. Because [it's] celebrity fans versus celebrity endorsement—and we're not paying anyone to endorse us.[4]

Indeed, these kinds of efforts have paid off. Sanrio boasts a dedicated following of celebrities, such as ice skater Tara Lipinski, model Tyra Banks, actresses Sarah Jessica Parker and Drew Barrymore, and pop singers Christina Aguilera, Mariah Carey, Mandy Moore, Brandy, and Lisa Loeb. What is more important, news of these celebrities' Hello Kitty fandom has been published in hundreds of articles in newspaper and magazines. For example, a 2002 story in *USA Today* lists Hollywood fans of Hello Kitty and pictures singer Mandy Moore holding up a sequined Hello Kitty coin purse. According to the article, singer Christina Aguilera, who wore Hello Kitty jewelry on the cover of *Teen People*, was spotted on a Hello Kitty shopping spree at posh mall Beverly Center in Los Angeles, and professed her love of Hello Kitty chewing gum on the "Tonight Show."[5] This kind of "news" is exactly what the marketing department at Sanrio works for and showcases in its news clippings. At Sanrio Inc., binders of these articles, photo spreads, and magazine covers spotlight the hard work of the marketing department in getting the word out, while not officially advertising. On the company's web site, one can find these same news clippings in a section entitled "Kitty in the News."[6] Sanrio's products have also been "placed" in television shows, such as the popular hits *Friends* and *Everybody Loves Raymond*, and movies such as the 2002 *Austin Powers in Goldmember*, for which actor Mike Meyers specifically requested a Hello Kitty storefront set.

The prospecting of celebrity outreach sometimes strikes gold, as Hensley explains:

> [t]ake our friendship with Lisa Loeb. We read in an article someplace her saying, "I really wish I had a Hello Kitty rice cooker." It's like—done—here's

the rice cooker! And then she gets back [to us], saying "I love your stuff. Can we do something?" . . . [We say,] "Why don't we do a story on your new album and on your Hello Kitty collection [using our company web site]?" So for her it's great exposure to have all the eyeballs that go to Sanrio-dot-com see something about her and her new album. For us, it's interesting content and implied endorsement.[7]

Loeb's collaboration with Sanrio resulted in a 2002 CD release entitled "Lisa Loeb—Hello Lisa."[8] The CD's pink-themed jacket embeds Hello Kitty in a series of cleverly nested identities: Kitty, sporting a trademark pink bow over her left ear, holds a CD jacket of singer Loeb; meanwhile Loeb, wearing her trademark 1950s wing-shaped glasses, dons white Kitty ears with a pink bow over her left one (just as Kitty does). Loeb holds a mirror whose reflection is an image of Hello Kitty wearing Loeb-style glasses and winking. In effect, the CD jacket shows Kitty holding Loeb (dressed as Kitty) holding Kitty (dressed as Loeb), each borrowing trademark accessories from the other. The CD jacket's wink references the tongue-in-cheek, linked identities of singer Loeb and product icon Kitty, exemplifying the adage, "You are what you buy."[9]

Kitty's wink may also reference what has been dubbed the "wink on pink" of Wall Street female executives and other businesswomen in the United States who consume and display Hello Kitty goods. As a 2005 *Fortune* magazine article proclaims; "[s]erious businesswomen are bringing Hello Kitty products into the boardroom. Is this in-your-face girliness the next edge in business?"[10] The article quotes consumer trends forecaster Faith Popcorn:

> Hello Kitty's popularity among adult women strikes me as kind of a "wink on pink.". . . It's like saying women are complicated—that we can't be contained. We can wear monochromatic Armani suits and whip out Hello Kitty notepads at a moment's notice. . . . Women are . . . fed up with doing all the self-denying things they have to do in order to make it in business. . . . So in defiance, they're bringing cutesy into the corporate sanctum. They're saying, "Screw you, [business] suits!" It's a small but very public act of rebellion.[11]

Popcorn herself admits to a personal fondness for Hello Kitty. But note the place of Kitty in this boardroom scheme: Japanese Cute accessorizes American corporate suits, but does not supplant them. The Kitty notepad works as a hidden weapon of femininity, a surprise attack of pink in what is characterized as a colorless masculine world. The women are toting (Japanese) cute into the (American) boardroom, but not necessarily making the boardroom cute. To the question of in-your-face girliness, the article contends that women bring with them new leadership styles that may be female driven, but not necessarily "girlie." It quotes a female vice president of a New York public relations agency: "My [Hello Kitty] ring [a cheap toy that opens to reveal a rubber-stamp image of Kitty], which I *love*, is definitely girlie . . . But in a way, what the ring represents—my ability to think and act creatively—certainly isn't. And that's what my colleagues and clients love."[12]

The wink would not work as well if the ring were an expensive piece of jewelry. Instead, it winks specifically as an inexpensive toy. The ring provides a playful, ironic, Japanese Cute commentary upon the seriousness of the corporate world. Furthermore, the ring is not only an inexpensive toy, it is also a toy that has a function: it can be used to imprint Kitty's face—small, postage-stamp sized—multiple times. Turning a Kitty stamping device into a piece of jewelry (or turning jewelry into a stamping device) marks nothing less than Sanrio genius. This female business executive, by way of her Kitty stamp-ring, thus flaunts Japanese Cute and her own cleverness in discovering and wearing it in the face of American big business. The wink on pink thus represents a small act of defiance in recuperating and asserting both the playful and the feminine using the kitsch of a Japanese icon in a masculinist world.

Female business executives are not the only ones wanting a piece of the Kitty wink. So, too, are New York socialites, who shop at a boutique featuring Kitty goods within New York's posh specialty store Henri Bendel. Tiffany Dubin, socialite, former director of Sotheby's fashion department, and founder of the boutique explains, "I am so allergic to pretentiousness in fashion, and I think everyone else is, too. . . . Now, having a sense of fun is where it's at, like wearing your Marc Jacobs coat with a plastic Hello Kitty purse."[13] Mariah O'Brien, a 30-year-old Hollywood-based actress who favors designer labels Miu Miu and Prada concurs: "[w]earing Hello Kitty is like wearing a designer logo, but cooler. . . . It says the person is hip, fun and doesn't take fashion too seriously. For sure, there is a cool factor to Hello Kitty."[14] It is exactly the "cool factor" that, according to these women, Kitty imparts that is at issue here. Kitty lends panache to high fashion, allowing these women to perform both their knowledge and acceptance of fashion's dictates, as well as their distanced stance from it. For these designer-conscious sophisticates, Kitty becomes a means of performing their own camp take on a rigidly froufrou world.

The monstrous phenomenon of Hello Kitty in the United States includes not only female celebrities, business executives, and fashionistas, but far more commonly the legions of "tweens"—girls between the ages of 8 and 12—who populate malls across the United States on weekends. Armed with their parents' money and growing independence as shoppers, tweens constitute the newfound darlings of marketers' campaigns. Sanrio's appeal to tweens catches them at the tail end of childhood, just entering the middle-school battleground of cool, after which they may snub anything hinting of infantile sweetness. According to Hensley, the typical consumer pattern of Sanrio goods is for young preschool girls to latch on to Hello Kitty, continue their consumption into elementary school with stationery goods, lunch boxes, and back packs, purchase Kitty goods as a tween in a dying gasp of lingering cute, and then drop Kitty goods once they enter middle and high school.[15] They may reenter Sanrio consumption as young adults in their twenties, and especially after they return to purchase items for their own children, completing the cycle through to another generation.

Hello Kitty has long been popular among Asian Americans, who constitute the first, largest, and most long-lasting market for Sanrio goods in the United States. One reason for this close tie is the fact that Sanrio goods were initially sold primarily in Asian-based stores, such as in Chinatowns and Japantowns. In fact, one Asian American female fan in her thirties from the Los Angeles area half-seriously laments the current widespread popularity of Hello Kitty, arguing that Kitty used to be "theirs"—that is, "belonging" to Asian American females. She recounts that Hello Kitty used to be such a symbol of being Asian American and female among her friends that one of them was even nicknamed "Hello Kitty" because of the shape of her head.[16] Even in the 2000s, the Asian American female component of Hello Kitty can be seen in many of the sales personnel, at least of West Coast stores. When I asked the manager of the Sanrio store in San Francisco why the great majority of her employees were Asian American (including herself), she replied that they are some of the best customers, know the merchandise well, and subsequently make the best employees.[17] The public face of Sanrio (and Hello Kitty) at many West Coast stores, then, is Asian American.

The private face of Sanrio is also Asian American, as a visit to their corporate headquarters in South San Francisco proves. Almost all female workers there are Asian American, from receptionists to designers to executives.[18] This includes Becky Hui, Chinese American woman who has served as Home Office Stores Supervisor. Hui is known in the office as a "Hello Kitty super fan." For someone such as Hui, working at Sanrio is, as she puts it, her "dream job."[19] In fact, her fandom gained global (virtual) renown when the company featured Hui and her Hello Kitty collection on their web site.

The second largest group of Hello Kitty consumers in the United States is Hispanics. Although Japanese Cute finds little resonance in the stereotype of the sensual Latina, Peter Gastaldi, executive vice president of Sanrio Inc. explains, "[Hispanic customers see Hello Kitty as reinforcing] family values, children at the center of the family, buying things for the children, things that will make children happy."[20] But do Hispanics see Hello Kitty as a particularly Japanese icon of cute? Gastaldi replies, "No, they're buying cute. In the case of Hispanics, I don't think that the fact that it's from Japan really has a whole lot to do with it. It's cute, it's colorful, it's child-oriented, it's whimsical. It's a gift, it's something for the child, and the child is . . . the center of the family."[21] Gastaldi's explanation tells only part of the story. Hispanic family members may buy Hello Kitty for their children, but this does not stop female teenagers and young adults from purchasing Kitty goods for their own consumption. Indeed, when I visited the Sanrio company store in New York's Times Square in spring 2003, the majority of the sales personnel were female Hispanics, including the manager who admitted to being a huge Kitty fan.

So what is the camp/cool of Kitty? Is it simply the irresistible appeal of cute? Or is there something that can be identified as Japanese Cute? Dan Peters, a tall, lanky 30-something with spiky hair and a ready smile, majored in graphic design and looks to know camp/cool when he sees it. He also works as senior promotions designer in the marketing department at Sanrio,

Inc. According to Peters, Hello Kitty consumers are not just buying cute. Rather, they're buying the quirkiness of Japanese Cute that contrasts with the treacly sweetness of Precious Moments, as well as, more importantly, the predictable, straightforward commercial appeal of Disney or Warner Brothers. Whether customers recognize the Japaneseness of it or not, Peters suggests that quirkiness marks Japanese Cute:

> Part of what I find to be of great appeal of Sanrio is the Japanese quality of it. . . . I love the fact that Sanrio is different. And so [in my work as the designer of Sanrio promotions] I could very easily edit things and smooth them out into [Disney's] Sleeping Beauty type, you know, kind of descriptions. But I love the quirkiness [of the Japanese products].[22]

Peters gives as examples of "quirkiness" marking an X for a stuffed animal's anus or having a canine character by the name of "Pudding" eating a cup of pudding. "Is he existentially eating himself?" Peters asks with a sly grin. It is the unexpectedly playful aspect of the product line that prompts Peters to comment in awe, "[t]his is brilliant! This is like—Disney would never do this! That kind of quirkiness I think is just really appealing."[23]

In August 2002, journalist Annalee Newitz wrote in the *San Francisco Bay Guardian* about "the apotheosis of cute," suggesting that "cute" has hit America with an unsettling force. She writes, "[t]he national [American] craze for cuteness has turned the innocent optimism of Hello Kitty into a hollow, cynical commercialism. . . . Today cuteness is starting to feel like fake, mall-bought conformity."[24] Newitz traces the evolution of this cute boom from the subcultural fringes of the United States to its mainstream. She explains;

> [b]y the end of the 1990s, nothing was cooler than Asian pop. And nothing was cuter. . . . These days cuteness has lost any subversive edge it might have had back in the days when raves and manga in the United States were still mostly the purview of underground culture enthusiasts. Cute is a consumer item, a mainstream aesthetic. . . . Asian-philia [is] at the heart of America's obsession with cuteness. . . . Cuteness—at least as it's consumed in America—reduces all of Asian culture to its more precious, infantile, and fluffy form.[25]

Characterizing all of the United States as hit with "Asian-philia" may be overstating the case, but certainly Japanese Cute by way of Hello Kitty has become normalized as part of mall fare, rather than exoticized as Chinatown trinket.

Monstering the Japanese Cute

The global trek of Japanese Cute with all its camp/cool quirkiness has not come without its detractors. Critics of Hello Kitty engage in what I call her "monstering." For many observers, specifically because of her long-lived appeal with steady popularity and name recognition in the United States and elsewhere, and because she is so seemingly benign, Hello Kitty has become the "monstrous cute." In the eyes of her foes, Kitty and the pink globalization that she leads represent a symbolic menace from Japan, far more insidious than a Godzilla or even Pikachu. Pink globalization may not generate World Trade Organization protests, but it possesses its own kind of exotic-yet-familiar provocation embedded in *kawaii*. To what, whom, or where does Hello Kitty's "monstering" point? What are the transgressions of Hello Kitty that have generated certain virulent responses? In short, what kind of global monster is she?

Whereas critics of Euro-American centered globalization have protested the cultural gray-out and buy-out of first McDonald's then Starbucks throughout much of the industrial world, the critics of Japan-based pink globalization express different kinds of concerns. They are not concerned with Kitty overtaking local cultures and economies; Sanrio's pink globalization does not threaten with that level of scale. Rather, Kitty's critics express a more subtle, yet no less emphatic critique. Some sneer that cute may have overstepped its bounds. British journalist Lesley Gillilan, for example, asks, "Hello Kitty overkill?" calling Kitty "mistress of the world's weakness for cute, collectable 'femorabilia' " and "a kitty-kitsch merchandising phenomenon. . . . fueled by nostalgia."[26] Gillilan's critique points to the fact that Hello Kitty is no longer just kid stuff, that she garners the continuing attention of adults, particularly women in their thirties who grew up with Kitty. These overgrown Kitty afficionados include well-heeled celebrities who, according to Gillilan, should know better, and sophisticated fashion designers, such as Samantha Chang (lingerie) and Tarina Tarantino (jewelry). In doing so, Hello Kitty has become matter out of place, and thus matter that no longer knows its place. "Hello Kitty overkill" suggests that Kitty has overstayed her welcome.

Others who monster Kitty find cause for alarm in the nature of what Hello Kitty stands for—that is, cute itself. These range from private, individual critiques to more public, media-enhanced, sometimes commercial ones. Some companies have embedded anti-Hello Kitty in their products. The most obvious of these is the Florida-based American company David and Goliath and its Stupid Factory stores, which specialize in humorous T-shirts and other paraphernalia.[27] Founded in 1999 by Todd Goldman, the company's Goodbye Kitty line is a direct spoof of the sweetness of Hello Kitty.[28] Although the David and Goliath cat is mouthless and wide eyed, it looks nothing like the abstract infantilized Hello Kitty with outsized head. Goodbye Kitty is drawn as a more realistic cat. Nevertheless, its name suggests that this character is meant to represent everything that Hello Kitty is not. Indeed, the 53 designs of Goodbye Kitty depict various nefarious ways to dispose off a cat. Kitty floats in an inner tube with an alligator approaching, mouth wide. Kitty sits in a bathtub into which is thrown a plugged-in toaster. Kitty stares out of the glass window of a front-loaded washing machine, tumbling round and round. Kitty in a blender here, Kitty in a microwave oven there. If Hello Kitty's world is one where nothing bad ever happens, then Goodbye Kitty's world is one where everything goes violently, disgustingly wrong.

In fact, dubbing something or someone "anti-Hello Kitty" has become a generic moniker to designate goods and images that counter cuteness, or at least Sanrio's version of it. For example, the commercial goth character Emily Strange has been called "anti-Hello Kitty" because of her reputation as the antithesis of cute.[29] A creation of former skateboarder and Santa Cruz, California native Rob Reger in 1992, Emily's goth world is full of cats, spiderwebs, and haunted houses, all depicted in a trademark palette of black and blood-red. If Hello Kitty's world is bright and sunshiny, then Emily Strange's world is dark and gloomy.

Another "anti-Hello Kitty" commercial character is the shiftless rabbit Mashimaro, which a web site calling itself geekgirlz-r.us describes as "the Anti-Hello Kitty in the shape of a fat conniving rabbit."[30] The web site points to Mashimaro's scatological humor and nasty deeds as part of what earns it the status of "anti-Hello Kitty." Ironically, Mashimaro is originally a Korean internet-based manga figure and now the central character in a Korean line of "cute" goods.[31] His trademark tool is a toilet plunger, which he often wears stuck to his forehead. In a figure such as Mashimaro, one can have your cute cake and eat it, too. The contrast with Hello Kitty extends pink globalization to include Mashimaro's anti-cute cute.

On-line, Hello Kitty comes under particularly venomous virtual attack. Part of this viciousness may be a function of flaming, the tendency of web-based interaction to easily fall into hyperbolic critique under the shield of anonymity. This critique may be expressed both verbally and visually through the use of fonts (styles, sizes, colors, bold, italics, underline), upper case letters, and other orthographic elements (especially exclamation marks). For example, one web site "Anti-Hello Kitty!!!!" begins with a tirade: "I've been trying to tell you all for years . . . the kitty is evil . . . pure evil i tell you. Just look into her beady little eyes and tell me you do NOT see PURE evil."[32] The site juxtaposes Hello Kitty holding a bouquet of flowers—"May be disguised as the following cute lovable . . . *yet very deceiving* little kitten"—with a pseudo-Kitty holding a sign reading "Kill" and "the kickers of ass." The web site includes the infamous Hello Kitty vibrator: "What appears to be a harmless childs [sic] toy . . . is in fact . . . a dildo!!!! . . . She's captured the children . . . now she's after the older ones." The webmaster critiques Hello Kitty for the deceptiveness with which she has hoodwinked the American public. The seemingly innocent children's icon seduces people—particularly vulnerable youth—to sexual pleasures, consumer activities, and more.

Another site, "Hell Kitty, the original anti-Hello Kitty site," begun in 2000 by self-dubbed "Evil Princess Chikako" says, "[w]elcome to my little Anti Hello Kitty shrine! Known as Hell Kitty! . . . Come on in, look around and find a fun way to kill the kitty everyone loves to hate!"[33] The site's motto is, "Everyone needs something to hate, start with Hello Kitty." This site, like many others, critiques Hello Kitty in vitriolic language, both semantically and visually, with extensive use of upper-case letters and vividly colored background shades of red to suggest a true hell.

According to these virtual critics, what is so hellish about Hello Kitty? First, she is *too* good, too cute, too much. The unremitting sweetness of Hello Kitty seems, at least for some Euro-Americans, saccharinely overdone. Second, her goodness is only a pretense. She plays upon the sly deceit of a cute facade to seduce consumers into her capitalist lair. *Kawaii* is, in effect, not only the devil, but what's worse, the devil disguised as an angel. Third, the devil-formerly-known-as-Kitty is a commodity. In fact, one might say that the devil is not Hello Kitty so much as Sanrio, successfully doing what it set out to do—that is, promote and sell its products globally. Fourth, Hello Kitty bastardizes childhood in ways that these web sites consider perverse through adult vices of money and sex. This says as much about cultural ideals of childhood as about Hello Kitty's perceived assault upon it.

One multidimensional anti-Hello Kitty site calling itself "Hello Kitty Perversions" provides a compendium of links to news articles, goods, and graphics that both document the spread of Kitty to the far reaches of the capitalist imagination (robots, pink laptops, toasters that imprint Hello Kitty's face on bread), as well as spoof that spread.[34] Webmaster "Mark Hughes" provides links to *seppuku* (ritual suicide) Kitty clothing, including T-shirts for men and women and thong-style women's underwear. One defender of Kitty wrote to Hughes, "God damn you. Hello Kitty is not a sex object! She's cute, she's fluffy, she's funny and most off [*sic*] all she's bloody cool!" to which Hughes responded, "You poor delusional bastard. Seek help now."[35]

Hello Kitty has become such a genre of empty cuteness that the American satire magazine *National Lampoon* created its own spoof entitled "Hello Jesus."[36] Imitating the simplified graphics of Sanrio, the *Lampoon*'s Jesus/Kitty sports a familiar large round head, this time with a halo replacing Kitty's trademark bow. Jesus/Kitty has two dark button eyes, a little round nose, a diamond-shaped beard, and still no mouth. The *Lampoon*'s treatment includes various Jesus/Kitty goods and poses: a card showing Jesus/Kitty carrying the cross ("Hello, bloody little Jesus. Thank you for dying for me"), a necklace with a little-girl pendant ("Here comes My Magdalene"), rubber "flip-flop" slippers with the figure of Jesus/Kitty ("Hello Jesus walks on water. Don't you try it!").[37] This spoof may not be specifically anti-Kitty, but provides an indirect critique of cute goods and their insidiousness. Hello Kitty here becomes the template and thus the target of exponential monsterings.

CONCLUSION: THE PLEASURES AND PERVERSIONS OF KITTY AS GLOBAL CUTE

For the thirtieth birthday of Hello Kitty, Sanrio issued 100 new products, such as a robot for 450,000 yen ($4,100) that will recognize and remember up to 10 faces, identify voices, hold conversations, and sing; limited edition pink and blue underwear decorated with Hello Kitty's face made up of Swarovski crystals selling for 6,000 yen ($55); and one diamond-encrusted

Kitty figure that sold for 10.5 million yen ($102,000). Kitty consumerism, apparently, seems to have no limits, in Japan and elsewhere. Hello Kitty has proven not only a global economic success, but also an international civic success in being named UNICEF's "special friend of children" to help raise funds for girls' education programs in 2004. However, it is the mixed messages that Hello Kitty sends out globally that prompted no less than the English-language Tokyo-based *Japan Times* to call for a halt to this proliferation. An October 2004 editorial entitled "Time for Goodbye Kitty?" laments Kitty's "potential to embarrass Japan abroad":

> As a cultural ambassador, Kitty presents Japan as the ultimate kingdom of kitsch. . . . Someone needs to explain how a kitty with no mouth can be a spokesperson for anything—especially girls' education—and how an image that embodies female submissiveness is supposed to help banish gender-based stereotypes. . . . The issue of Hello Kitty's potential to embarrass Japan abroad got another twist this month with MasterCard's announcement that the kitty will adorn a new debit card . . . [that] would target American girls aged 10 to 14. The card . . . has already sparked controversy in the United States. . . . Imagine trying to be a UNICEF ambassador *and* a capitalist tool at the same time.[38]

According to the *Japan Times,* Hello Kitty proves an embarrassment abroad because of its ties to kitsch, blatant consumerism, and antifeminism. This editorial is written not only in the spirit of criticism of one of Japan's most popular global icons, but also with an eye to international opinion of Japan itself.

So what is the nature of the pink globalization of which Hello Kitty is a part? Is this Joseph Nye's "soft power"—"the ability to attract" and "shape what others want" through such means as popular culture?[39] Is she Godzilla gone soft, fuzzy, and ultimately, consumer-lusting sexy? Indeed, soft power seen in the newfound global sense of Japanese Cool (including Cute) is a growing source of national pride for Japan. Cuteness, as Anne Allison argues, is "Japan's Millennial Product."[40] The Japanese government, recognizing the place of such cute/cool-based soft power, is showing increasing interest in and support for these informal cultural ambassadors.[41] *Japan Times* editorial opinions are in the minority in a country in which both *kawaii* and consumerism separately and together are met with relatively little critique.

Pink globalization soft power seduces precisely through its image as benign. Fans call Hello Kitty's cuteness "irresistible." They are powerless amid her charms: walking into a Sanrio store, they can't help but buy at least one item. Of course, the staging of the seduction has been carefully crafted by Sanrio through offering new products every month and selling a range of goods at a range of prices so that there is always something temptingly affordable. The pinkness of the product line—its sweetness, cleverness, quirkiness, inventiveness, seeming harmlessness—makes this globalization more palatable than most. Child media and product specialists do not raise warning flags at the first sign of cute in the same knee-jerk manner that they do violence or sex.

But what can we conclude about the boundaries being policed by those minority legions of anti–Hello Kitty vigilantes? At least some of the critiques can be lined up alongside antiglobalization forces growing worldwide. According to these, Hello Kitty has gone too far, infiltrating malls and department stores throughout the United States. More importantly, she has leapt beyond the bounds of Asian enclaves and landed in mainstream shopping carts. Indeed, some of these anti–Hello Kitty critiques shade over subtly into racialized anti-Asian or anti-Japanese sentiment. Japanese Cute does not inhabit the global marketplace with the same kind of authority or birthright that McDonald's and Mickey Mouse do. Hello Kitty thus becomes not only the outsider to the global club, but also its yellow-peril nemesis.[42]

Furthermore, Hello Kitty enacts the transgressiveness of kitsch. For some, including the editors of the *Japan Times*, she represents pandering emotionalism and lower-taste cultures. Stallybrass and White write of "a striking ambivalence to the representations of the lower strata . . . in which they are both reviled and desired."[43] The desiring of Hello Kitty—youth, females, emotionalism—is but the flip side of her being reviled. Cuteness morphs into kitsch when it oversteps its bounds: what is right for the child is kitsch for the adult. In the same way that Kitty oversteps its racial/cultural bounds when it moves from Asian enclaves to mainstream malls, so, too, does it become kitsch when marketed to adult females. The kitschiness of Hello Kitty, then, does not inhere in the object so much as in the hand that grabs it. It also inheres in sheer volume: one lone Hello Kitty cell phone strap may not incite hostility; but when that strap is the twentieth or fiftieth or hundredth Kitty item that one sees in a given day, then the ubiquitousness of the image can drive at least some people to virtual trashing. Kitsch rests not only in the tasteless, but also in the ubiquitous. Placed on a national scale, Japan as the Kitty-led "ultimate kingdom of kitsch" suggests both its infantilization and feminization.

This is where the soft power of pink globalization breaks down and national-cultural-racial imaging enters. Koichi Iwabuchi asks the question, when does "cultural odor" of global goods become "cultural fragrance"?[44] I argue that the shift from odor to fragrance—from a neutral or even negative image of a country transforming to a positive, desirable one that enhances the global marketability of its goods—is not a one-way street. In other words, the imaging of both product and nation-culture go hand in hand, and back and forth in shifting dialectics. Hello Kitty's cute/kitsch becomes Japan's global face; Japan's economic might frames Kitty's purr (or Godzilla's roar). Hello Kitty treads warily for the monstering of the pinkness she inhabits, provoking fans and critics to draw battle lines around her mouthless appeal. She becomes the Godzilla not so much of the kindergarten set, but of their mothers hovering nearby in Kitty thong underwear.

NOTES

1. Douglas McGray. "Japan's Gross National Cool." *Foreign Policy* (May/June 2002).
2. Quoted in Parja Bhatnagar, "Hello Kitty's a Whisker Away from 30," *CNN Money*, http://money.cnn.com/2003/11/14/news/companies/hello_kitty/index.htm. Accessed November 14, 2003.

3. Ibid.

4. Personal communication, June 19, 2002.

5. Kelly Carter, "Female Celebrities Can't Get Enough of Hello Kitty," *Honolulu Advertiser*, May 1, 2002, p. F-1.

6. http://www.sanrio.com/main/happytimes/kittynews.html. Accessed December 2, 2005.

7. Ibid.

8. "Lisa Loeb—Hello Lisa," CD, Artemis Records 751151-2 (2002).

9. Herbert Marcuse, *One-Dimensional Man* (London: Sphere, 1968); cf. John Clammer, "Aesthetics of the Self: Shopping and Social Being in Contemporary Urban Japan," in *Lifestyle Shopping*, ed. R. Shields (London: Routledge, 1992), p. 195.

10. Megan Othersen Gorman, "The Office Kitty," *Fortune* (January 5, 2005), http://www.fortune.com/fortune/print/0,15935,361079,00.html. Accessed January 24, 2005. This article is a slightly updated, revised version of an earlier one that Gorman wrote for *Fortune* (February 7, 2002) by the same title, http://www.fortune.com/indext.jhtml?channel=print_article.jhtml&doc_id=206404. Accessed November 2, 2002.

11. Ibid.

12. Ibid.

13. Jill Gerstow, "Feeding the Kitty," *Los Angeles Times*, December 27, 2002, Calendar, part II, p. 1.

14. Ibid.

15. According to a mother of a 19-year-old coed, many of these "sophisticated" high schoolers may playfully and somewhat ironically reembrace their childhood stuffed animals, including Hello Kitty, just as they are leaving home for college, as if to say, "I'm leaving home, but somewhere inside me there still exists a little girl."

16. Personal communication, December 5, 2003.

17. Personal communication, July 10, 2004.

18. Male workers, including several of its executives, are primarily white, creating both a gender- and race-based hierarchy.

19. Personal communication, May 1, 2003.

20. Personal communication, June 13, 2002.

21. Ibid.

22. Personal communication, June 30, 2002.

23. Ibid. What Peters describes as Japanese Cute may perhaps more accurately be called an Asian or East Asian Cute, especially as similar products and characters at lower prices have been coming out of Korea (e.g., Morning Glory Company). In recent years a Japanese company known as San-X takes the quirkiness of Sanrio one step further, including many food-themed characters out of burnt bread (Kogepan), rice balls (Omusubiya-san), tangerines (Mikan Bouya), cheese (Cheese Family), sweets (Sugar Recipe), and even beer (Beer-chan). Some of San-X's nonfood characters, such as Nyan Nyan Nyanko (kittens), often dress up as food items (e.g., grilled fish, hamburger, hot dog, Chinese *gyoza* dumplings, milkshake, french fries, watermelon, beer, crepe, cafe latte), http://www.those happydays.com/nyako/nykeychains.htm. Accessed February 2, 2005.

24. Annalee Newitz, "The Apotheosis of Cute," *San Francisco Bay Guardian*, August 3, 2002.

25. Ibid.

26. Lesley Gillilan, "Hello Kitty Overkill?" *Financial Times*, January 24, 2004, p. W11.

27. For more information, see http://www.davidandgoliathtees.com

28. Company spokesperson Lauren Siktberg says, "GBK [Goodbye Kitty] is definitely seen as an anti-Hello Kitty, but it was not meant to be, believe it or not. . . . He [Goldman] just doesn't like cats. That's all there is to it. He just thought it was funny." Personal communication, February 9, 2005. This disavowal concurs with the company's motto, which is, "[W]here being stupid is smart!" Even though Goldman says that Hello Kitty was not a direct target, the company draws upon knowledge of Sanrio's Kitty to amplify the pointedness of their humor. In other words, the Goodbye Kitty series may be considered humorous regardless of the context, but set against the cuteness of Hello Kitty, its humor is particularly barbed.

29. Lorraine Carpenter, "Stranger in the Night," *Montreal Mirror*, December 19, 2002, http://www.montrealmirror.com/ARCHIVES/2002/121902/fashion. html. Accessed February 9, 2005. For more information on Emily Strange, see http://www.emilystrange.com.

30. http://www.geekgirlz-r.us/links.html/. Accessed February 9, 2005.

31. For more on Mashimaro in Korean, see http://www.mashimaro.co.kr/.

32. http://www.geocities.com/lindsy0287/evilkitty.html. Accessed May 1, 2003.

33. http://www.geocities.com/kill_kitty_here/main.html. Accessed May 1, 2003.

34. http://kuoi.asui.uidaho.edu/~kamikaze/sanrio/. Accessed May 1, 2003.

35. Ibid.

36. http://www.nationallampoon.com/flashbacks/wg/hj00.html. Accessed February 11, 2005. Hello Jesus is a creation of Fred Graver and Philip Scheur, and was published in the April 1984 issue of *National Lampoon*.

37. Ibid.

38. http://www.japantimes.co.jp/cgi-bin/getarticle.p15?ed20041010a2.htm. Accessed February 11, 2005.

39. Joseph S. Nye, Jr., *Soft Power: The Means to Success in World Politics* (New York: Public Affairs, 2004), pp. 6, 7.

40. Anne Allison, "Cuteness as Japan's Millennial Product," in *Pikachu's Global Adventure: The Rise and Fall of Pokémon*, ed. Joseph Tobin (Durham, NC: Duke University Press, 2004), p. 34.

41. Ryuji Iwasaki, personal communication, November 7, 2004.

42. For comparisons with anti-Pokémon critique, see Christine Yano, "Panic Attacks: Anti-Pokémon Voices in Global Markets," in *Pikachu's Global Adventure*, pp. 132–133.

43. Peter Stallybrass and Alton White, *The Politics and Poetics of Transgression* (Ithaca, NY: Cornell University Press, 1986), p. 4.

44. Koichi Iwabuchi, "Japan as a Global Cultural Power," in *Pikachu's Global Adventure*, p. 57.

12

KIKAIDA FOR LIFE: CULT FANDOM IN A JAPANESE LIVE-ACTION TV SHOW IN HAWAI'I

Hirofumi Katsuno

INTRODUCTION

Change! Switch on! 1–2–3!! After a brief moment of silence, the mighty red-and-blue android, Kikaida, appeared on stage, raising a storm of excitement in the crowd of several thousand. It was April 12, 2002, a cool, breezy day at the Japanese Cultural Center of Hawai'i in Honolulu. For the first time in over two decades, fans would see a Japanese *tokusatsu* (live-action) superhero on stage in Hawai'i.[1]

During the 1970s, KIKU-TV, a Japanese-language station in Hawai'i, broadcast a series of Japanese *tokusatsu* shows.[2] In February 1974, two years after its original broadcast in Japan, *Kikaida* made its debut in Hawai'i, achieving overnight popularity.[3] *Kikaida* started a craze among young fans, especially boys, garnering higher ratings than any American children's television programs.[4] Its success was amplified by a merchandising bonanza of related products such as dolls, T-shirts, books, and recordings from Japan.[5] Twenty-six years later, in November 2001, KIKU began to rebroadcast the series and issue related collectibles at the request of diehard adult fans. This generated a second *Kikaida* boom in Hawai'i. The original fans from various ethnic backgrounds, now in their thirties and forties, were dubbed "Generation Kikaida" by KIKU.

This essay examines how the nostalgic hyperconsumption of *Kikaida* products in Hawai'i has developed from a small-scale cult fandom to a new direct-marketing strategy following the redeployment of *Kikaida* by KIKU in the 2000s. The *Kikaida* phenomenon traces a different path from other major *tokusatsu* shows such as Godzilla films and the Power Ranger television series that have become globally popular.[6] The *Kikaida* phenomenon is specific to Hawai'i, constituted by a liminal geography between the continental United States and Japan, combined with youthful nostalgia for 1970s Japanese-influenced media culture and canny marketing by a local production company.[7]

THEORIZING CULT FANDOM

One problem in discussing this revival fandom is that cult fans, regular fans, and more general consumers mingle within a given fandom. Making a distinction between "fans" and consumers is relatively easy. I can recognize the degree of intensity in terms of fans' relationships with *Kikaida* texts, secondary productions, and fan organizations. Still, under this standard, "cult" fans and regular fans are interchangeable. Matt Hills considers the essence of cult fandom to be its duration, "especially in the absence of 'new' or official material in the originating medium."[8] In other words, by Hills' definition, the 1970s *Kikaida* craze in Hawai'i is not cultic since it did not acquire cult status until diehard followers appeared after the end of the official broadcast.

The interviewees I focus on in this essay were longterm, diehard fans long before the revival campaign started in Hawai'i or they had become possessed by the superhero within the year before the revival campaign started. In either case, these fans can be distinguished from general consumers or even those who self-identified as fans only after KIKU's campaign started. However intense their consumption during the campaign, they left Kikaida fandom in early 2005 after the end of KIKU's campaign. By contrast, cult fans appeared independently from the market-oriented revival campaign, although they influenced its participatory culture.

The word "cult" is loosely applied by the media to describe films and television shows that seem to have some features in common. Generally, they fall into a particular genre (e.g., horror, monster, fantasy, science fiction, Japanese anime, B-movies); present a flagrant disregard for "good" taste or blatant and vulgar anarchy; are produced, distributed, and aired by small, peripheral companies outside the commercial film studios and TV stations; and are repetitively watched and collected by an enthusiastic niche audience. However, not every horror movie or low-budget movie is considered a cult film. For a show to achieve cult status requires a "full circuit of communication, that is, text, production/distribution, and audiences, rather than . . . an overvaluation of any one or two of these three factors."[9] J.P. Telotte calls this circuit of communication "supertext" in distinguishing cult films or television shows from conventional genres.[10] That is, "cult" is not a genre in which a set of films or television shows can be identified by a common quality of style. The similarity between cult shows can be better explained through Wittgenstein's concept of "family resemblances": it appears as a total phenomenon articulating quality of text, circulation, and enthusiastic spectatorship.[11]

Kikaida is characterized by a large "metatext" consisting of "seriality, textual density and the nonlinearity of multiple time frames and settings." These "create the space for fans to revel in the development of characters and long, complex narrative arcs both within the commercial texts and their own, noncommercial spin-offs."[12] As I will demonstrate, *Kikaida* shows have a complex internal logic, partly because they transgress multiple generic aspects as children's shows, science fiction, hero action, monster shows, and comedy. These shows combine realistic and imaginary characters in both utopian and dystopian modes, developing a contradictory world of fantasy where philosophical questions can be explored. Fredric Jameson accounts for how popular culture strategically and simultaneously arouses a utopian dream and contains the ways that the aroused desires can be acted out.[13] This feature in *Kikaida* is constituted by a nonlinear narrative. The text contains multiple storylines and settings and emphasizes each character's background. Consequently, the narrative readily deviates laterally, encouraging fans to make multiple emotional investments and creating a potentially infinite metatext that brings about continuous discussion on the authentic message of *Kikaida* among cult fans. *Kikaida* fans emphasize the show's quality, particularly the philosophical questions posed by robot battles, thereby celebrating the contradictory complexity of the text.

Kikaida fans are somewhat different from what Henry Jenkins calls "textual poachers," who appropriate texts from the dominant culture to create an alternative, resistant participatory culture.[14] *Kikaida* cult fandom runs against the dominant American discourse and aesthetics by valuing a quality of text that is opposed to the dominant aesthetic within the American mediascape. Kikaida ostensibly looks cheesy and old-fashioned compared to current commercial television. Fans use *Kikaida* texts to legitimate "their sense of distinction and identity from, and superiority to, those who are damned by their preference for the mainstream and commercial: those who do not know better."[15]

In the following sections, I will discuss how fans construct this antimainstream taste by reference to (1) socially structured access to economic and cultural resources, that is, their middle-class background; (2) nostalgia based on their generational background; and (3) Hawai'i's geo-political liminality between the continental United States and Japan.

CIRCULATION AND MARKETING

Jenkins's idea of "textual poachers" is grounded upon Michel de Certeau's model as a kind of metaphorical space that is being fought over.[16] Inherent to the notion is a separation between the roles of owner and poacher. Jenkins recognizes that development of interactive media, primarily the Internet, forces the media industry (the owner) to be accountable to its audiences (potential poachers).[17] Consequently, according to Jenkins, the media industry actually coopts audience resistance into the commercial economy. Mark Jancovich and Nathan Hunt similarly comment that the increased rise of cult television shows (e.g., *Babylon 5, Twin Peaks, X-Files*) in the last couple of decades has influenced the production and marketing strategies of local television stations and network television: "Despite the rhetoric of [British and American] audiences declaring their opposition to the media and cultural industries, they are rather intimately and intricately related to them."[18] *Kikaida* fans and marketers/distributors of *Kikaida* products have mutually influenced one another, particularly in the context of the *Kikaida* revival in Hawai'i. KIKU, a small television station with an ethnic audience base, may have found it necessary to integrate this bottom-up labor force into the marketing process in order to manage the campaign and develop a broader audience. *Kikaida* fandom therefore provides an interesting case study for considering the relationship between marketers and fans in contemporary media.

Kikaida fandom in Hawai'i started after some fans launched unofficial fan clubs or personal web pages in tribute to the classic *tokusatsu* Japanese superhero. Before the advent of the Internet, cult activities drew on unofficial, personal connections to Japan. Some fans bought books, VHS tapes, or CDs while visiting Japan; others asked their Japanese friends to ship such products to Hawai'i. Ronnie, a 38-year-old Spanish and Portuguese American, born and raised in Hawai'i, described the beginning of her involvement in *Kikaida* fandom:

> In the 1990s, I started music full time, here and mainland. What I used to do was, when we had Japanese visitors, we thought they [would be aware of] the Kikaida song. We sang the whole song. . . . I created a Kikaida song and the whole band played it, too.[19]

To a large degree, the fandom in Hawai'i was made possible by the fluid circulation of products, ideas, and people between Japan and Hawai'i.

Web sites increased around 1998, just after the twenty-fifth anniversary of *Kikaida* had been celebrated in Japan in 1997. Cult fans in Hawai'i started purchasing *Kikaida* tribute products such as books, action figures, and CDs over the Internet. Collector's events were soon held. Fans then began to pressure KIKU through email and telephone calls to rerun the show. In May 2001, Joanne Ninomiya, president of JN-Productions (JNP), a company closely affiliated with KIKU, decided to reacquire broadcasting and merchandising rights. A DVD series with new English translations and commercial goods such as T-shirts and posters were produced locally by JN-Production under the logo "Generation Kikaida."

What characterizes *Kikaida* fandom is fans' closeness not only to the media industry but also to their stars and robotic superheroes. Most events are supported by fans, some as volunteers and others employed for the job. They regulate lines and clean up venues, as well as create costumes, arrange and perform music, and act as extras on stage. JNP often invites actors Ban Daisuke (who plays Jiro in *Kikaida*) and Ikeda Shunsuke (Ichiro in *Kikaida 01*) to fan events. They appear in costumes made by fans that accurately reproduce the superheroes from *Kikaida*, *Kikaida 01*, and other classic Japanese *tokusatsu* TV shows that have been aired in Hawai'i. Ronnie and Nila, a 36-year-old Filipino American raised in Hawai'i, explain how proximity to the stars and costumed superheroes plays a significant role in *Kikaida* fandom in Hawai'i:[20]

Nila: Waruda and Bijinda, it's the first showing of these costumes in Hawai'i.[21]
Ronnie: Not even in Japan, according to my friend in Japan. He never saw Bijinda and Waruda costumes in Japan. We created it.
Nila: So, it's sort of like for us, Generation Kikaida, history making.
Ronnie: Yeah, that's [what] we call history. Because even back in the 1970s, Kikaida came several times for appearances here, but not Bijinda and Waruda.
Nila: It's the first time. And, it's first time, too, for the new generation, the new kids to see the live characters up front in person, you know. We never had that chance as children. Only just the main characters, but never like the secondary or supporting characters. This is the first time I can. So, real treat for the newer ones and their parents, who are our generation. They let kids watch the show.
Ronnie: Fans and kids today are more lucky to see Kikaida because it's more available.
Nila: Yes!!!
Ronnie: Back then [in the 1970s], Joanne [Ninomiya] hired actual, real people from Japan. Back then, it was so crowded, it was so hard to get close to them. It's like superstars, really hard to get close to them. Long lines, crowds . . .
HK: So, do you think in the 1970s there was a certain distance between Kikaida and fans, but not so much now?
Ronnie: Yeah, I think so. People tend to be more personally touchable. They shake hands.
Nila: Yeah, yeah.
Ronnie: Because of this fan base, like Rhein, Miura-san, they made the costumes.
Nila: They feel more closer to the characters today, I think. Because they can touch them and take a picture with them. They can shake hands with Ban-san. When I met him like two years ago, it was like, "You are my idol. I can touch you!" you know. So, now, just touch him and speak to him. For me it's like a childhood dream comes true. I never, when he first arrived, I couldn't see him because line was too long and tickets were sold out. But, now it feels more personal, means more to me now. Especially for adult growing up in childhood watching your superhero.
Ronnie: Yeah, more accessible.

Samantha Barbas asserts that the construction of celebrity is in a large part grounded upon making stars appear "from reel to real."[22] Fans desire a connection to stars that feels in the flesh instead of merely on the screen. This commercially created closeness between fans and their heroes has contributed to making *Kikaida* a cult television show in Hawai'i.

Most fans recognize that Hawai'i is the only place where *Kikaida* is such a phenomenon today. Some fans even told me that people in Hawai'i understand *Kikaida* more than do the Japanese. Presenting Hawai'i as a sacred place for *Kikaida* is an integral part of JNP's marketing strategy. JNP incorporates *Kikaida* into Hawai'i state government events, including the declaration of *Kikaida* days on April 11, 2002 and October 29, 2004. This brought about a rebound in Japanese *Kikaida* fandom. One major Japanese travel agency, Kinki Nihon Tourist, created a pilgrimage tour for Japanese fans to participate in the *Kikaida* events in Hawai'i in April 2002. Thus, in this cult fandom, fans and the media industry share a relationship of mutual power and influence.

THE KIKAIDA TEXT

Kikaida Narrative

Kikaida was originally produced by the Japanese TV and film production studio Tōei in 1972, during the heyday of *tokusatsu* superhero programming that ran from the late 1960s to the beginning of the 1980s. The script was written by a well-known *manga* (comic book) author, Ishinomori Shōtarō, who created numerous superheroes with Tōei. One of his masterpieces, *Kamen Raidā* (Masked Rider) established *henshin* (metamorphosis) as a key concept in Japanese *tokusatsu*. *Henshin* is a central theme in the *Kikaida* series as well, posing philosophical questions that I will discuss later.

Kikaida plotlines center on an epic battle against a villainous organization, Dark, which is attempting to conquer the world using androids. At the beginning of the series, the organization captures Dr Kōmyōji, an authority on robotics, and his assistant and daughter Mitsuko, and tries to force them to build androids. While imprisoned by Dark, Dr Kōmyōji secretly creates a conscience circuit and puts it into a mechanical man. The result is Jiro, a motorcycle-riding, guitar-playing, denim-clad human figure who can transform into Kikaida, a red and blue android that fights evil. Evil Professor Gill, the head of Dark, finds out what Dr Kōmyōji is up to. He stops him just before the final piece of the conscience circuit can be installed, so Kikaida's conscience remains incomplete. Kikaida rescues Mitsuko and they escape from Dark. Dr Kōmyōji also manages to escape from Gill, but suffers a severe case of amnesia. The brilliant scientist wanders from town to town in a mental fog, taking jobs varying from gardening to driving a cab, even tending bar. The 43 episodes of *Kikaida* follow Jiro/Kikaida's journey with Mitsuko and her younger brother Masaru as they track down Dr Kōmyōji.

According to Hal Blythe and Charlie Sweet, the traditional superhero narrative moves through six stages: (1) introduction of a powerful menace; (2) appearance of a superhero; (3) pursuit; (4) confrontations between superhero and supervillain; (5) victory achieved through the superhero's intelligence; and (6) restoration of order.[23] In this genre, superheroes cannot exist without foes. Similarly, each *Kikaida* episode follows a conventional format: (1) Professor Gill introduces a robotic monster to perpetrate a sinister plan; (2) Mitsuko and Masaru somehow get involved in trying to stop the crime; (3) the robotic monster and drone androids attack, but are interrupted by the familiar strains of Jiro's guitar music. Jiro appears in a quarry, denounces the monsters, flings his guitar away, and plunges into the fray; (4) the destructor monster and drones retreat, and Jiro rides off on his bright yellow motorcycle, Sidemachine. A shaken Mitsuko and Masaru, along with any innocent survivors, are left to carry on with their angst-ridden search for their father; (5) the destructor and drones mount a second attack, and again Jiro appears. Unfortunately, Jiro's weakness, an incomplete conscience circuit, renders him vulnerable to Professor Gill's mind-controlling flute. Jiro suffers excruciating pain resisting the flute's shrill strains wooing him to the Dark side; (6) invariably, a fortuitous explosion or ear-splitting noise will momentarily block out the evil flute, providing Jiro the window of opportunity to perform a transformation sequence "Change! Switch on! 1–2–3!!" The pulsating Kikaida theme song plays in the background; (7) Jiro transforms into Kikaida to save the day, then rides off on his motorcycle, once again leaving Mitsuko and Masaru behind.[24]

These contrived and predictable narrative rules enable Kikaida fans to develop a sense of community as they act out responses to such key points of the show in fan events. In a *Kikaida* stage show, for instance, fans make noises to block out the sound of Professor Gill's flute. They also sing the theme song together in Japanese when Jiro escapes from the evil flute and successfully transforms into Kikaida. Such performative, ritualized collective reactions at predictable points are part of the attraction. The fandom consists of both text and fan participation. Their special knowledge of the plotlines is a kind of unofficial cultural capital that discourages newcomers from taking part.

Metatextuality of Kikaida

According to Ōtsuka Eiji and Sasakibara Gō, in the traditional superhero narratives, it is always foes who bring drama to the show.[25] Superheroes solve problems caused by villains. The superhero's position is autonomous, stable, and absolute. The TV show can therefore continue a long run based on a simple didactic pattern. In the case of Ishinomori's work, however, the relationship between the superhero and the foe reverses. Ishinomori's superheroes are always robots, cyborgs, or mutants submitting to relentless fate. Drama is elicited by problems internal to the superheroes. Given such internal dilemmas, as Ōtsuka and Sasakibara point out, Ishinomori's superheroes are not suitable for long-term series, since the stories end when the superheroes solve their problems.

In the case of *Kikaida*, most fans agree that the "conscience circuit" is the underlying dramatic problem. Dr Kōmyōji intended the conscience circuit to enable Kikaida to act autonomously, rather than at the command of humans. But because Dr Kōmyōji had to activate Kikaida with the circuit still incomplete, Jiro cannot transform into Kikaida when Professor Gill plays his cataleptic flute until he finds a way to drown out the evil sound. Once Jiro changes into Kikaida, the flute is ineffective in controlling him. The strong, immortal body of the robot is normally an object of modern desire. The audience experiences a utopian state by fantasizing themselves as Kikaida in the action scenes. Ironically, however, Jiro's powerful mechanical body is the object of aversion, affliction, and even a feeling of inferiority. Because of his incomplete conscience circuit, Jiro is always in danger of being controlled by an evil force. What makes the narrative even richer in meaning is that the more robotic monsters Jiro battles, the more he shies away from getting the complete conscience circuit installed.

Kikaida episodes sometimes turn out to be profound, even contradictory, despite targeting children as the prime audience. This complexity makes the genre ambiguous and draws out multiple readings from adult fans. For example, fans usually react to the *Kikaida* storyline in two ways. Jason, a 35-year-old, 75 percent Filipino and 25 percent Portuguese American who teaches at an English language school in Honolulu, pointed out, "Jiro didn't want to be a complete robot . . . because if his conscience circuit is incomplete, it will give him a freedom to decide between what is good or bad. In this sense, he is a lot more human."[26] In a similar vein, Nila commented, "Jiro wanted to be more human. He didn't want to be perfect, because I think it is his imperfection that made him strong."[27] By contrast, Ed, a 36-year-old Japanese American shopkeeper told me that "Jiro knew machine is machine after all, even if he got a complete conscience circuit."[28] Jason and Nila see a modern humanism in Kikaida's inner struggle; they essentialize mind as the core of humanity. Ed's reaction is more critical. He sees the body as determining humanity. These contradictory reactions to the same text do not mean either reading is right or wrong, since the contradiction is already embedded in the text. In other words, fans' reactions involve factors both in the text and in the individual, although the ways in which fans choose particular readings are complex.

Another enduring storyline in the *Kikaida* text is the relationship between Jiro and the heroine, Mitsuko. Almost all the fans, male and female, mention that their enthusiasm for *Kikaida* in part owes to this romantic relationship. Fans emphasize Mitsuko's devotion to Jiro, despite knowing that her love can never find fruition. Their reactions are gendered, however. Male fans describe an infatuation with the heroine; some even call Mitsuko their "first love." Anthony, a 39-year-old Portuguese, Spanish, Hawai'ian, and Puerto Rican American triathlete, said that Mitsuko strongly influenced his concept of the ideal woman:

> I liked Mitsuko. I liked her. She influenced my ideals of what real women should be like. . . . Honestly, I have no attraction to white women. I am serious. . . . When I look at Japanese women, they look exciting, enjoyable, lovable, and attractive. But looking at other types, they don't attract me at all. I'm not prejudiced or anything, but I'm telling the truth. . . . Japanese women make the best mothers, too. Most of them are loyal to their men. They don't cheat on their men. They don't look at the other men.[29]

Anthony's ideal woman is a racial and cultural narrative. He finds in the *Kikaida* show an old-fashioned, heterosexual, romantic ideal of femininity that relates to a stereotypic image of Japanese women.

In contrast, the reactions of female fans center on unrequited romantic feelings for Jiro. Nila, for instance, emphasized how she wished Mitsuko and Jiro could get together. Lynn, a 35-year-old Japanese American shopkeeper, described their waffling relationship as "very Japanese" in that they do not express themselves directly.[30] Lynn also pointed out Jiro's lack of overt sex appeal compared to traditional American superheroes. Ban Daisuke, who plays Jiro, stands about five-feet-six-inches tall and is very skinny and emotionally unexpressive. Lynn attributed the ambivalent relationship between Jiro and Mitsuko to Japanese cultural stereotypes.

Although female fans did not mention this, the "waffling relationship" is partly due to an incest taboo. As the creator of Jiro, Dr Kōmyōji is symbolically his parent, so Jiro and Mitsuko are structurally in a brother-sister relationship. At the same time, they are decisively different in terms of physicality, since one is robot and the other human. Their ambivalent relationship appears in concrete form primarily whenever Mitsuko has to fix Jiro's mechanical body. While Mitsuko is happy to get closer to his "mind" through his body, Jiro shies away from showing his mechanical body to her. Again, the issue of mind and body become controversial, delaying the resolution of the narrative hermeneutics.

Characters

The metatextuality of *Kikaida* is also grounded upon the uniqueness of each character, including the monster robots. The monster robots are modeled upon animals and insects (e.g., praying mantis, flying squirrel, rhinoceros, starfish) that are dying out due to the environmental disruption caused by the uncritical worship of science and civilization. Creatures facing human-driven extinction gain revenge against human beings by means of scientific technology, which implicitly symbolizes the dark side of human civilization. Ironically, it is a robot, Kikaida, who protects humans from the robot monsters.

The fact that each robotic monster has some degree of uniqueness increases the metatextuality of *Kikaida*. The nonlineality of the series encourages fans to make an emotional investment in particular characters, including the evil monsters. Among 42 robotic characters created by Dark, Hakaida (or Hakaider) is inordinately popular. Hakaida only appears in the last five episodes, but it is recognized as one of the most popular villains in the history of Japanese *tokusatsu*. Its cultic status resulted in the production of an original film, *Hakaider*, in 1995.

Hakaida appeals to fans because it is the only humanoid robot created by Dark, aside from Kikaida. The body of Hakaida was made by Dr Kōmyōji at the direction of Dark in order to destroy *(hakai)* Kikaida. Hakaida is black from head to toe, an expert gun-slinger, and rides a 750 cc Kawasaki motorcycle. Many fans note a resemblance both in terms of visual and internal character between Hakaida and Darth Vader in *Star Wars*, suggesting proudly that Hakaida inspired George Lucas.[31] More importantly, fans are fascinated by the background drama involved in this character. Unlike most other robotic monsters, Hakaida is not one-dimensional. He doesn't blindly follow the whim of his master. His evil circuit is the counter to Jiro's conscience circuit. Hakaida is a cyborg, part machine, part human. The living part is his brain, which is actually Dr Kōmyōji's brain, revealed within a transparent head. In what seems to be a side effect of being programmed as the essential Kikaida killer, Hakaida swallows this as his own personal agenda, regardless of the wayward tactics assigned to him by his master. Some fans regard Hakaida as Kikaida's younger brother, because he was created by Kōmyōji. However, it is technically Kōmyōji himself. Kikaida can't kill Hakaida or Kōmyōji dies, and if he doesn't fight back he will fall victim to the tenacity of his enemy. These are the kinds of dilemmas this series sets up so well.

In episode 42, when Kikaida is defeated by another evil android, Hakaida loses control, saying "What am I? What purpose was I created for? . . . What is left for me to live for?! What is my purpose? How will I live from now on? . . . I despise Professor Gill for creating me!"[32] Many fans agree that such complexity in a robotic character is one of the biggest appeals of this TV program. For instance, Saburo, a 38-year-old local comic book distributor and Chinese male born in the Philippines, explained: "Hakaida is not like . . . that bad guys are just straight on bad guys. Then, nobody will sympathize with that. But if you make him complicated, if you give a motivation, give a reason, people then like the character."[33] Jason pointed out that "a deep existentialism underlies *Kikaida*."[34]

Another character that has given rise to heated debate among fans is Gold Wolf, which appears in episode 11, "Tormented Howls from Hell." Like Kikaida's reaction to Hakaida, this episode triggers a string of moral dilemmas. Gold Wolf appears more or less human, is one of Dr Kōmyōji's robots (thus also Jiro's brother), and is equipped with a conscience circuit (although less complete than Jiro's). He acts friendly to Mitsuko and Masaru in his human form because of his conscience circuit. However, on a night with a full moon, Gold Wolf transforms into an evil monster. Near the end of the episode, Jiro hesitates over killing Gold Wolf because of their connection and because Gold Wolf also has a "mind," however incomplete. Finally, after destroying Gold Wolf, Kikaida cries.

Nila told me that this scene is understandable "because Kikaida did have a heart."[35] For Nila, the tears symbolize the humanity inside Kikaida. Ed reacted to the scene more cynically, suggesting with a laugh that the tears are "just coolant discharge."[36] Ed confessed that he does not like this particular scene, since it constitutes an obstacle to the consistency of his reading of the text. Dramatization of characters in interconnected story lines thus extends beyond any single episode to become a metatext that leads fans to close textual analysis.

NOSTALGIA, GENERATIONAL IDENTITY, AND COMMUNITAS

In interviews, fans repeatedly emphasized how the collective actions at fan events strengthen their sense of unity. I assert that the solidarity felt by fans is not generated through passive absorption. Rather, by actively participating in collective events, they create "communitas." As Victor Turner puts it, "Communitas is almost always thought of or portrayed by actors as a timeless condition, an eternal now, as 'a moment in and out of time,' or as a state to which the structural view of time is not applicable."[37] Communitas allows fans to pursue what Roger Aden calls "symbolic pilgrimage," which "features individuals ritualistically revisiting powerful places that are symbolically envisioned through the interaction of story and individual imagination."[38] According to Aden, the symbolic pilgrimage in popular culture is grounded upon complex feelings for "home" in that "we seek to leave it, yet paradoxically we yearn for it as we find ourselves between places or in other places. Consequently, our symbolic pilgrimages leave us longing for a return to a comforting standpoint even as we enjoy the view from other places."[39]

The idea of symbolic pilgrimage is useful for understanding the formation of *Kikaida* fandom as communitas for those who grew up with Japanese *tokusatsu*, particularly *Kikaida*, in 1970s Hawai'i. Through relishing this classic TV show in the current context, cult fans are led to romantic yearning and longing for home, "returning to a time and place they know reaffirms a sense of who they are by reminding them of who they were."[40] For example, Nila's excitement about reconnecting with the past is made possible only through interacting in the present with other fans from the same generation. She says,

> I guess *Kikaida* was always in our hearts. But, this revival sort of opened our hearts. And, I guess it helped . . . reconcile childhood dreams to the present, make it kind of come together for us. . . . It's sort of like you lock away your precious toys and memories. And then something triggers it. You meet the right people who have the same interest and excitement toward it. . . . And then you realize you are not alone. It kind of unifies our generation in that sense, who have the same enthusiasm, who have the same passion for the sense of past, the childhood memories. . . . I was thinking, why *Kikaida* is so popular now and why we are getting back into it, [is] because it lets you feel like a child again. It gives you the same spirit, energy, enthusiasm, innocence, and, ah, so many memories, wonderful memories.[41]

For Nila, *Kikaida* is a path through which she can symbolically return to the good old days. For fans, this sentimental attachment to *Kikaida* legitimizes the internal structure of this generational group and provides a claim to a collectively shared past. In the ever-changing postmodern reality, their imaginary home becomes fixed in their fandom, allowing fans to experience communitas as a liminal state between adult and child.

Their yearning for home reflects their reality as middle-class adults. They create communitas by consciously or unconsciously establishing themselves as insiders through a set of rules (e.g., predetermined reactions to the predictable plotlines in stage shows) and anti-mainstream aesthetics based on transgressive, cheesy, and peripheral elements. These may not make sense by the commonsensical standard. In this sense, *Kikaida* cult fans are conformists in their own way. Their *Kikaida*-centered-cocoon is the product of economic and emotional investment in the text and related products. Thus, the formation of fan community is also intimately connected with ways in which KIKU has marketed and distributed *Kikaida* in Hawai'i.

CONCLUSION

The logic of the *Kikaida* phenomenon in Hawai'i is different from the normal global consumption of Japanese popular culture in that it is not based on a marketing strategy generated by a Japanese corporation or Hollywood. *Kikaida* has been appropriated by a local marketer in Hawai'i and fans making their own meanings out of it. Whereas fans actively celebrate the quality of text and create a space of communitas, KIKU/JNP attempts to turn Kikaida into a local icon through nostalgia marketing. Different *Kikaida* fans read the text differently. They continually poach their own meanings. However, unlike Jenkins's poachers, *Kikaida* fandom has developed in close relation to KIKU's commercially created participatory culture.

Although fan relations to *Kikaida* operate within a particular sensibility connected to the pleasure of fantasy, the contexts in which their actions take place are embedded within an intricate macrodynamics of sociocultural, historical, economic, and geopolitical forces. In this fandom, the mix of personal and collective fantasies transforms the media text into consumer identities for a particular generation.

NOTES

1. Although *tokusatsu* literally means "special effects," it is generically used to refer to live-action cinema or TV show *kaijū* (monsters, such Godzilla and Gamera), *henshin* (transforming superheroes such as *Kamen* [masked] *Rider* and *Kikaida*), and *sentai* (battle team shows such as *Go Ranger* or *Battle Fever J*). Subgenres include *robotto* (robot) fantasy series (e.g., Robocon) and *metaru* (metal) heroes (e.g., Space Sheriff Gavan and Galaxy Wolf Juspion).
2. These included *Kamen-Rider V3, Go Ranger, Robocon, Diamong Eye, Inazuman*, and *Battle Fever J*, as well as *Kikaida*.
3. The official title of the TV show is *Jinzō Ningen Kikaida* (Mechanical Man Kikaida, also called Kikaida in Hawai'i). Kikaida made its continental U.S. debut in 1975 on San Francisco's Fuji Television, but the show never caught on as it did in Hawai'i.
4. *Time* magazine reported that *Kikaida* and other superhero programs favoring martial arts moves were the top children's programs in Hawai'i in 1975, even surpassing *Sesame Street* in the Nielsen ratings. *Time*, May 5, 1975, pp. 61–62.
5. In January 1975, Shirokiya, a Japanese department store in Honolulu, reported Christmas holiday sales of over 6,000 Japanese superhero dolls. Shirokiya also sold 48,000 *Kikaida* T-shirts in about six months. Another Japanese supermarket, Daiei, sold more than 4,000 *Kikaida* soundtrack albums in a single month in 1974. *Honolulu Magazine* (November 2000), pp. 134–136.
6. For details on the marketing and consumption of the Power Ranger series in the United States, see Anne Allison, "Sailor Moon, Japanese Superheroes for Global

Girls," in *Japan Pop! Inside the World of Japanese Popular Culture*, ed. T.J. Craig (Armonk, NY: M.E. Sharpe, 2000).

7. This study is based upon fieldwork conducted between April 2002 and May 2003 in Honolulu, Hawai'i. Methods included participating in fan events, monitoring fan-based web sites, and conducting one or more hour-long interviews with a total of 15 fans and marketers of *Kikaida* at KIKU. Follow-up research was conducted until November 2004.

8. Matt Hills, *Fan Cultures* (London: Routledge, 2002), p. x.

9. Sara Gwenllian-Jones and Roberta Pearson, "Introduction" in *Cult Television*, ed. Sara Gwenllian-Jones and Roberta Pearson (Minneapolis: University of Minnesota Press, 2004), p. x.

10. J.P. Telotte, "Introduction: Mapping the Cult," in *The Cult Film Experience: Beyond All Reason*, ed. J.P. Telotte (Austin: University of Texas Press, 1991), p. 8.

11. Hills, *Fan Cultures*, pp. 131–143.

12. Gwenllian-Jones and Pearson, "Introduction," p. xvii.

13. Fredric Jameson, *Signatures of the Visible* (New York: Routledge, 1992).

14. Henry Jenkins, *Textual Poachers: Television Fans & Participatory Culture* (New York: Routledge, 1992).

15. Mark Jancovich and Nathan Hunt, "The Mainstream, Distinction, and Cult TV," in *Cult Television*, ed. S.G. Pearson (Minneapolis: University of Minnesota Press, 2004), p. 42.

16. Jenkins, *Textual Poachers*; Michel de Certeau, *The Practice of Everyday Life* (Berkeley: University of California Press, 1984).

17. Matt Hills, "Henry Jenkins" (interview), *Intensities: The Journal of Cult Media*, 2 (Autumn/Winter 2001).

18. Jancovich and Hunt, "The Mainstream, Distinction, and Cult TV," p. 38.

19. Personal communication, January 25, 2003.

20. From an interview conducted January 25, 2003. HK is Hirofumi Katsuno.

21. Both Bijinda and Waruda are characters from *Kikaida 01*.

22. Samantha Barbas, *Movie Crazy: Fans, Stars, and the Cult of Celebrity* (New York: Palgrave, 2001), p. 9.

23. Hal Blythe and Charlie Sweet, "Superhero: The Six Step Progression" in *The Hero in Transition*, ed. R.B. Fishwick (Bowling Green: Bowling Green State University Popular Press, 1983), pp. 182–184.

24. See the Generation Kikaida Hawaii web site by JN Productions (http://www.generationkikaida.com) for details on the Kikaida storyline.

25. Ōtsuka Eiji and Sasakibara Gō, *Kyōyō to shite no "manga, anime"* (Tokyo: Kodansha, 2001).

26. Personal communication, March 24, 2004.

27. Personal communication, January 25, 2003.

28. Personal communication, May 5, 2003. The interview with Ed was conducted in a combination of Japanese and English, although English is his first language. I have translated the Japanese terms.

29. Here "Japanese" means Japanese nationals, not Japanese Americans. Personal communication, April 15, 2002.

30. Personal communication, April 13, 2002.

31. George Lucas once admitted in an interview that Darth Vader was based on Hakaider, a villain from the superhero TV series, *Jinzō Ningen Kikaida*, which he saw while he was in Japan.

32. At this point, Hakaida does not know that he is a creation of Dr Kōmyōji.

33. Personal communication, January 10, 2003.
34. Personal communication, March 24, 2004.
35. Personal communication, January 25, 2003.
36. Personal communication, May 5, 2003.
37. Victor Turner, *Dramas, Fields, and Metaphors: Symbolic Action in Human Society* (Ithaca, NY: Cornell University Press, 1974), p. 238.
38. Roger Aden, *Popular Stories and Promised Lands: Fan Cultures and Symbolic Pilgrimages* (Tuscaloosa: University of Alabama Press, 2001), p. 10.
39. Ibid., p. 101.
40. Ibid., p. 43.
41. Personal communication, January 25, 2003.

13

Apocalypse in Fantasy and Reality: Japanese Pop Culture in Contemporary Russia

Yulia Mikhailova

Introduction

Scholars of Russo-Japanese affairs often note that in contrast to political relations, abundant in confrontations and disagreement, the cultural encounters between Russia and Japan have always been mutually enriching and fruitful. Suffice it to say that in the first half of the twentieth century, Japanese intellectuals were fascinated with Russian literature, seeking in it a means for individual and national identity.[1] The cultural flow has now taken the reverse course and many young Russians are captivated with Japanese popular culture. Some even say that Japan is no longer exotic because its cultural presence in contemporary Russia is becoming a part of everyday life. Indeed, sushi bars, *yakitori* shops, Doraemon, and Hello Kitty goods may be spotted everywhere. The year 2004 was proclaimed the year of Japanese culture, paving the way for numerous art exhibitions, musical performances, and cinema festivals. Whereas such exhibitions and performances could be enjoyed mainly by the citizens of large urban centers, the majority of Russians, especially the youth, see Japan through the lens of anime and manga.

This phenomenon is, of course, a part of the general process of globalization, as since the second half of the 1980s, Japanese anime and manga began to spread rapidly around the world and communities of their fans, known as *otaku*, also appeared in many countries. The popularity of these genres may be explained by the variety of topics and story lines that they offer, their striking visual difference from Western comics and animation, and by their ability to address problems that contemporary youth is concerned with. According to Susan Napier, these problems of universal significance for youth include technological development (together with the anxieties it brings to human beings), shifting gender identities, and relations between the sexes, as well as the reconsideration of history.[2]

However, is there something specifically Russian that makes Russian anime and manga fans different from their counterparts in other countries? This essay aims to examine *otaku* youth subculture in Russia, which developed around the interest in Japanese anime and manga, and to discuss what needs of Russian youth are satisfied through this interest. This essay is based on information about the activities of Russian anime and manga fans gained through numerous personal observations made during meetings and interviews with them conducted between 1996 and 2004; the results of a survey of 500 *otaku* carried out in March 2004 in St. Petersburg; materials and discussions by *otaku* broadly available on the Internet; their own drawings in the manga style; and the contents of magazines that popularize Japanese pop culture in Russia.

This essay argues that in the process of coming to terms with contradictions of social reality, brought about by the collapse of the previous forms of social and cultural identities in the Russia of the 1990s, and because of the failure of the political and intellectual elite of the country to offer a new national idea or new system of values, some groups of Russian youth found a meaningful system of identification in a culture of foreign origin, namely Japan. It is emphasized here that, although in their graphic works Russian *otaku* try to follow Japanese patterns as closely as possible, their creative and organizational activities reflect the specific social and cultural context of the local society. This offers a possibility for understanding the correlation between the global and the local in contemporary pop culture.

RUSSIAN YOUTH CULTURE IN CHANGE

The official Soviet ideology, formed in the 1930s, vested the young people of the country with the faith that "the happy future lies in the construction of communism" and managed to bring forth an unprecedented enthusiasm for its achievement. However, as Soviet society moved into stagnation in the 1970s and 1980s, this faith and enthusiasm evaporated. The lives of young people and the population in general became sharply divided into official and private spheres. The official sphere was supervised by Komsomol (Young Communist League) and targeted at the organization of youth toward "socially useful activity," such as participation in socialist competition, "shock" construction work[3] and student work brigades, or engagement in officially sanctioned cultural practices.[4] In the private sphere, these official directives were despised and young people were attracted, along with other forms of entertainment, to Western culture as represented by music, style, dance, fashion, sport, and so forth. The authorities, in turn, regarded the influence of Western culture on youth as disruptive, diverting young Soviet men and women from their main task of "building socialism."

Interestingly, although on the level of official Soviet propaganda Japan was treated negatively as an ally of the United States and the possibility of the revival of Japanese militarism was not excluded, even during the cold war the Soviet mass media looked at Japan more sympathetically than at other "capitalist" countries: Japan, in a way, was regarded as the "victim of American imperialism." This idea was clearly expressed, for example, in several jointly produced Soviet-Japanese movies.[5] However, the Japanese film *Gojira*

(1954), which explored the nuclear victimization of Japan by the United States, was never released to the broad public in the Soviet era.[6]

During the years of *perestroika* (1986–1991), when democratization and the pluralism of society were declared as the main goals to be achieved, the dominance of Komsomol was undermined and the former culture of private life flourished in the form of the so-called unofficial organizations (*neformaly*).[7] The Russian people enjoyed previously unimaginable opportunities to read books of formerly forbidden or ignored authors, both native and foreign, to see new movies, and to visit foreign countries. A powerful deluge of information prepared the Russian public for the acceptance of new forms of contemporary culture, including the popular culture of Japan. Young people, by their very nature, became the leading social (and age) group participating in intercultural exchange. They willingly opened their minds and hearts to new information and cultural forms.

The mass media of the time carried information about the activities of punks, bikers, hippies, admirers of hard rock, new religious organizations, and so on. Most of these groups were overtly apolitical in nature and were interested mainly in new forms of culture. At the same time, many young people were preoccupied with semilegal or illegal economic activities such as profiteering in foreign currency exchange, buying and selling Western goods, or setting up small business enterprises. They developed a particular culture of their own that admired consumerism and the accumulation of money (often associated in the mind of Russians with American influence), and that incorporated elements of violence and brutality.

The collapse of the Soviet Union in 1991 had a dramatic effect not only on the elderly people who lost their savings, but on the youth as well. It is well known that the "adolescent/youth state is of particular importance for the identity formation process because of its transitional, or liminal, quality in relation to the other stages in the life course."[8] In post–Soviet Russia this identity search, common to youth in general, coincided with the national identity search process of Russian society as a whole and hence was even more dramatic.

Ironically, it was the former members of Komsomol or children from the families of Soviet *nomenklatura* (high-ranking bureaucrats) who were most successful in their new lives. They were among those who managed, for example, to get grants for studying abroad or to start their own businesses in the process of privatization, owing mainly to the privileges they had through connections in official circles. However, the majority of young people found themselves unemployed, suffering from a lack of sustainable living conditions and financial resources, or simply lost in the rapidly changing reality and unable to adapt quickly to a new lifestyle.[9] The erosion of civil society resulted in the undermining of social safety nets and support systems that had previously provided some sustenance and hope for youth. The Russian mass media and academics characterized the young generation of Russians in the 1990s as deserted by the state and occupying a marginal status in society.[10] This tendency would continue into the next century.[11]

From 1992, a market economy opened new opportunities for social mobility and rapid achievement of success, which was understood as enrichment primarily in the sphere of trade and services. The road to this goal often went through criminal activities, for example, racketeering, whereas education was losing its former prestige. The economic and social instability of Russia brought the problem of mere physical survival to the forefront of priorities of young people.

Anomie and disorientation also pushed young people to search for new sources for their social and cultural identity, for new forms of collectivity, and for expression of their aspirations and sensitivities. As noted by G. Murdock, young people everywhere are always in search of the available symbolic resources that they can draw upon in their attempts to make sense of their specific situations and construct viable identities.[12] The increasing polarization and pluralization of Russian society brought forth a broad variety of youth subcultures. However, the loss of norms and values essential for social unity and normal identification became the cause of rapid growth in delinquency and of subcultures associated with the criminal world. Presently, young people comprise 53.6 percent of all criminals in the country.[13]

At the same time, other young Russians have attempted to build their identity on the basis of borrowings from foreign cultures, especially in the spheres of music, dance, and games, embracing forms such as rave, hip-hop or even using the famous novels of J.R.R. Tolkien's *The Lord of the Rings* for costume playing. What is apparently common to many of these groups is the search for an atmosphere in which their members could at least temporarily forget the harsh realities of coming of age in the Russia of the 1990s and early 2000s and withdraw to the fantastic worlds of imagination.

It is important to notice that in the post–Soviet Russia these youth subcultures appeared not in rejection of one dominant adult culture (as it was in late Soviet times), but in opposition to the emptiness of values or the mere lack of them in society in general. It was in this social and cultural context that fans of Japanese anime and manga began to appear in Russia. It should also be noted that their emergence would not have been possible without the process of informatization of the Russian society and the spread of the Internet.

THE BIRTH OF *OTAKU* SUBCULTURE IN RUSSIA

Foreign animation was little known in the Soviet Union until the very last years of the empire because it was officially forbidden along with other forms of foreign culture. In the late 1980s, Disney's *Duck Tales*[14] and similar cartoon movies started to carve a niche in the sphere of entertainment for children. Among them were films of Tōei Animation and Studio Ghibli. Since then, animation of Japanese origin has become a regular feature of TV programming and Japanese movie festivals organized in Russia.[15] However, animation of any sort was regarded as a form of entertainment suitable only for children.

Manga was completely unknown to the Soviet people. Its dissemination outside Japan had just begun in the second half of the 1980s, but there were specific hindrances to its entry into the Soviet Union. As opposed to rock music, for example, which could rather easily make its way into the lives and minds of the Soviet people because sound recording equipment was available to the population in general, comics were less accessible. Pixel-perfect copying of an artwork required at least a photocopier, but such devices were under state control in Soviet times and only began to show up at some joint-venture companies at the very end of the 1980s. It is difficult to say now when the first manga books or magazines appeared in Russia, but it is possible that they were brought to Russia by students studying in Japan, whose number increased in the 1990s, or else entered the country in English versions through the United States and Western Europe.

Some conscientious manga and anime fans had already appeared in Russia in the early 1990s. Through observations and interviews conducted in the mid-1990s, it seems that Japanese animation and comics first attracted those who could draw pictures themselves, offering them a challenging opportunity to try their own abilities in a new sphere of art. However, the 2004 survey demonstrated that only 10 percent of respondents were interested themselves in drawing, 15 percent of respondents to the 2004 questionnaire gave preference to manga in comparison with anime, and 23 people out of 500 had attempted to translate manga into Russian. At present, anime is obviously more popular than manga and not only because it is more easily available through TV, movie theaters, video, and CD. It requires less knowledge of the Japanese or English languages for understanding because moving characters are more comprehensible than those just drawn on paper. Besides, as P. Osborne noted, in our age "all genres of communication (including the novel) have subsequently been subject to cinematization, the logic of montage and the image."[16] In other words, animation as a cinema genre corresponds to the requirements of the time and has more potential for becoming an international cultural form.[17] Susan Napier argues as well that anime is probably "the ideal artistic vehicle for expressing the hopes and nightmares of our uneasy contemporary world."[18]

As mentioned above, an important source for getting acquainted with anime and manga was the Internet. However, in the mid-1990s it was available only to some 10 percent of Russians, mainly businessmen, academics working at universities or research centers, and members of their families. Besides, anime and manga sites were in Japanese or English, which required some knowledge of those languages. This partly explains the greater spread of this genre among more educated youth, that is, those who knew foreign languages, could use the Internet, and consequently could interpret the content to their friends. *Otaku* call themselves "advanced, but not fashion-conscious," meaning that they are up-to-date with innovations in technology and new information, but are not particularly concerned with clothing-related fashion.

Since the opinion survey was not carried out at the initial stage of *otaku* activities, it is difficult to give a clear-cut answer to the question of what the social composition of members at that time was. Interviews and observations created the impression that parents of many *otaku* were affiliated with artistic professions and had passed such interests on to their children. Most *otaku* were college or university students or those who had intended to become students but failed at exams or withdrew from universities for some reason (including financial difficulties). It is interesting that some fans came from families of recent migrants to Russia from the former Soviet republics, that is, they were people who had no established relationships in Russian cities, and sought through their interaction with *otaku* a new group of belonging.

Observations demonstrated that anime- and manga-related activities comprised the major part of *otaku*'s time, far more than an average person would usually spend on a leisure activity. None of the interviewees, however, clearly expressed the intention to connect their future careers with anime or manga. In other words, in the middle of the 1990s, anime and manga provided a psychological niche and means of identification for educated representatives of youth coming from the families of intelligentsia who could not adapt themselves well to the rapid changes in Russian society, but found business activity—and the atmosphere of criminality associated with it in Russia—to be distasteful.

At the present time some *otaku* of the first generation have become professional designers, translators, cinema and art critics, or pursue other intellectual professions. In this sense it is quite possible that fascination with cultural forms from Japan further stirred their creative activities. As *otaku* themselves acknowledge, now they belong to the growing middle class of Russia: "We are people who have some extra money for entertainment, but are not rich enough to spend our free time traveling from Hawai'i to the Bahamas resorts," that is, behave in the style of rich new generation Russians.[19]

LIVING WITH ANIME AND MANGA

It took several years before Russian *otaku* realized that some organized form of activity would better suit their needs. Such an organization appeared in Moscow in the autumn of 1996 under the name RAnMa (an abbreviation of Russian Animation and Manga Club, although the word definitely has associations with the famous anime *Ranma 1/2*). RAnMa sought to spread anime and manga in Russia and assist beginners in the field in obtaining materials. RAnMa also wanted to create a market in Russia that would be ready to accept anime and manga not as an "exotic Oriental perversion," but as a valuable part of entertainment, one which could enjoy as much popularity and commercial success in Russia as the mass culture of the West.[20]

Otaku view American comics and animation as "too sweety and pink," suitable only for small children and unable to address any serious problems or stimulate the imagination. To cite one opinion, "American cartoon movies always have a happy ending which can be predicted from the beginning, while in Japanese anime the end is far from clear, leaving opportunities for imagination."

In late 1996 and early 1997, similar *otaku* organizations appeared in other cities of Russia, such as St. Petersburg, Rostov-on-Don, Perm, and Voronezh. Their membership consisted of two levels: regular members, the backbone of the movement, who paid membership fees, and all those who did not pay fees but were simply interested in anime and manga. Nowadays some kind of club or organization uniting anime and manga fans exists practically in every city or town in Russia, and small *otaku* communities may be found even among residents of a block of neighboring houses. The average age of a Russian *otaku* is 22 years old, with most between 16 and 35, and the proportion of male and female fans is approximately equal.[21]

The most regular form of communication for Russian *otaku* is *animka*, that is, gatherings of several fans at someone's flat or studio to watch videos, DVDs or PlayStation, to discuss recent news of the anime world, or to prepare costume play for later demonstration to a larger audience. The latter may be based completely on the contents of some anime or manga, but may also be a further development of an existing story where new characters are introduced. In the beginning, costume play compensated, to some extent, for the lack of original Japanese anime available in Russia, but it was also an important means of expressing creativity, providing a space for the sense of collectivity and building group identity (figure 13.1).

Gatherings in public spaces, *tussovka*, are another form of activity. Fans come to *tussovka* to buy and sell CDs, DVDs, videos, pictures, and other products related to anime and manga, such as badges with characters, as well as just to communicate with each other. *Tussovka* may become a space for performing costume play. Until quite recently most *tussovka* had to be conducted outdoors because local authorities viewed them with suspicion. However, since the autumn of 2003, *otaku* have managed to establish good relations with local authorities, which allows them to organize festivals and other gatherings in public buildings. This proves that anime and manga fandom has begun to receive some level of official recognition.

All *otaku* agree that *animka* or *tussovka* occupy an important part of their lives, even being a sort of "second family." They present not only an opportunity for exchange of videos and games and the passing of leisure time, but are also the place where fans meet close friends, people with the same interests and affections.

During their gatherings *otaku* do not consume much alcohol (some beer is allowed) or drugs, and do not resort to physical force, though many of them are familiar with the martial arts. Female *otaku* often stroke each other over the hands and shoulders while talking, but allegedly do not regard this as the expression of sexuality. *Otaku* particularly emphasize the peaceful nature of their gatherings and in this way contrast themselves with the culture associated with criminal activities, violence, drugs, and alcohol. They think that "it is high time to realize that anime and manga are the only alternative to the drugs and hooliganism dominant in Russia."

Unlike the members of many other subcultures, anime fans do not have any special clothing or hairstyles (except those for costume play) that would

Figure 13.1   Russian otaku prepare for costume playing of *Ranma 1/2*. Photograph by Yulia Mikhailova.

make them immediately recognizable in a crowd. However, each of them has a nickname based on the name of a favorite anime or manga character. Sometimes they try to reproduce features of those characters in their behavior, and their language—at least when they talk to each other—is rich in citations from anime. *Otaku* appreciate the ability to tell an interesting story, either based on anime or on one's own imagination; the subject itself does not seem to matter so much. The thrill comes merely from intellectual conversation, costume playing, or karaoke singing.

The number of Internet sites supported by *otaku* is growing and, with the spread of the Internet in Russia, information on anime and manga is becoming more and more available to an increasing number of people. *Otaku* purposefully advertise information only in Russian, targeting the Russian-speaking audience who cannot access information on Japanese popular culture in English or Japanese. Now it is possible to buy not only pirated videos,

CDs, and DVDs, but licensed ones as well. More and more Russians are affluent enough to engage in electronic shopping and a Russian company, MC-entertainment, releases CDs with Russian translations of most famous anime.

Two special magazines on anime- and manga-related topics are published in Russia, *Anime Magazine* and *Banzai*. They feature overviews of various animated movies and games, describe events in the lives of Russian *otaku*, organize contests based on the knowledge of anime, and also provide some information on Japanese culture. Among cultural topics, those involving Japanese history, religion, and traditional culture prevail. The publication of these magazines gives evidence to the fact that there is an audience large enough to support them commercially.

Since 2000, anime festivals have become another important feature of anime and manga subculture in Russia. Voronezh, a city in central Russia, was the first place to organize such a festival in 2000. At that time the program was limited to the presentation of anime movies in a local movie theater and only 100 fans attended. Now, in addition to annual festivals in Voronezh, similar events are held in Moscow and St. Petersburg at least twice a year. An important event was the festival MAniFEST held on November 2, 2003 in St. Petersburg and supported by the local Committee of Youth Organizations and the Japanese Consulate. It was attended by more than 1,000 people.

Answers to the 2004 questionnaire administered to 500 *otaku* demonstrated that 46 percent preferred romantic comedies centering on relations between characters, 31 percent fantasy, 18 percent sci-fi, and 5 percent Japanese history and other topics. It is difficult to determine precisely whether "romantic comedy" is a euphemism for anime with sexual themes, but some *otaku* emphasized during interviews that it is the dialogue in *hentai* (sexual perversion) products, rather than the pornographic content, that is of main interest for them. Another group of interviewees held the opinion that there definitely exist male anime fans who prefer *hentai*, but, as they put it, "you should not think that everyone is like them, because the world of anime is much more diverse." Research on other subcultures confirms that nowadays, with the increase of AIDS and other sexually transmitted diseases, young people tend not to regard their gatherings as "pick-up joints."[22]

When asked to specify what factors in particular attract young people to anime and manga, many said that they "just love anime" or "love them because they are so cool." In their answers to the multiple-choice questionnaire, respondents mentioned the following reasons: an opportunity to understand problems of contemporary youth (43 percent), an interesting leisure-time activity (22 percent), artistic style (18 percent), an opportunity to learn more about Japan (8 percent), an alternative to movies with violence and crime (7 percent), and other (2 percent). As is obvious from these answers, fans treat anime and manga rather seriously, and not as mere entertainment.

Generally speaking, *otaku* equally like various genres of anime because, according to the opinion of several interviewees, "all of them pose problems related to the meaning of our lives." One group of female *otaku* noted that they like anime because it gives space for fantasies and liberates them from restrictions set up by parents or traditionally formed stereotypes of sexual relations. Another group confessed that anime-related contradictions with parents exist because all parents dream of their "daughters marrying a good guy," although the girls themselves do not think of marriage at all. For them anime and manga can even be a means of expressing the feeling of freedom. One girl represented her friends as Amazons in a manga she drew, commenting that "Amazons can do what they want and are free from restrictions imposed by men." These interviewees were second-year university students of 19–20 years of age. For the generation of their parents it was quite common to marry at this particular age. At the same time, parents of some *otaku* enjoy this cultural genre too, so it cannot be generalized that anime and manga present an open defiance of a younger generation to an elder one.

After ten years of Japanese animation having a presence in Russia, the general attitude to it seems to be changing in the sense that anime is no longer viewed exclusively as a form just for children, but is now seen as a kind of popular culture with the potential of broader influence on the masses. Whereas in the beginning the RAnMa club saw its main goal as collecting examples of anime and manga (most of them pirated versions) and in familiarizing the public with them, this goal has now been partially achieved. This is the result not only of the *otaku*'s own activities, but also of the joint efforts of TV (especially channels 2×2 and NTV), cinema, Japanese consulates in Russia, and some business corporations, as well as the fact of Russia's increasing integration into global popular culture.

However, although the number of fans and the popularity of the genre are growing, some *otaku* are worried that fandom and the genre itself are losing their elite status in becoming an entertainment for the "crowd." They now tend to classify anime themselves into elitist and refined or populist and simplistic, but cannot work out any common criteria for this division.[23] This trend, ironically, goes against the very notion of pop culture, but is common to other subcultures too.

As mentioned above, business corporations have recently begun to exhibit an interest in financing projects dealing with the purchase of Japanese anime, translating them into Russian, and thus making them available for a broad audience. However, *otaku* do not like translations into Russian, saying that the attraction of the original *seiyu* voice becomes lost.[24] They also consider their own interest in anime as "pure," if not professional, and feel apprehensive that the wide popularization of anime will somehow make it "dirty" or "profane." Thus there is an inherent contradiction between the imagined exclusiveness of *otaku* subculture and their efforts to make it a part of mass culture.

CREATIVE ACTIVITIES OF RUSSIAN *OTAKU*

Members of RAnMa are also engaged in their own creative activities, the so-called fan art. The most widespread form of it is *fanfik*, literary or graphic

Figure 13.2 Felix Torchinov's Amadeus Bernstein, a character created during the development of the video game *The King of Fighters*. Used with the permission of Felix Torchinov.

works produced for noncommercial purposes in manga style. They are usually based on the plots, ideas, and characters of Japanese works, but may also contain additions to existing stories where new characters are introduced, may create new narratives using Japanese characters, or may even be a parody. Their authors try to reproduce the Japanese manga style as much as possible. When asked about the differences between their pictures and Japanese manga, they plainly replied that their pictures were not as perfect as the Japanese ones. New graphic heroes are often invented by *otaku* themselves. For example, Amadeus Bernstein (figure 13.2) is a character created by Felix Torchinov in the process of development of a video game *The King of Fighters*. Amadeus is thought to be one of the sons of Rugal Bernstein, the main villain in this series. The drawing is characterized by a rather sophisticated graphic style.

There are also cases when manga drawings are used to reveal the personal feelings of their authors without any connection to original Japanese stories and are done because "drawing in manga style brings fun and pleasure." For example, the artist of figure 13.3 was inspired to it during a sea voyage when, as she said, the wind was blowing and she had a feeling that she was about to rise up into the sky.

The first work of Russian *otaku* in the manga genre was published in *Klassny zhurnal* (Schoolroom Magazine) in 1999–2000.[25] It was called *Nika*, which was the name of the main heroine. The author of the text was Vyacheslav Makarov and the drawings were by Bogdan Kulikovsky. *Klassny zhurnal*, founded in April 1999, targets mainly schoolchildren of various

Figure 13.3   Jane Smirnova's "Freedom." Used with the permission of Jane Smirnova.

ages. It is published under the auspices of the National Russian Organization of Scouts and contains a variety of forms of entertainment for children from the description of video games, including explanations of their technical use, to detective stories, comics by foreign and Russian authors, crosswords, and puzzles. The magazine also organizes photo competitions and once even celebrated Barbie's jubilee.

In 2002, the first part of *Nika* was published as a book.[26] As the first serialized manga story officially published in Russia, *Nika* deserves detailed description and analysis, in spite of the fact it was created by amateur artists and is far from being a masterpiece. This also provides a good opportunity for understanding the ideas, images, and sensitivities which the authors wanted to share with their readers, and thus affords some insight into the Russian *otaku* world. Although *Nika* is an original story, needless to say it contains many references to Japanese anime and manga, along with sci-fi and books for children such as the Harry Potter series.

The main character, Nika Novikova, is a 15-year-old Moscow schoolgirl. Her parents perished in an automobile accident and left Nika a video-recording firm. The girl is rich, beautiful, smart, and ambitious, in a word an object of envy for many teenagers. However, Nika herself feels unhappy because she has no friends. Her guardian takes care of the video firm and looks after Nika, but she would rather practice martial arts than go to school. Nika is obsessed with the idea of becoming stronger than all the boys in her neighborhood, with whom she often fights. She definitely belongs to the *shōjo* (young girl) type of character.[27] Like many heroines of Miyazaki Hayao or other authors, she combines strength and independence, assertiveness and risk-taking, with magic powers. Her obsession with empowerment through magic is the same as, for example, that of *Sailor Moon* heroines.

The manga consists of three parts, with the last one published only electronically. In part one, Nika becomes the owner of a detective agency and thanks to her own wits manages to find the lost treasures of a famous archaeology professor. As a reward she receives an old book of magic compiled by a famous magician, Oleg, who later appears to be her grandfather. No one in the world except Nika can use the book as long as she is alive. The girl patiently masters magic spells to acquire superpowers, but soon finds out that magic may turn from a blessing to a curse. Various "evil forces," represented by Unit J9, want to take the book away from her. They fail, but not because of Nika's magical powers. She manages to survive only due to the help of two boys who protect her for "the sake of justice." Finally, Unit J9 is defeated and all three return to their normal lives.

This first part of the story is rather "Russian" in content and character. Its main theme may be described as the struggle for survival in a semifantastic reality saturated with criminals, violence, and danger. Many elements—the collection of weapons owned by a member of Unit J9 Red (who later defects from it to protect Nika), security guards, business corporations stealing commercial secrets from one another, hackers, nepotism, and betrayal—remind us of contemporary Russian life and are associated with the adult world that teenage heroes resist and overcome in the end thanks to their solidarity. It also portrays the life of the Russian youth who seem to be willing to live independently from their parents, a trope characteristic of many Japanese anime and manga too. Many features of the story may be viewed either as borrowed from Japan or of Russian origin. Thus, Unit J9, which attempted to attack Nika, may remind the readers of section 9 from *The Ghost in the Shell* or Nerd from *Evangelion*, but may also be associated with the former Soviet KGB, an organization that even now is by no means dormant. In general, the first part may be read as aversion toward contemporary Russian reality, especially if we take into consideration that *Nika* was created soon after the financial crisis that hit Russia in 1998.

Part two takes place in Japan or some other Asian country. Here Nika undertakes a trip to a remote monastery high in the mountains. Her purpose is to master a new magic technique called "gy," a probable allusion to Zen meditation. The building of the monastery and the scenery around it are portrayed as Japanese. It appears, however, that the insidious and uncanny Father Superior whom Nika meets there is not very willing to share his secret knowledge with anyone. He is more eager to get rid of a small girl, Asana, who is an orphan like Nika and happened to wander into the monastery when she was a child. The peculiar feature of Asana, and the reason no one likes her, is her unique ability to break everything that gets into her hands, be it a simple compass, a toaster, or a radio set. Father Superior casts a spell and as a result Nika and Asana are doomed to stay always together, bound by electricity (figure 13.4). After a series of misfortunes the two girls reach Moscow at last, only to discover that they are to be persecuted by the Goshi brothers, who allegedly received the command of some secret office from the wicked "other world" to get hold of the magic book. Only after Nika resorts to a

Ника и Асана (2 том)

Figure 13.4 Bogdan Kulikovsky, Nika and Asana, from *Nika, Volume 1, "The Magic Book"* (Moscow: Russian Publishing House, Ustico, 2002).

very strong spell do they manage to escape from the Goshis, an exercise that takes all Nika's strength. Exhausted, she falls into a long and deep sleep.

This part of *Nika* conveys a rather ironic attitude to "things Japanese." Already in the first part it became clear that martial arts, often associated in Russia with Japan, are not a sufficient means of self-protection. Father Superior is a far cry from a wise and benevolent Oriental sage. He is selfish, uncanny, and mischievous, and resembles the numerous proponents of various religions, of both Western and Eastern origins, that inundated Russia in the 1990s, often pursuing not purely religious goals. The Goshi brothers persecuting Nika are portrayed as overweight sumō wrestlers wearing huge Russian fur caps. They are slow-thinking and faint-hearted, and are finally taken by ambulance to a mental asylum. The funny little girl Asana with a seemingly Oriental name may only be pitied for her awkwardness. The irony expressed by the authors may seem strange in a story inspired by and imitating Japanese manga, and may be read as expressing counter-attitudes to the exoticization of Japan.

In the third part the narrative revolves around Nika and Asana traveling through numerous "other worlds," weird, mysterious, and always wicked (figure 13.5), while their constant struggles with the ominous and ugly denizens of these lands seem to have no end. However, if in the first part of the story the enemies of Nika and the purpose of fighting at least seemed to be clear, now it becomes meaningless, as the "other worlds" are portrayed in an apocalyptic mode as a result of destruction that took place many years

Figure 13.5   Bogdan Kulikovsky, "A Wicked World," from *Nika, Volume 1, "The Magic Book"* (Moscow: Russian Publishing House, Ustico, 2002).

before. Nika and Asana travel across a desert, dying from thirst and hunger. There they learn that the universal time consists of two periods, the good and the bad one, that interchange like sand in an hourglass. Some strange animal-like creatures mill stones into sand to extend the period of the good era, but it appears that no one has ever been able to achieve this goal. Nika and Asana give way to despair as their friends in Moscow fail to rescue the girls through the computer window; they are afraid they will never get back home, a quest that becomes their only dream. Here the authors convey the anxiety that technology cannot save humanity. The story has no clear end, but the authors pose the question of whether it is better to live in an artificial world full of technological calculations and computations, or to return to a past when the world was inhabited with mermaids, wood-goblins, and other fantastic creatures.

It is a matter of general knowledge that the interest in miracles, mystery, spiritual power, and control over ghosts is a feature of the "new age" concept, popular in Japan and around the world. According to Ian Reader, who studied this issue in relation to Aum Shinrikyō, it presents an emotional counterbalance to the heavily technologized contemporary world, the feeling that science cannot find solutions to all problems.[28] The authors of *Nika* seem to share this concern.

As mentioned above, the story contains many overt references to Japanese manga and anime. The magic book may remind us of *fushigi yugi*, pancakes of *Kiki's Delivery Service*, and the electric shocks that bind Asana and Nika together may have come from *Urusei Yatsura*. But it is rather through more general ideas, such as the euphoric state of power, fascination with magic, dystopia wrought by technology, nostalgia for a normal life, and anxiety about the future that we see the similarity between this Russian manga story and Japanese ones.

At the same time, some elements seem to betray more clearly the Russian origins of the story. These are the criminal debauchery in Moscow, the depiction of life as a constant struggle for survival, the strong sense of the insecurity and vulnerability of people, and also the idea that wealth is no replacement for the warmth of human relations. As represented in this story, young Russians feel uncomfortable whether surrounded by contemporary reality, technology, or magic. They look for an escape from each of them and are longing for friends. We see Nika's face with manga-style big eyes full of pain and angst, rage and frustration. It is so difficult to survive in this world, or so this face seems to cry out. At the same time, Nika is strong, always ready to fight, to protect herself, and to resist evil.

Such feelings of loneliness, anxiety, uncertainty, and diffidence over the ways young people can become happy in the society they inhabit are by no means characteristic of Russia alone, but represent universal adolescent fantasies of transformation into adulthood, expressed, among other means, through anime and manga. The youth of contemporary Russia may experience these feelings more strongly than people of the same age in other countries because of the unpredictable state of Russian life. This also stands in sharp contrast to the security and predictability that the parents of contemporary Russian youth enjoyed in prior decades.

CONCLUSION

Anime and manga youth subculture formed in Russia out of necessity to fill in the ideological and psychological gap that appeared as a result of the collapse of the Soviet Union and subsequent difficulties in the transition to new lifestyles. The adoption of these Japanese cultural forms in the 1990s became possible due to Russia's openness to new cultural trends and its involvement in the process of globalization. Russian *otaku* saw in anime and manga not only a new form of creative activity, but a means of escape, through their imaginations, from the "Godzillian" reality of Russian life.[29] Moreover, the ability of anime and manga to speak in an easy-to-comprehend way about the problems common to youth everywhere added to their popularity.

Nowadays this popular culture in Russia plays the role of an identity marker mainly for those who see themselves as intellectually, rather than commercially, oriented. Some *otaku* believe that anime and manga may play an important social role by presenting a good alternative to drugs, alcohol, and the various forms of delinquency that are so widespread among Russian youth. However, the dissemination of anime and manga in Russia actually resembles the fate of many other subcultures. Initially RAnMa club members wanted to turn anime and manga into a branch of popular culture in Russia. But now, when this objective seems to have been realized, the fans are afraid of losing their exclusive status as "intellectual elites." They regard the process of popularization of anime and manga as vulgarization, trying to protect in this way their self-constructed identity as experts and arbiters of taste.

Although a detailed comparison of *otaku* subcultures in Japan and Russia is beyond the parameters of this essay, a few disparities between these two communities are worth noting. In Japan *otaku* have a rather negative reputation as people who are so obsessed with their hobby that they sever relations with society.[30] Many *otaku* in Japan prefer online communication to personal interaction and feel apprehensive of close human contacts in real life. They are people who sense their own "deficiency" or inferiority, and purposely put themselves into a marginal position. They lack social consciousness and escape from society into the world of their hobbies.[31] *Otaku* in the Japanese context may be regarded as a part of the broader phenomenon of *hikikomori* (staying indoors) that gained force especially with the spread of the Internet.

In Russia anime and manga *otaku* are rather active socially and more open to society in general. Their gatherings (such as festivals) are widely advertised and everyone is welcome to participate. Although, as mentioned earlier, some *otaku* fear that the culture they regard as sophisticated and elitist may lose these characteristics as it is popularized in Russia, nevertheless, their goal is to "enlighten" the "masses," not to isolate themselves from the larger society. In this sense it may even be said that *otaku* have inherited some features traditionally characteristic of the self-consciousness of the Russian intelligentsia. The more public spirit of Russian anime and manga fans may also be explained by the communitarian traditions of Soviet society that have not yet evaporated in spite of the advance of a market economy. In contrast to the totally middle-class society of Japan, Russia is more socially stratified, and fascination with anime and manga, that is, objects of Japanese culture held in high esteem in Russia, serves as a vehicle for elevating one's social image through symbolic means.

NOTES

My attention to the topic of anime and manga in Russia was first attracted by now deceased Professor Evgeny Torchinov of St. Petersburg State University who made a presentation on the topic "Japanese Manga in Russia" at a symposium organized at Hiroshima City University in 1999.

1. N. Shomu and A. Katsumaro, *The Russian Impact on Japan: Literature and Social Thought, Two Essays* (Los Angeles: University of Southern California Press, 1981); J. Thomas Rimer, ed., *Russian and Japanese Cultural Encounters, 1868–1926* (Stanford, CA: Stanford University Press, 1995).
2. Susan J. Napier, *Anime: From* Akira *to* Princess Mononoke (New York: Palgrave Macmillan, 2001), pp. 10–11.
3. "Shock" construction work is the mobilization of youth to labor at large-scale construction sites.
4. Hillary Pinkinton, " 'The Future is Ours': Youth Culture in Russia, 1953 to the Present," in *Russian Cultural Studies,* ed. Catriona Kelly and David Shepherd (Oxford: Oxford University Press, 1998), pp. 369–370.
5. Irina Melnikova, "Representations of Soviet-Japanese Encounters in Co-production Feature Films, Part 2. From Romance to Competition," *Doshisha Studies in Language and Culture* 5:2 (2002), pp. 207–230.
6. The *Godzilla* series was released in Russia in 1993–1994 and now some *Godzilla* fandom exists, as is evident from the sites of several Internet chat groups. In the Soviet Union Japanese monster movies were represented only by Kurata Junji's film *Kyōryū: Kaichō no densetsu* (The Legend of Dinosaurs, 1977).

7. *Petersburg of Youth: Movements, Organizations, Subcultures (An Attempt of Sociological Description)* (St. Petersburg: Institute of Sociology, 1997).

8. Robert Sardiello, "Deadhead Subculture," in *Youth Culture: Identity in a Postmodern World*, ed. Jonathan S. Epstein (Oxford: Blackwell, 1998), p. 121.

9. Elena Omelchenko, *Youth Cultures and Subcultures* (Institut Sotsiologii RAN, 2000), p. 8.

10. V. F. Lukov, "Specific Features of Youth Subcultures in Russia," *Sotsiologicheskiye issledovaniya* 10 (2002), p. 80.

11. In 2002 youth comprised of 37.7 percent of the unemployed and 21.2 percent of those whose income was below the living wage. Ibid.

12. G. Murdock, "Mass Communication and the Construction of Meaning," in *Reconstructing Social Psychology*, ed. N. Amstead (Harmondsworth: Penguin, 1974), p. 213.

13. V. F. Lukov, "Specific Features of Youth Subcultures in Russia."

14. Soon after World War II, Disney movies were screened in the Soviet Union, but disappeared after the beginning of the cold war.

15. The first Japanese movie festival was conducted in 1960 and by autumn 2003 their number had reached 37. See the homepage of the Japanese Embassy in Russia for the titles of films offered to Russian audiences: www.embjapan.ru/culture/embfilms.html.

16. Peter Osborne, *The Politics of Time: Modernity and Avant-Garde* (London: Verso, 1995), p. 197.

17. Susan Napier suggests that anime is probably "the ideal artistic vehicle for expressing the hopes and nightmares of our uneasy contemporary world." Napier, *Anime*, p. 10.

18. Ibid.

19. http://anime.dvdspecial.ru/Articles/otaku.shtml.

20. These aims were stated at what was then the homepage of RanMa, http://ranma.anime.ru/. Presently the main homepage of RAnMa is http://anime.dvdspecial.ru/.

21. This is slightly different from Japan, because the Japanese tend to lose their obsession with anime as soon as they graduate from school.

22. Lori Tomlinson, " 'This Ain't No Disco' . . . or Is It? Youth Culture and the Rave Phenomenon," in *Youth Culture*, p. 200.

23. http://manga.ru/general/view and http://www.ulver.com/valhalla/showthread.

24. Originally *seiyu* meant the voice of an actor (or actress) who dubbed Western films into Japanese. In anime it means the voice of an actor (or actress) who speaks for anime characters.

25. The full version of *Nika* exists in electronic form at http://www.comics.aha.ru and in the magazine *Klassnyi zhurnal*, nos. 1–48 (2000).

26. Bogdan, *Nika, Volume 1, "The Magic Book"* (Moscow: Russian Publishing House, Ustico, 2002). The analysis of Nika in this article is based on the electronic and magazine versions, because the book version is shorter and probably more removed from the original ideas of the author.

27. Napier, *Anime*, p. 119.

28. Ian Reader, *Religion in Contemporary Japan* (Honolulu: University of Hawai'i Press, 1991), p. 236.

29. In fact, "Godzilla" is now often used as a metaphor for Russia. For example, Andrei Levkin in his story "Gypsy Romance"(in *Stories and Novels* (St. Petersburg: Amfara,

2000)) compared the horrors of contemporary Russian society with Godzilla, whereas other authors remark that all Russian revolutions are Godzilla-like.

30. Sharon Kinsella, *Adult Manga* (Richmond: Curzon, 2000), chapter 5, "The Movement against Manga."

31. For example, one *otaku* community called *Fujoshi* (spoiled girls) emphasizes on the top of its homepage that only those who share its views are recommended to continue reading it. See http://page.freett.com/sweethell/ or http://n-39.net/.

Epilogue: He Did the Stomp, He Did the Monster Stomp

Theodore C. Bestor

The big green guy has legs! Fifty years and still winning hearts and minds; still flattening cities after all these years.

How does the radioactive reptile stay cool? Nothing about him (him?) is cuddly, and his manners are atrocious. But he resonates and reverberates both with Japanese and with people around the world, with people in the 1950s and with those in every decade since. He is all monsters to all people for all seasons; he is Everyzilla!

Like any good symbol, he travels well and keeps company with many, many meanings. As Jorge Luis Borges put it (although probably not with Godzilla directly in mind): "We are ignorant of the meaning of the dragon in the same way that we are ignorant of the meaning of the universe, but there is something in the dragon's image that fits man's imagination, and this accounts for the dragon's appearance in different places and periods."[1]

Certainly, the origins of Godzilla fit a particular imagination of the primitive unleashed, destroying that which he cannot understand, moving from the south (the tropical other of enchantment, allure, mystery, and primordial danger, as much for mid-twentieth-century Japanese as for their Western counterparts) toward the cosmopolitan north. In *Gojira* (1954), Godzilla is first encountered by a vessel from the "Nankai" (South Seas) shipping line. The South Seas (also known as the "Nanyō") had been the site of Japanese ethnological investigations of primitive others, colonial exploitation, and the subtle struggles of Empire, since well before World War II (the "Pacific War" to the Japanese). Also, from earliest contacts in the sixteenth century, Europeans were known to Japanese as "Southern Barbarians," and of course it was from the south, from the South Seas, from the Pacific, that island-hopping Allied troops approached, besieged, and then wrecked havoc on the Japanese home islands, especially their modern infrastructure, which was as incapable of withstanding the Allied onslaught as it was (later) of repelling Godzilla. (And, in the early Godzilla films, the Japanese military or self-defense forces are valiant but futile in their ultimately discredited efforts to protect the homeland.)

But Godzilla is not only an intruder from the outside, he is also a primordial "other" from the inside. He is Japanese! After all, he is known to the inhabitants of the remote fishing village where he storms ashore, at least to the toothless old man of the island, who growls that in the past they sacrificed young girls to placate him. (Japanese dragons in tradition *do* live under the sea, and folklore does recommend sacrifices to them.) These villagers perform a rite, a traditional *kagura*-like dance, at the local Shintō shrine, to ward Godzilla off (although, tellingly, in postwar Japan, Shintō rituals apparently have lost all efficacy against dragons).

From religion, the Godzilla issue turns political. Left and right disagree what is to be done; populist female members of the Diet argue that the public must be informed, conservative male politicians argue to suppress news of Godzilla. Godzilla, of course, outtakes political debate, making his presence extremely public, defying the conservative establishment as well as the armed forces.

And so, from the murky depths of Japanese tradition rooted in remote rural life, the dragon sets forth to attack Japan's urban core. The awakened monster of the deep/of deep tradition cannot be vanquished by Japan's most advanced science and industrial technology.

This clash, in the original Godzilla film, is brought into high relief by the clash of humanistic and scientific values—themselves set in an almost explicitly Japanese versus "Western" context—by the differing perspectives of Professor Yamane (Shimura Takashi) and Dr Serizawa (Hirata Akihiko), both scientists but one an observer, naturalist, and taxonomist, the other a technological experimentalist; Professor Yamane embedded in a warm nexus of human relations, Dr Serizawa a tormented individualist; the former living in a comfortable Japanese-style home, the latter listening to Western classical music in an oddly Gothic castle somewhere in Tokyo (no doubt in the western part of the city). Professor Yamane of course wants to preserve and study Godzilla, but Dr Serizawa's anguish is that can destroy Godzilla but only by revealing that he has created the ultimate weapon, one which can annihilate all life itself.

What to do, what to do? Dr Serizawa turns out to be Japanese after all.

(Stop here if you haven't seen the movie yet. . . .)

Dr Serizawa takes Godzilla, his scientific discovery, and himself together to a watery self-sacrificial grave.

Myths are matrices of intelligibility, according to Claude Lévi-Strauss. But, he argues, myths are definable only within the context of their own rules of construction. In a sense, a myth makes itself through its structure, and deciphering its structure gets one not to the meaning of the myth per se, but to the meanings of images, motifs, symbols, social institutions, history, and our consciousness of and questions about these. These meanings arise out of the myth's structure that necessarily relies on juxtapositions, contradictions, conflations, and coincidences of motifs and questions.[2] Godzilla raises all the right questions: east and west; south and north; primitive and modern; rural and urban; tradition and cosmopolitanism; left and right; religion and science; war and peace.

However, what is intelligible in one mythic context—a reading of clues to potential Japanese interpretations of the original Godzilla film—cannot account for the intelligibility of the same mythic texts by entirely different audiences.

It is one thing to attempt a post hoc cultural reading of Godzilla in 1954 in Japan, and perhaps a different thing altogether to attempt a transnational reading of Godzilla across different (cultural) audiences, across different productions, across different generations.

To attempt this audacious step, or stomp, one has only to consider this: Godzilla—whether seen as a product of war or a force of nature, as primitive or primordial, as mindless or vengeful—does one thing well and does it over and over again.

He brings modern civilization to its knees. He brings devastation to those most intricate social, cultural, and physical creations of human societies—he is the destroyer of cities. As an urban Shiva, his destructive potential simply reaffirms what we know all too well: that cities and the fabric of social, cultural, medical, economic, and spiritual life that are required to sustain them are among the most fragile of human creations.

The nuclear menace is loud and clear in Godzilla; his awakening as a result of nuclear testing; his destruction a clear evocation of Hiroshima and Nagasaki. More direct references may escape most non-Japanese viewers. *Gojira* opens with a blast that bathes a ship's crew in explosive light. On March 1, 1954, the *Daigo Fukuryū Maru* (the *Lucky Dragon No. 5*), a Japanese tuna fishing vessel, was caught in an American atomic bomb test on Bikini Atoll. When the ship returned home, the story of its brush with nuclear death consumed Japan (and spawned the production of *Gojira*). Fish markets across the nation brought out Geiger counters (a bit character in the film has a brief line about radioactive fish), and the antinuclear movement in Japan received an enormous and lasting increase in support. (Today, the hull of the *Lucky Dragon* is in a small antinuclear museum in Tokyo, located at water's edge, directly east of the city's center; the proper location for a dragon in Japanese versions of feng shui.)

But it is not merely nuclear. *Gojira* deliberately evokes the destruction of Tokyo by fire bombing, and by extension urban destruction, the terror of urban warfare among civilians. Any adult (or adolescent) Japanese viewer in 1954 could vividly recall, often from personal experience, the horror of aerial bombardments that left more dead than the atomic bombings: "scorched, boiled, and baked to death," as General Curtis LeMay put it.[3]

If this lesson was taught in the mid-twentieth century by World War II, and the instructive list is almost endless—Rotterdam, Warsaw, Coventry, Leningrad, Stalingrad, Dresden, Berlin, Nanjing, Auschwitz, Tokyo, Hiroshima, Nagasaki—it has certainly been reaffirmed in the last years of the twentieth and the opening years of the twenty-first centuries: cities are targets of the most vicious destruction mankind is capable of (or in the cases of Auschwitz, Bergen-Belsen, Birkenau, and too many others, cities can be created as intentional killing machines).

Chernobyl, the Kobe earthquake, Bhopal, the sarin gas attacks in the Tokyo subways, the World Trade Center, the European heat wave, the

Madrid trains, the Southeast Asian tsunami, the London subways, the levees of New Orleans—destruction is all around us, some of it wrought by nature, some by humans, often compounded by the incompetence (or arrogance) of humans who think they have conquered, tamed, or contained the furies of nature or the furies of their fellow human beings.

As John Dower has pointed out, iconic terms and images of war (as well as other kinds of catastrophic events) linger on, for example, as convenient shorthand for comparison ("Pearl Harbor") or subtle elisions (as the referent "Ground Zero" transfers easily from Hiroshima to lower Manhattan).[4] "Shock and awe," as well, first used in reaction to the first wartime nuclear tests in New Mexico, was made famous by Donald Rumsfeld in the lead-up to a different war.

The ability of mass media and popular culture to encapsulate these iconic terms and images from real world events and carry them in some sort of only partially suspended animation across generations (whether Godzilla and Hiroshima, or "Mary, Mary, quite contrary" and the conflicts between the Tudors and Stuarts) must ultimately leave us to wonder, what monuments will be erected in popular culture to the events, either political and natural, of our own present day—Aum Shinrikyō, Kosovo, 9–11, Tora Bora, Guantanamo Bay, Baghdad, Beslan, the Bali bombings, the tsunami of 2004, Abu Ghraib, the Gaza Strip, Hurricane Katrina—and how will these be reflected in global popular culture half a century from now?

When Godzilla storms ashore at the fishing port of Shimizu, in *Godzilla, Mothra, and King Ghidorah: Giant Monsters All-Out Attack* (2001), a poster in the harbormaster's office reminds alert viewers to "Remember the *Lucky Dragon No. 5*," the tuna vessel whose homeport was Shimizu.

Just as a fleeting glimpse of the *Lucky Dragon No. 5* connects the viewer to American nuclear testing, which fragments of which contemporary events will be echoed by whom in the future? Where will images of the World Trade Center or Abu Ghraib or the Madrid bombings appear and in what contexts? Certainly they will not be propelled only by Hollywood's versions of things, but also by the myriad media—both new and old—of the twenty-first century, produced who knows where? In 1954, the struggling Tokyo film industry inscribed Godzilla onto global popular culture. Fifty years from now, which new global center of media will have emerged to reconnect events of our day to the global imaginary: Bangalore, Kandahar, Jakarta, Madrid, Havana, Pyongyang, Manila, Qatar, or . . . ?

NOTES

1. Jorge Luis Borges with Margarita Guerrero, *The Book of Imaginary Beings*, trans. Norman Thomas di Giovanni (New York: Dutton, 1969), p. 13.
2. Claude Lévi-Strauss, *Myth and Meaning* (New York: Schocken Books, 1995).
3. Quoted in John W. Dower, "Cultures of War: Pearl Harbor, Hiroshima, 9–11," Paper presented at Harvard University, September 20, 2005.
4. Ibid.

INDEX